MASTERS
OF
DISASTER
THE TEN COMMANDMENTS
OF DAMAGE CONTROL

CHRISTOPHER LEHANE,
MARK FABIANI,
AND BILL GUTTENTAG

palgrave
macmillan

First published in 2012 by PALGRAVE MACMILLAN® in the United States—a division of St. Martin's Press LLC, 175 Fifth Avenue, New York, NY 10010.

Where this book is distributed in the UK, Europe and the rest of the world, this is by Palgrave Macmillan, a division of Macmillan Publishers Limited, registered in England, company number 785998, of Houndmills, Basingstoke, Hampshire RG21 6XS.

Palgrave Macmillan is the global academic imprint of the above companies and has companies and representatives throughout the world.

Palgrave® and Macmillan® are registered trademarks in the United States, the United Kingdom, Europe and other countries.

ISBN 978-0-230-34180-7

Library of Congress Cataloging-in-Publication Data is available from the Library of Congress.

A catalogue record of the book is available from the British Library.

Design by Letra Libre

First edition: December 2012

10 9 8 7 6 5 4 3 2 1

Printed in the United States of America.

CONTENTS

PART I
CRISIS AS A STATE OF NATURE

PROLOGUE
NOT A QUESTION OF IF, BUT WHEN

IN THE INFORMATION AGE, THERE ARE TWO KINDS OF PEOPLE, TWO KINDS OF INSTITUTIONS, two kinds of organizations: those who have been hit with a crisis and those who haven't been around very long.

Whether you are a multinational corporation such as BP responding to oil gushing into the Gulf of Mexico or the neighborhood restaurant dealing with a bad Yelp review, confronting a crisis is not a question of *if* but of *when*. And of those who have looked a great crisis squarely in the eye, there are similarly two kinds of people, two kinds of institutions, two kinds of organizations:

Those who were able to be masters of their disasters, and those who failed.

The landscape is dotted with a few winners but crowded with many losers who simply did not have what it took to survive the crisis.

For every Bill Clinton—who left office with the highest presidential job approval rating in history despite having been impeached—there are disgraced former politicians like Gary Hart and John Edwards.

For every Goldman Sachs—which, despite being widely portrayed in the wake of the 2008 financial meltdown as a pack of real-life Gordon Gekkos savagely trouncing all in their path in the service of the bottom line, has continued to have great success—there are companies like Lehman Brothers, Enron, and Arthur Andersen, consigned to the ash heap of Wall Street.

For every franchise athlete like Yankee's star Alex Rodriguez—who in 2009 went from being the spring training goat of ridicule over revelations about his use of performance-enhancing drugs to being the 2009 World Series hero—there are disgraced former superstars like Barry Bonds and Mark McGwire.

These same battles play out every day not just in *The New York Times* and *The Wall Street Journal,* but also in the *Peoria Journal Star* and *Palo Alto Online.* The names may not be known to all, but the problems are just as serious to those in the vortex, such as:

- The local bed and breakfast that suddenly discovers it has been reported to BedBugRegistry.com;
- Your colleague who inadvertently left his resume in the printer and is being called in by his boss to address whether he is applying for another job;
- A neighborhood fast-food franchise that is suddenly dealing with a so-called foreign particle in its hamburgers that may or may not have been planted there by a spiteful customer or a disgruntled employee;
- A principal at a private school who is trying to explain the dip in the latest test scores to a group of angry parents;
- A guy in the adjoining cubicle who inadvertently hits "reply all" when sending his best friend a scathing criticism of their boss.

All of these examples are, in fact, real-life cases—and versions of them happen every day. And while these crises may not be leading national news reports, when they happen to you or your organization, it's personal, it's profound, and it will have an enormous impact on you, your family, and your future.

It's like what Ronald Reagan said about the economy when running against Jimmy Carter—when your neighbor's out of work, it is a recession; when you're out of work, it is a depression.

Similarly, when your neighbor faces a crisis, it is someone else's scandal; when *you* face a crisis, it is a disaster that you *must* master.

We are often asked how to identify a crisis. A crisis can manifest itself in a seemingly infinite number of ways: It could be a legal problem, such as when a Fortune 500 corporation is sideswiped by an accounting scandal; it could be an economic challenge, such as when a restaurant is losing market share to a competitor because of poor Yelp reviews; it could be a personal issue, such as when a spouse is caught cheating on their partner; or it could be organizational in nature, such as when a high school principal removes a teacher for inappropriate conduct. In whatever for the crisis appears, the most accurate way for you to know whether it is, in fact, a crisis is to apply one very simple test:

Is there something that is putting you or your organization's trust at risk with those very audiences—be they shareholders, consumers, your spouse, or your superior—whose trust you must maintain to be able to survive and thrive?

Simply put, *crisis is everywhere and impacts everyone,* whether you are big or small, established or less established, powerful or not so powerful. Crisis is a constant state of nature in our Information Age. And in the modern spin cycle, whether you are a business protecting a brand, a public figure guarding your image, or that guy in the cubicle defending your reputation, *if you do not fight back—even after a short, nasty, or brutish experience—you will no longer have your brand, your image, or your reputation.*

Successfully fighting back—whether it is fending off a national story or your neighborhood blogger—involves the application of a set of basic principles of crisis survival coupled with the execution of field-tested tactics.

This is the survival of the fittest.

This is the black art of damage control.

And this is what we do.

For more than twenty years, Chris Lehane and Mark Fabiani have manned the frontlines of scandal patrol. In the 1990s, the two of us helped lead a team of lawyers who were responsible for representing President Bill Clinton, First Lady Hillary Rodham Clinton, and the White House on various scandals related to Ken Starr's investigation of the president. During that time we became publicly known as the "Masters of Disaster." Since leaving the White House in 2000, our crisis communications firm, Fabiani & Lehane, has represented global Fortune 500 companies, high-profile CEOs, elected officials, celebrities, and athletes.

Our partner in this, Bill Guttentag, a lecturer at the Stanford University Graduate School of Business, comes from the journalism side of the damage control house. Bill is a filmmaker who has made films and television programs for ABC News, HBO, NBC, CBS, PBS, and others. He has worked with multiple national network news anchors and has won two Oscars, three Emmys, a Peabody Award, and other awards. And he's spent enough time inside the networks and other media to know what works in deflecting a crisis and what throws gas on the fire.

When we began to write this book in June 2011, the United States experienced a month that saw record-high temperatures, matched only by what seemed like a record-high number of breaking scandals—from Congressman Anthony Weiner's salacious tweets to teenagers and a porn star and revelations about Arnold Schwarzenegger's love child, to French political star Dominique Strauss-Kahn's being charged with sexually assaulting a New York City hotel maid.

And then things *really* heated up and July brought even hotter temperatures and even more scandals—from News Corporation's British cell phone hacking scandal; to a high-stakes fight over the debt ceiling that roiled the markets; to an Oregon congressman with an odd penchant for dressing up in a tiger suit who admitted to a having sex with the teenage daughter of one of his fundraisers.

In reality, while the sizzling summer temperatures were indeed at record levels, the skyrocketing scandal meter was merely reflecting that, in the times in which we live:

Crises have become the normal state of nature.

In fact, to illustrate this point, you just have to look back to the previous summer, where you would be reminded of another set of crises: the BP explosion; WikiLeaks; the Greek banking crisis; Toyota's recall; NPR's firing of Juan Williams; a sex scandal within the Vatican; Google pulling out of China; the Ground Zero Mosque imbroglio; the Icelandic ash cloud grounding international air travel; and the Chilean mine workers rescue—to name a few.

And, whenever you are reading this book, we are confident that even a cursory glance at the daily news will reveal a whole new series of scandals erupting. Scandal is an endlessly self-renewing resource.

Our hope is that this book will serve as a manual both to help you understand why crisis is a state of nature and, more importantly, to help prepare you to *manage* the crisis—whether it is national news or news in your neighborhood.

And the first step to managing a crisis is understanding the five fundamental elements responsible for why a state of crisis has become the new normal.

ONE
CRISIS AS A STATE OF NATURE

IN OUR AGE, SCANDALS ARE LINED UP LIKE PLANES CIRCLING TO LAND AT NEW YORK'S
La Guardia airport at rush hour, raising the question: Why is it that crisis is a
state of nature in the Information Age? The reality is, to err is human—and
that hasn't changed since Eve went for the apple and she and Adam were ban-
ished from the Garden of Eden.

Human behavior has not changed.

What has changed is that information is created, conveyed, and consumed
in a completely different way than it was a generation ago—or even a decade
ago. The five elements at work are: the vast proliferation of outlets communicating information, the light speed at which information moves, the erosion
of trust in the quality of the information received, the capacity of individuals
to selectively identify and leverage information, and the evolving communal
nature of information.

Moreover, the way in which information is created, conveyed, and consumed in this day and age means that scandal does not distinguish between
brand name or no name, national news or local gossip, a Fortune 500 company
or a mom-and-pop shop—when it comes to scandal, there is a level playing
field in how information moves, with perhaps the biggest difference being the
resources the big boys can throw at a challenge while the little guys are left to
fend for themselves.

THE PROLIFERATION OF OUTLETS—IF A TREE FALLS IN THE FOREST, IT DOES MATTER

On April 6, 2008, a little more than two weeks before Democratic primary voters were to go to the polls in Pennsylvania, Senator Barack Obama, who was

locked in a bitter and protracted campaign against Senator Hillary Rodham Clinton for the Democratic presidential nomination, hustled into what was thought to be a "closed press" fundraiser at a private home in San Francisco's elegant Pacific Heights neighborhood.

The then senator stood before the well-heeled wine-and-latte crowd and tried to explain the resentment of some small-town American voters, who at this point in the campaign had not yet fully warmed to his candidacy. The senator observed of the people of rural Pennsylvania:

> You go into these small towns in Pennsylvania and, like a lot of small towns in the Midwest, the jobs have been gone now for twenty-five years and noth-ing's replaced them. And they fell through the Clinton administration, and the Bush administration, and each successive administration has said that somehow these communities are gonna regenerate, and they have not. And it's not surprising then they get bitter, they cling to guns or religion or an-tipathy toward people who aren't like them, or anti-immigrant sentiment or anti-trade sentiment as a way to explain their frustrations.

Unbeknownst to our future president, his campaign staff, donors, and the professional press corps cooling their heels outside of the event, in the crowd was Mayhill Fowler, a sixty-one-year-old "citizen journalist" from across the bay in Oakland, who was a progressive, had a ticket, and was recording the speech on a small digital recorder. Fowler posted the transcript online shortly thereafter—and within days created a major crisis for the Obama campaign. In fact, this incident served as one of those defining moments for Obama that has contributed to the narrative that he has been dealing with ever since: of being perceived by some as an elitist.

And as Obama had a hidden recording crisis, so too did his 2012 op-ponent, Governor Mitt Romney. At a private $50,000 per person fundrais-ing dinner in Boca Raton, Florida, Romney was secretly filmed saying that his campaign would not try to appeal to 47 percent of the American public who he said paid no income taxes and are "dependent upon government, who believe that they are victims, who believe the government has a responsibil-ity to care for them. . . . And so my job is not to worry about those people. I'll never convince them they should take personal responsibility and care for their lives." The comments hit like a bombshell, generated an enormous amount of attention from the public and media, and produced widespread criticism across the political spectrum. The statements played into an existing narrative that many voters already believed about the candidate, and given what had happened four years earlier to his opponent at another closed door event, this secretly recorded video was an enormous and unforced tactical error in his campaign.

The bottom line is that even in a time when news organizations face serious financial challenges, there are still hundreds of television channels available through cable or satellite; a vast number of print outlets, from national and local newspapers to trade magazines covering the most specialized of subjects; and countless online platforms, including websites, blogs, Facebook pages, and Twitter feeds that have given *everyone* the tools to report news—all leading to the inescapable fact that there are no longer any real "closed press" events.

When coming up in politics, we were taught never to put anything in writing that you would not want to see on the front page of *The New York Times.* Well, today, you shouldn't say or do anything—*anything*—that you would not want to see boiled down to a 140-character tweet blasted for all the world to read.

In this era where anyone with a smartphone can break news, information can be just as easily communicated by professional reporters who have spent years perfecting their craft (and whose reporting is reviewed by multiple layers of editors) as by a citizen-journalist blogging from their back porch in their pajamas.

News still comes from conventional sources, such as a front-page *New York Times* investigative story by a prize-winning journalist exposing the depth of News Corporation's phone hacking in the United Kingdom. But it also comes from the ground up, as with George Allen, running for senator in Virginia, filmed at a campaign stop referring to an Indian American with the racist slur "macaca"—an event that helped doom his candidacy. Or it could be through the use of advanced technology, as was the case in the BP oil spill, when an underwater web camera documented the unending gush of oil spewing into the Gulf of Mexico.

Or it could be Mayhill Fowler and her digital recorder.

Today, it truly does matter if a tree falls in a forest.

And the result is that in today's media landscape *every* event, *every* comment, *every* activity is virtually guaranteed to be reported—with great potential for negative consequences.

SPEED KILLS

In 1992, the successful Clinton campaign was branded as cutting edge for the development and execution of the "War Room"—a room in Clinton's Little Rock campaign headquarters that was manned around the clock by caffeine-fueled twentysomethings who operated according to the new imperatives of rapid response: getting in front of the news, hitting back harder then you have been hit, and pre-butting the attack.

The Clinton campaign's fundamental insight was that there were at least three news cycles a day—morning, day, and night—and that a campaign could effectively shape the coverage of the evening news and morning papers by driving a story and a message through all these news cycles and beyond. No longer would information begin with the morning newspapers and end with the evening news.

In 1992, the Clinton campaign's War Room was considered so revolutionary that Hollywood even made a film of it. Today, the idea of *just* three news cycles a day would be akin to thinking that dial-up is the quickest way to surf online. We no longer have conventional news cycles but cycles within cycles within cycles, where platforms like Twitter, YouTube, blogs, and Facebook are akin to the small wheels of a clock that turn the bigger wheels.

Information moves at such a pace that the public makes decisions and takes actions before it is even known whether the information being disseminated is accurate—which on some level makes the ultimate accuracy irrelevant, as people have already acted on the perception. In 2008, Bear Stearns, Merrill Lynch, and Lehman Brothers suffered enormous consequences when information on the state of their finances sped around Wall Street at lightning speed, and the market moved on the information before they were able to effectively respond.

Just look at the velocity with which information moved throughout the Middle East during the Arab Spring. Many commentators and Middle East specialists observed that the spread of ideas and the capacity to organize were a direct function of the so-called liberation technology of Facebook and Twitter. The news traveled so quickly that the traditional state security organs, which had so successfully repressed dissent in the past, were overwhelmed. And the world witnessed a fundamental change—in some of these situations a tweet proved to be more powerful than an AK-47.

Marshall McLuhan—the visionary media theorist who saw long before others where the world was heading due to the proliferation of mass media—coined the term "global village," which conveyed the notion that modern communications were going to lead to the replacement of individual cultures with a collective identity, as the world began to receive the same information from the same sources at the same time (supplanting local customs and localized information sources). Well, today, the way information moves is producing a type of global village on speed, with a collective identity that is constantly being bombarded with still more new information.

The result is that information now moves at a dizzying rate; as a consequence, news can go around the world numerous times before you even have a chance to take a breath and figure out what is going on, whether it is accurate, and what you should say to deal with the story at hand.

And thus, *speed kills.*

SKEPTICISM MEETS CYNICISM—THE NEGATIVE FEEDBACK LOOP

I'm not a crook.

—President Richard Nixon, November 17, 1973

It is a crisis of confidence.

—President Jimmy Carter, July 15, 1979

Mistakes were made.

—President Ronald Reagan, January 27, 1987

Mission Accomplished

—Banner displayed during President George W.
Bush's aircraft carrier address, May 1, 2003

If one used each of the above defining presidential moments as part of a connect-the-dots drawing for children, it would produce an illustration vividly documenting the erosion of trust in the institution of the presidency. And what has happened with the presidency has also occurred with nearly all of society's traditional institutions. Over the past fifty years, beginning with America losing its innocence over Vietnam and continuing through Watergate, there has been a steady and relentless breakdown of public trust in the nation's political leaders, business sector, churches, and press. The historic gatekeepers—the esteemed institutions to which society looked to be its arbiters of disputes—have lost their credibility and no longer hold sway over the public in the way they once did, when they were looked to as impartial umpires who would fairly and accurately call balls and strikes.

Moreover, as the United States was rocked by a series of major events that were covered in vastly different ways—whether it was the 2000 presidential election recount, 9/11, Iraq and weapons of mass destruction, or the 2008 financial meltdown—the nature of the coverage has been growing more skeptical, and the public's perception of the information they are receiving has become far more cynical.

Stan Greenberg, a leading Democratic pollster, has written about how voters today have grown "estranged from government," as the public increasingly distrusts the government's ability to deliver on its promises. Similarly, over the last twelve years the global public relations giant Edelman has tracked levels of trust across key sectors of society, including business and governments, in the United States and internationally. In its annual global survey, the Edelman Trust Barometer, the firm has documented stunningly low levels of trust across nearly all sectors.

What is especially problematic about the low levels of trust is that they come at a time when the public believes we are on the wrong track and wants some answers—but simply does not have faith in the ability of the traditional gatekeepers of society to solve these problems. And this only reinforces the skepticism of those reporting and spreading the news, such as the mainstream press or social media, and so the cynicism by which it is consumed by the broader public swells.

This cycle, of skeptics reporting skeptically to a cynical audience that consumes the information cynically, perpetuates itself—and deepens the skepticism and cynicism by creating an enormous feedback loop of distrust.

Speaking about U.S.-Soviet arms treaties, President Ronald Reagan used the Russian phrase *doverai, no proverai*—trust, but verify.

Nowadays, reporting—across the spectrum of how news is delivered— starts off without trust, and the public in turn seeks out information to confirm their distrust of our leaders and institutions. And the cycle repeats.

LEVERAGED INFORMATION, SELECTED SOURCES—TUNE IN, SEARCH IN, OPT OUT

Let's go all the way back to the summer of 1995.

At the time, we were working at the White House and began to increasingly receive calls from mainstream media outlets asking us to respond to various bizarre items related to the late Vince Foster, a lawyer in the White House counsel's office who had tragically taken his own life in the summer of 1993. At first, we ignored the calls, as there was nothing to the story beyond the terrible loss of one of the president and first lady's friends. However, as the calls continued without letup, and the nature of the questions became even more bizarre—to the point where we were asked to comment on alleged eyewitness sightings of Foster—we knew we had to get to the heart of the matter and began asking the reporters the basis for their questions.

All roads led to a mysterious source—the newly exploding Internet.

One Saturday morning in the midst of an oppressively hot D.C. summer weekend, we found ourselves squirreled away in a stuffy room on the fourth floor of the Old Executive Office Building, where there was a bank of computers from which you could access the "World Wide Web." Eight hours later, we emerged from our warren having seemingly been transported to a parallel universe. Online we found early versions of chat rooms, postings, and other information showing there was an entire cottage industry devoted to discussing conspiracy theories relating to the death of Vince Foster, including numerous online reports of people claiming to have seen him, followed by self-identified news sources that at the time most Americans had never heard of—conservative outlets such as Eagle Publishing's *Human Events* or Richard Mellon Scaife's the *Pittsburgh Tribune-Review*—to right-leaning outlets we were familiar with, such as the *New York Post, The Washington Times,* and the editorial pages of *The Wall Street Journal*—and from there to traditional news reports.

What we learned in those eight hours became the basis for a 332-page report we authored shortly thereafter that documented how various right-wing conspiracy theories against the Clintons moved from fringe Internet sites into conservative publications, and then journeyed from there into mainstream outlets. The document was created so that we could provide the information to reporters asking us about Foster and other related questions, journalists who at the time were even more ignorant of the World Wide Web than we were.

What the eight hours in the White House's computer room in 1995 tipped us off to was that the world was moving to a place where the public could use the power of technology to actively seek out information and leverage it—and they could selectively determine where they could go for their information.

Now, of course, this technology has spread to where anyone with a Wi-Fi connection is able to select from whom, how, where, and when they receive information and then leverage that information. News no longer comes from

three networks and the morning paper, but from tens of thousands of potential sources. By using Google, Bing, or another search engine, it is possible to
instantaneously seek information and swiftly make decisions based on sources
the user selects. People can and do opt out of receiving information from
specific media outlets, while opting in to others. In fact, the Edelman Trust
Barometer recently found trust in information conveyed through self-selected
social media sites—social networking sites, content-sharing platforms, blogs,
and micro-blogs—actually surged 75 percent.

This opt in/opt out dynamic has resulted in the fragmentation of information whereby large segments of the population can believe in completely
ungrounded conspiracy theories—such as that President Obama was not born
in the United States—despite a massive trove of assiduously documented evidence to the contrary.

Moreover, the fragmentation of information and what the public trusts to
be accurate are presented against a backdrop of a fragmentation in where we
physically live (at least in the United States). As detailed by former columnist
Bill Bishop and sociologist Robert Cushing in their 2008 book *The Big Sort*,
and subsequently reported on by *The New York Times*, America has become
a nation that self-segregates. According to Bishop, people self-select "their
neighborhoods and their churches, to be around others who live like they do
and think like they do—and, every four years, vote like they do."

To make this point, Bishop determined that in the 1976 presidential election, where the Democrats squeaked out a victory with 50.1 percent of the vote,
26.8 percent of people lived in so-called landslide counties, where the voters
voted for either the Democratic nominee (Jimmy Carter) or the Republican
nominee (Gerald Ford) by 20 percent or more. In the 2000 election where Al
Gore won the popular vote by 543,895 votes, 45.3 percent of the public lived
in landslide counties. And in 2008, which was a landslide victory for President
Obama, more than 47 percent of the country resided in landslide counties.

We indeed live in a red and blue America—as much by neighborhood
as by state. And in these different neighborhoods the public consumes information from vastly different news sources. Just watch Fox News and MSNBC
cover the same political story—you don't need a sociology degree to understand that the self-selection of information is a very real phenomenon.

A generation ago, we had "tune in, turn on, drop out." Today, we have
"tune out, search in, opt out." You get the information you want and rarely
have to hear a dissenting voice.

THE COMMUNITY NATURE OF INFORMATION—YELP VERSUS ZAGAT

We travel a great deal. And we all enjoy a good meal (we especially enjoy a good and expensive meal when Mark is springing). In our view, there is no better way to cap a good day's work of damage control than with fine food complimented by an appropriate libation. And when we first began a life where we spent too much time getting on and off planes, we would typically turn to a Zagat guide, or seek the counsel of a concierge to help us pick a restaurant. We all had friends, especially in places like New York City, who considered their Zagat book to be amongst their most precious reading possessions and who welcomed each year's new edition as if they were bring home a new baby.

Today, Zagat is looking for ways to just survive. Why? One world: Yelp. Yelp, the user-generated restaurant-and-more guide has quickly supplanted Zagat through the use of crowdsourcing—creating a view of a particular place through the aggregating of many reviews by a vast army of citizen reviewers.

The community-based nature of information has altered how information is created, moved, and shared. We have gone from passively sitting in our living rooms and watching TV, or driving in our car and listening to the radio, to interactively engaging with information as activists. Instead of reading a newspaper story reflecting someone else's reporting, we can blog our own reflections.

Rather than just digesting the opinions of the talking-head so-called experts, we blast out our own opinions on web chats or in tweets.

As opposed to watching the six-second sound bytes cable TV gives us, we create and share self-produced YouTube videos—over four billion YouTube videos a day are viewed. And over sixty hours of new video is uploaded onto YouTube every minute.

Just a few years ago, political campaigns sought families watching a thirty-second spot on the living room Zenith. Today, we have meet-ups, flash mobs, and tweet-ups.

Not only do we tweet. We re-tweet.

We go to the crowdsourced Wikipedia as our first stop for information on anything and everything.

Given that there are far more eyeballs on Twitter than *The New York Times*, *The Washington Post*, and *The Wall Street Journal* combined, a 140-character tweet can be more powerful than what is on the front page of a major national newspaper.

The number of Facebook users is approaching a billion (one in seven of everyone on earth), and as discussed, the role the platform played as liberation technology in the Arab Spring showed just how powerful social media has become. While it has been debated for years whether the pen is indeed mightier than the sword, social media has proven that it has the power to help knock down the most entrenched of despots, no matter how many troops they had under their control.

And when we have worked up an appetite with all of this tweeting, retweeting, and blogging, we go to our smartphone to find a restaurant by clicking on our Yelp app. It works.

And managing this can be our greatest problem and our greatest asset.

THE THREE PRINCIPLES OF SURVIVAL

Building from a foundational understanding of the above elements, we now wish to present the Three Principles of Survival, which will determine whether or not one survives in such a threatening environment:

1. Do No Harm
2. Take a Disciplined Approach
3. Preserve Your Credibility

We will then provide a prescriptive, step-by-step operational approach to managing one's way through a crisis. In our Ten Commandments of Damage Control we will explore specific rules as they relate to key aspects of successfully mastering a disaster.

This is the art of damage control.

For each of these Ten Commandments of Damage Control, we will provide case studies of those who have not mastered the art of damage control and those who have, focusing on examples of how the commandments were successfully applied.

By considering, analyzing, and reviewing these commandments, an elected official or voter, a CEO or board member, a professional ballplayer or fan, a nonprofit or contributor, a small business or customer, a publicly traded company or shareholder, a philanthropy or donor, a neighborhood restaurant or patron—or any other person or entity caught in the vortex of a crisis—will be able to plan accordingly and survive.

Many of the cases in the chapters ahead represent situations in which we had some involvement. Some involve nationally known, high-profile crises, while others feature smaller, more local matters. Through the prism of the case studies we hope to show a crisis is often a make-or-break moment for the afflicted individual or organization and must be addressed.

Simply put, as a general proposition, the failure to honor the principles of survival or apply these commandments of damage control will translate into the failure to master a disaster.

A crisis is like a knife fight in a telephone booth. And to come out on top, you will need to become your own Master of Disaster when it comes to the art of damage control.

We'll help you learn what it takes to win.

PART II
IT'S A MATTER OF LIFE OR DEATH
THE PRINCIPLES OF SURVIVAL

TWO
STOP DIGGING

THE MISSION OF DAMAGE CONTROL—RESTORE TRUST

In the years since the book and movie *All the President's Men* portrayed the events leading to President Richard Nixon resigning in disgrace for participating in the cover-up of a "second-rate burglary," it seems far more attention has been paid to the identity of the writers' secret source, Deep Throat, than to the overarching lesson of Watergate, namely:

It's not the crime, it's the cover-up.

President Nixon was ultimately forced from office because the actions he took after the break-in of the Democratic National Committee headquarters at the Watergate Hotel led the American people to lose their basic trust in him. His participation in the cover-up confirmed the public's long-held suspicions—as exemplified by his nickname, "Tricky Dick."

And while the Watergate-era phrase "it's not the crime, it's the cover up" has seeped into the American lexicon, its *true* meaning seems to continue to elude the public consciousness—or at least people lose sight of it when facing their own crises.

Time and time again, whether it is the most powerful man in the world engaging in illegal actions to cover-up the Watergate break-in or the guy in the cubicle down the hall who just mistakenly hit "reply all" in an email castigating his employer and then curling up in the fetal position under his desk, individuals, businesses, and organizations far too often make basic mistakes of both commission and omission in their immediate response to a crisis. These actions only serve to further erode trust at the very moment when everything you do needs to be about one crucial question: *How do you go about restoring trust?*

As seen in the preceding chapter, the mission to restore trust is made much more challenging given our current information ecosystem. The burgeoning number of news outlets, online sites, and social media platforms guarantee that everything gets covered in some form or fashion; the speed in which information moves is a game changer; and we live in an era of enormous public distrust, where the burden of proof is higher than ever.

Watergate and its aftermath offers a stark lesson in what the mission of damage control is truly all about: When you find yourself in a hole—*you need to stop digging and start restoring the public trust.*

The reality of life in the Information Age is that:

- To err *is* human.
- Mistakes *are* made.
- Crises *do* happen.

Sooner or later, you *will* find yourself in a deep hole that you can't dig yourself out of through more spin.

When you land in such a hole, you must drop your shovel, *stop digging,* and start figuring out how you are going to climb out of the hole.

Simply put, you are *not* going to be able to put the genie back in the bottle, the oil back in the ruptured pipeline, the steroids back in the syringe, or the tweet back in your Twitter account.

You have to understand that what went wrong cannot be corrected with the wave of a wand, which is why you will be evaluated not just on the basis of the crisis itself but, in particular, on *how* you respond to the crisis *after* it has happened.

Your response to the crisis must demonstrate that going forward, despite the crisis, you can be trusted.

Therefore, when responding to a crisis, the *mission* is to *restore trust.*

The *response* to the crisis is what is known as *crisis management.*

The *tale of what you do* to manage the crisis—and, in particular, how fairly you are treated going forward by those audiences who will be judging you—is called *damage control.*

The operational steps you must execute in pursuit of the mission of restoring trust are what we call the Ten Commandments of Damage Control.

However, before you can most effectively use the operational guide section of this book, it is vital to understand three principles that govern the Ten

Commandments. These guiding principles of damage control do not exist in isolation. They are complementary, with one building upon the others. These principles are the foundational blocks upon which all of the Ten Commandments of Damage Control are built. Therefore, to apply the Ten Commandments, you first must understand these three principles:

1. Do No Harm
2. Take a Disciplined Approach
3. Preserve Your Credibility

THREE
DO NO HARM

ONE OF OUR ALL-TIME FAVORITE MOVIE SCENES OCCURS IN QUENTIN TARANTINO'S *Pulp Fiction,* where Harvey Keitel's character Winston Wolf, the mob equivalent of a crisis management consultant, is brought in to help two hit men, John Travolta's Vince Vega and Samuel L. Jackson's Bible-quoting Jules Winnfield, dispose of the body of the college drug dealer they inadvertently shot in their car.

The tuxedo-wearing, coffee-drinking man called "The Wolf" calmly, self-assuredly, and clinically advises the two hit men to clean up the car, put the body in the trunk, and follow him to a junkyard disposal site, collecting a well-earned consulting fee for his damage control expertise:

THE WOLF: Now boys, listen up. We're going to a place called Monster Joe's Truck and Tow. I'll drive the tainted car. Jules, you ride with me. Vincent, you follow in my Acura. We run across the path of any John Q. Laws, nobody does a fucking thing unless I do it first. What did I just say?

JULES: Don't do shit unless.

THE WOLF: Unless what?

JULES: Unless you do it first.

THE WOLF: Spoken like a true prodigy.

The genius of employing the character of The Wolf is that it is a spoof of consultants, and as good satire it is based on getting at a central truth and then going just a little further. The truth here relates to the damage control imperative of not engaging in action that is going to make a bad situation worse (with the over-the-top element being it is damage-control counsel being dispensed by criminals for criminals).

Like the Victorian-era physicians whose prescriptions of bloodletting doomed their patients far more than the ailment they were being treated for, all too often, the initial crisis response from the modern spin doctor results in *imperiling* the fundamental issue of trust—the opposite direction you need to go—and frequently ends up being a bigger challenge than the actual crisis that precipitated the response.

Therefore, the first principle of damage control—the crisis management expert's equivalent of the physician's Hippocratic Oath—Do No Harm.

Time after time, those who find themselves in a hole not only do not stop digging—they take actions that are the equivalent of calling in the backhoe so they can dig an even deeper hole for themselves.

In the immediate moment of a crisis, this Do No Harm principle is typically undermined in one of three ways:

1. It wilts under the inevitable extreme external and internal pressures to *chase the story* and provide an instant response that proves to be unsustainable and detrimental.
2. It's overrun by the instinctive reflex to *spin the story* in the best possible way.
3. It succumbs to the desire to *lay the blame on others.*

DON'T CHASE THE STORY

The most common way in which the Do No Harm principle is put at risk is when one reacts to the intense heat they are feeling from internal and/or external audiences to address the breaking story and issues a response that does not prove to be tenable over the long run. In other words, to avoid more harm, *don't chase the story.*

Depending on your situation, the pressures to respond could be felt any number of ways.

It could be the press, investors, and lenders banging away for information as short sellers celebrate a run of your company, and your firm feels obligated to release information that only serves to accelerate the run—as Bear Stearns experienced in March 2008.

It could be a business owner who responds to a poor Yelp review by attacking the customer and creating even more negative coverage—as a New York City dentist did when she sued a patient for writing a negative review on Yelp.

It could be subpoenas arriving as if they were holiday cards in December, lawsuits piling up like leaves in autumn, and corporate officials suggesting that employees should erase emails—which only serves to increase the company's legal exposure.

The impulse is to extinguish the fire before it gets out of control, but it is critical to understand that releasing inaccurate or incomplete information is akin to throwing more fuel on the fire.

When you are in the throes of a crisis it is critical to remember: *It is not about winning the battle of the news cycle, it is about winning the war of the news story*—and the war of the news story is won by rebuilding trust.

Chasing the news is a futile effort, because in this day and age you simply *will not* catch the news—rather, given the nature of a crisis situation, where one most likely does not have a complete grasp of all the facts or is not in a position to provide a comprehensive response, it is more likely that you will release information that will turn out to be inaccurate or counterproductive. Audiences are looking for information they can trust, and a hurried and inadequate response in the face of external or internal pressures will, in fact, *erode* trust.

Consider the case of former New York congressman Anthony Weiner and his infamous tweets to at least six women, which included the posting of close-up photos of him in his Jockey underwear, from the waist down and knees up.

Given that Weiner was a young congressional star, a New York City mayoral front-runner, and a ubiquitous cable talk show presence in Washington, D.C., when news first broke over a weekend, "Weinergate" initiated a feeding frenzy involving the press corps of both cities. The dynamic was akin to two pit bulls pulling on the congressman from opposite ends, and over the course of the weekend the media pressure built to a fever pitch. There were endless loops of the changing story on cable TV; the networks did segments; the New York tabloids were in full scandal mode; and online political sites from Politico to Drudge Report provided virtual real-time reporting.

Everyone recognized that there were three basic questions that needed to be addressed:

1. Were those indeed photos of him?
2. Did he tweet the photos?
3. If they were photos of him that he indeed tweeted, did he have any physical contact with the women?

If the answer was "no" to all of these questions, the congressman needed to be cleared.

If the answer was "yes" to questions one and two and "no" to question three, he needed to offer an abject apology and be able to draw the line between questions one and two and question three.

And, if the answer was "yes" to all three, he needed to apologize and evaluate whether he should remain in office.

The congressman, in a futile effort to chase the successive waves of news cycles, issued a series of curious statements that only became more curious as additional information surfaced and raised even more questions than they answered, including:

- "I can't say with certainty very much about where the photograph came from." (Reported in *The New York Times.*)
- "Tivo shot. FB hacked. Is my blender gonna attack me next?" (Tweet.)
- "The wiener gags never get old, I guess." (An email to a reporter for Politico.)
- "Anthony's accounts were obviously hacked." (Statement from Weiner's congressional office.)

Ultimately, Weiner went on CNN and sat down with the network's Washington, D.C., eminence gris, Wolf Blitzer, and categorically denied sending the tweets to the women and intimated that perhaps someone had hacked into his various accounts and, presumably, misappropriated private material (Weiner went as far as retaining a lawyer to investigate the alleged hacking). And, predictably, this response was shredded in subsequent news cycles as more and more women went public with their tweets. Even his friend *The Daily Show* host Jon Stewart weighed in with the memorable quote, "I'm not certain about a lot of things. But there are three things in this world I do have certitude on: *Empire Strikes Back* is the best *Star Wars* movie. O.J. killed those two people. And the third one is what my erect penis looks like in my own underwear, from a bird's-eye view."

The congressman, under attack from the leadership in his own party, other prominent Democratic officials, the press corps in two cities worked into a frothing frenzy, and voters in his district upset *over his misrepresentations as much as the tweets themselves,* had little choice but to resign from office.

And while this was a highly embarrassing situation, given that he purportedly did not actually have any physical contact with the women in receipt of his "brief" tweets, had Congressman Weiner not attempted to chase the news cycle, which led to the issuing of misleading and, ultimately, inaccurate representations, Weinergate would have been a survivable crisis. But the former star politician had a spectacular fall. After twelve years in Congress, less than three weeks after the first tweets appeared, Congressman Weiner faced the cameras and an army of media at a massive press conference and resigned from office.

An abject apology along with the acceptance of full responsibility in the opening days of the crisis—even if multiple news cycles went by before it was provided—would have afforded Congressman Weiner the best shot at remaining in Congress.

Instead, by *chasing the story*, he put out inaccurate information that did even more harm and, in doing so, lost the war for control of the story. And he lost his seat in Congress.

YOU DON'T WIN THROUGH SPIN

The second most common way in which the Do No Harm principle is violated is a function of the very human instinct to try to put the best face on a bad situation, which results in an effort to spin the story in the most favorable way possible by highlighting exculpatory information, while simultaneously not disclosing the more problematic facts. It may feel natural—but it is far from the right strategy. Simply put: *You don't win through spin.*

Further reinforcing this rapid response reflex is the prevailing communications philosophy and related communications systems infrastructure that puts a premium value on rapid response.

Whether it is a political campaign, a CEO under fire or, a corporate branding campaign—in this era of Twitter trend lines, viral videos, Facebook postings, and micro-blogs, everyone is educated on the need for speed, but some confuse speed with efficacy.

In fact, this need-for-speed dictum translates into a *Guns of August*–type crisis management dynamic where organizations automatically spring into action the moment they believe that are about to be fired upon, regardless of whether it makes strategic sense. Racing into the fray are war-room staffs of PR professionals eager to demonstrate their worth, platoons of social media bloggers and tweeters with itchy fingers, and the professional spin doctors ready to speak on your behalf. All of these tactical assets are focused on playing a game of Whac-A-Mole, where their very function is to respond to every issue that pops up with an instantaneous mallet blow.

And like a boomerang version of the law of conservation, which states that every action prompts a reaction of equal energy, each and every one of these spin actions often leads to a *reaction*—aimed right back at your head and typically with more force than the initial action.

Thus, be warned:

- If you seek to sweep the incident under the rug by downplaying the seriousness of the issue, when the "rest of the story" becomes public, whatever you failed to release, no matter how minor, takes on a much larger significance.
- If you offer up an explanation designed to put on the best face by self-selecting what information you release, you will be hit with accusations of engaging in a cover-up once the less exculpatory information is discovered.
- If you avoid accountability by offering excuses, once the excuses become riddled by scrutiny, it will make it *more* likely, not less likely, that you will be removed from your position.

And, given that a crisis can often involve legal exposure, each of the courses of action in these examples would only serve to increase your legal exposure.

Over the years, we have repeatedly seen the basic patterns play out in situations like the following:

- The call from the general counsel of a publicly traded company involving the issuance of back-dated options to a CEO, after the company releases a statement asserting that the compensation was approved with the full knowledge of the Board, a claim that turns out not to be entirely supported by the actual board-meeting minutes.
- The call from a sports agent involving a failed drug test by a professional athlete who has already vehemently proclaimed via Twitter his innocence, citing a prescription drug that he was prescribed, which turns out to be a women's fertility drug.
- The call from a campaign manager involving an elected official's relationship with someone other than his spouse, after an outright denial has already been issued to the reporter investigating the story—who inconveniently has proof of the affair.

In the moments after a crisis hits, it is very unlikely that you can ever be in a position to understand what has truly happened, be in possession of all the facts, appreciate the motives of all the parties, or be able to ascertain variables of which that you may not even be aware.

Even in a situation where you *think* you have all the answers, it is usually the case that you *do not*.

Any answer you provide is going to be poked and prodded by the audiences you care about with an extraordinary level of scrutiny. And the slightest discrepancy will be seized upon and magnified. To be brutally frank, any response you provide will be examined with the rigor of a colonoscopy—without anesthesia.

At this moment, you need to ditch the spin—and focus on counter-spin. Communicating in a way that makes it clear you are not engaged in spin will help rebuild trust.

Instead of emphasizing the positive and de-emphasizing the negative, recognize the value of transparency.

Rather than releasing self-selected information to the public, commit to openness when you have information that is ready to be released.

As opposed to blanket denials, make clear that you are fully cooperating with any inquiry.

Unless you are in a position where you can proffer an explanation with the absolute certitude that it will be sustainable, it is almost always better to remember that less can be more when it comes to providing the initial explanation. This is because less information that is accurate is going to do far more good in addressing trust issues over the long haul than an in-depth answer that looks good on paper but does not hold up under the inevitable close scrutiny ahead.

The bottom line is that you simply cannot allow the pressure of the situation to lead to spin that does more harm than good.

We cannot even begin to count the number of times where we have been retained by a large corporation, high-profile individual, or major organization facing a crisis, where the introductory meeting begins with a proud walk through their "war room"—typically adorned with clocks for multiple time zones; a bank of television sets tuned to different cable channels; cutting-edge communications equipment allowing the principals from the far-flung corners of the nation or world to talk with one another; and massive screens featuring websites, Twitter accounts, and YouTube channels—but those in charge have no understanding that what they need to do first is *nothing*—unless it is designed to accomplish the strategic mission of restoring trust.

We want to be clear: These communication tools can be enormously powerful in servicing and supporting the communication of information and ought to be deployed—but *only* when you have absolute confidence that the information you intend to disseminate on these platforms is consistent with restoring trust.

One of the more recent and high-profile examples of the failure to understand that you cannot win through spin was evident in BP's crisis management approach to the 2010 Gulf Coast oil spill.

It is nearly certain that a company of BP's size that operated in the high-risk business of oil exploration and had experienced various crises in the past—from a 2005 refinery explosion in Texas City, Texas, to a 2008 pipeline explosion in Prudhoe Bay of Alaska—must have spent significant time considering the damage control approach it would pursue in response to a possible explosion of one of the company's offshore oil drilling platforms.

And on April 20, 2010, when the Deepwater Horizon oil drilling platform in the Gulf of Mexico exploded, BP indeed appeared ready with a plan. In the days and weeks following the explosion BP moved into a rapid response mode: They created a tag line ("We will make this right"); posted significant website content; launched a Twitter account; flooded the zone with online advertising to impact search engine results; and even established an underwater web camera, providing a live feed of the oil spewing forth from the ruptured pipe.

And through multiple communications response tools, BP's CEO, Tony Haywood, began issuing regular, positive statements about the actions BP was taking to cap the spill and downplaying characterizations of the environmental impact of the disaster.

In particular, the company under Haywood made what proved to be overly optimistic predictions on its ability to contain the spill, including a failed effort to repair the blowout preventer with a robotic submarine, a failed effort to cap the spill with a containment dome, and then a failure, after indicating it was having "some success," with its so-called top kill approach (involving heavy liquids and cement to seal the leak).

Then, in contrast to what everyone else was seeing, Haywood blithley asserted that the damage would be limited, claiming "the environmental impact of this disaster is likely to have been very, very modest" and that "the Gulf of Mexico is a very big ocean. The amount of volume of oil and dispersant we are putting into it is tiny in relation to the total water volume."

But the oil continued to flow, doing enormous harm to the Gulf and the communities that depended on the Gulf for their livelihoods. And as each statement issued by BP crumbled upon itself, the webcam continued to show oil spewing unabated into the Gulf. (BP's own webcam soon became part of a citizen-journalist-produced split-screen video that showed the amount of oil BP said was spilled that day compared to what the webcam actually revealed was being released.) BP's damage control only increased the harm the company was doing to itself. And the company's tactics led to the erosion of trust.

While BP had virtually unlimited funds as well as the full menu of twenty-first-century cutting-edge communications tactics and tools, it was lacking a fundamental understanding that spin alone cannot build trust—and that spin that is not accurate can, in fact, do far more harm than good.

DON'T LAY THE BLAME ON OTHERS

The third way in which the Do No Harm principle is typically challenged is when the party at the center of the crisis appears to *lay the blame on others,* which frequently backfires and in a variety of ways—all of which do additional harm.

If you choose to play the blame game:

- You inflict harm on yourself by trying to duck whatever role you may have had.
- You lose the opportunity to be perceived as honest by dodging the need to be perceived as accountable.
- And you inevitably end up picking a fight with whomever you blamed.

Above and beyond the fact that throwing an individual under the bus undermines your crucial ability to rebuild trust, this move can lead to picking a fight that you cannot win. The person you blamed has nothing to lose in turning the tables on you. It's like picking a fight in a pub with the crazy-looking guy drumming his hands on the corner of the bar—rarely a good idea.

Absent some pre-arranged separation agreement (usually, a generous severance package) or dead to rights proof (such as the YouTube video of Dominos employees putting nasal mucus on sandwiches they were preparing), the person who is being let go has every incentive to fight back and often nothing to lose—where as you have a lot more to lose.

In such a scenario, the disgruntled employee can also raise questions on what you knew and when did you know it. They can also work with investigative entities, from law enforcement to reporters—without you having any knowledge of what they actually know, and what accusations they are making behind closed doors.

And they can become a lasting thorn in your side going forward—complicating your efforts to rebuild trust. They will forever be questioning, disputing, and contradicting information you are putting out or actions you are taking. All of which is antithetical to your goals.

They can become a debilitating nuisance like Frank Bailey, the former aide to then Alaska governor Sarah Palin. Bailey was put on administrative leave from his state government post in 2008 and went on to blast Palin in a tell-all book.

They can become a highly motivated chief witness against you, like Victor Conte, the founder of the San Francisco Bay Area Balco Laboratory, which provided performance-enhancing drugs to professional athletes, and who became a prime source of information in the wide-ranging Balco investigation, which involved Barry Bonds and other star athletes.

They can be a legitimate whistleblower like Sherron Watkins, whose actions helped expose the Enron scandal.

And these are all fights being picked at the moment you are least prepared to fight.

As the person in the eye of the media storm, you are the most vulnerable; there is typically far greater public interest in what drugs Barry Bonds did or did not use than in why Victor Conte is dishing on him.

And you are extremely exposed because when government oversight bodies are investigating a publicly owned company for wrongdoing, regardless of any assertions designed to question a whistleblower's motives, the government and the public have good reasons to want to hear from the person making the charges.

Simply put, *you will lose* this fight, even in cases where the individual retaliating is far from legitimate, because you simply do not have a necessary reservoir of trust with which you can fight back.

Thus, in order to minimize your harm, instead of pointing fingers it's crucial to guard against *Laying the Blame on Others*.

But also, it's very possible that as part of rebuilding trust—and because real fault does often lie with specific individuals—you will have to hold people fully accountable for their role in what happened. This can necessitate demoting, suspending, or firing people involved. However, these actions require that:

- *You are clear in admitting an organization-wide mistake,* as Coca-Cola did when it turned lemons into lemonade by swiftly recognizing the error it had made with introducing New Coke, publicly acknowledging the mistake, and turning the entire situation into a new opportunity to market its products.
- *The top of the organization takes personal responsibility in a meaningful way,* as reflected by Citibank CEO Vikram Pandit's pledge in the wake of an economic meltdown that he would only accept $1 in annual salary until the bank returned to profitability.
- *You make clear that a company is taking actions designed to put the best interests of its customers first, above all else,* which is exactly what Odwalla did in addressing the *E. coli* contamination of its drinks in 1996 by owning up to the problem relatively quickly, cooperating openly and fully with government authorities, and thoroughly explaining what it was going to do to prevent such problems in the future.
- *You initiate a credible review process to understand how a company took a wrong direction (ideally, with all or some portion of the review being made widely available to explain and contextualize),* which is what Nike did at the direction of its founder Phil Knight in the form of a 2001 "corporate responsibility report," following harsh criticism of the company's off-shore labor practices, and in which Nike admitted that it "blew it" when it came to employing children in third-world countries.
- *You do not shirk from a crisis but step in aggressively to take charge of a situation and hold yourself out as the accountable party to solve the problem,* as Chile's President Sebastián Piñera did in taking immediate control of the rescue operations for trapped miners. The president's focus was constantly forward looking and he communicated regularly with the media on the efforts underway and the innovative approaches being taken (including working with NASA). Not only was the rescue successful, but there was relatively little focus during

the crisis on the failures in government regulation that might have contributed to the crisis in the first place.

- *You take specific, detailed, sound, prophylactic actions based on internal investigations designed to make sure the problem does not happen again.* This is what the National Football League has managed many times over the years. They have turned the traditional rule that little good usually comes from investigating yourself (an investigation that will be seen by many as simply not credible) on its head. The NFL has succeeded where most fail because in most cases it acts very quickly in response to damaging revelations and is able to rely on the tremendous credibility of the NFL commissioner. As a result of aggressively holding itself accountable, the NFL has been able to deal successfully with issues such as performance-enhancing drugs, teams spying on one another, player bounties for injuring opponents, and off-the-field misconduct.

Following these approaches will provide a bulwark against judging too quickly and accusing too soon, and allow you to hold both the organization and specific individuals responsible in a manner that will contribute to the rebuilding of trust.

Some of the most powerful and profitable companies in the world fail to heed these lessons. James Murdoch's 2011 testimony before the British Parliament on the hacking of cell phones by the News Corporation–owned *News of the World* tabloid was a textbook case of the perils of being too quick to judge and too soon to accuse.

Murdoch's testimony effectively laid the blame on a number of *News of the World* executives, including the paper's former editor Colin Myler and former legal advisor Tom Crone. Not surprisingly, these officials—out of their jobs and purportedly irate at being pointed to publicly by a boss who appeared to be seeking to absolve himself of any wrong-doing whatsoever—subsequently provided highly damaging testimony against Murdoch.

As a result, Murdoch found himself embroiled in subsequent investigations for his testimony before Parliament and had to resign from the Board of News International. By seeking to *blame others*, Murdoch certainly did himself more harm than good.

In your quest to manage the crisis and come out ahead, never lose sight of the principle of Do No Harm. As the email, tweets, and calls are all flying, keep your focus on the three crucial parts of the principle:

1. Don't chase the story and provide an instant response that proves to be unsustainable and detrimental.
2. Don't rush to spin the story for short-term gain and long-term loss.
3. Don't succumb to the desire to lay the blame on others.

With this under your belt, it's now time to focus on discipline, which will take you to the next level of success.

FOUR
DISCIPLINE

It's not personal, Sonny. It's strictly business.
—Michael Corleone, *The Godfather*

WE BELIEVE THAT ALMOST ALL THE CRITICAL LESSONS OF CRISIS MANAGEMENT (AND THERE is a good argument for life in general) can be derived in some form or fashion from Francis Ford Coppola's *Godfather* series.

One of the most memorable scenes in *The Godfather* is a conversation between Michael, the youngest son of Mafia don Vito Corleone; Sonny, the eldest son and heir apparent to the don; and Tom Hagen, the family consigliere (the mob equivalent of a crisis manager). The talk occurs in the charged aftermath of a failed effort by a rival mob family to murder the don that involved a corrupt police officer, and it centers on whether in hitting back at the rival family it would violate some sort of code to kill the crooked cop.

MICHAEL CORLEONE: Where does it say that you can't kill a cop?

TOM HAGEN: Come on, Mikey . . .

MICHAEL CORLEONE: Tom, wait a minute. I'm talking about a cop that's mixed up in drugs. I'm talking about a dishonest cop—a crooked cop who got mixed up in the rackets and got what was coming to him. That's a terrific story. And we have newspaper people on the payroll, don't we, Tom? And they might like a story like that.

TOM HAGEN: They might, they just might.

MICHAEL CORLEONE: [to Sonny] It's not personal, Sonny. It's strictly business.

The scene shows how preternaturally calm, cool, and collected Michael is, despite the extreme duress of his father having just been shot, and the knowledge that he may have to kill the corrupt cop. And it demonstrates that when under attack, no matter how extreme the situation, you can never personalize the situation, but rather must be *committed to a disciplined approach.*

It's not personal, Sonny. It's strictly business.

In the preceding chapter, we discussed the need to take the crisis manager's equivalent of the physician's Hippocratic Oath by vowing to Do No Harm. The violation of this Do No Harm principle essentially constitutes acts of commission—whether it's putting out bad information, engaging in overspin, or blaming others—that can result in doing more harm than good when it comes to restoring trust.

But there is another extreme that can produce similarly bad results in restoring trust, and that's an act of omission: the failure to take appropriate action when hit with a crisis.

When a crisis hits, the Do No Harm principle should not be interpreted as a license to have no response. You should not act like the proverbial ostrich and stick your head in the ground and behave as though *nothing* happened.

We often see such a non-response in cases involving legal exposure. An individual's or company's concerns about doing or saying anything that even hints at increased legal exposure can prevent them from responding effectively to a crisis. And this failure to mount an aggressive response and demonstrate that you can be trusted can lead to even more harm over the long run.

Research in Motion (RIM)'s handling of the company's BlackBerry network outages provides a cautionary tale for those who think that hiding in a closet and hoping that the storm will pass is the best way to handle a crisis. Their most notorious outage—dubbed the Great Berry Crash of 2011—lasted four days. And for most of that time, Research in Motion was silent—silent despite the fact that 70 million customers relied on their BlackBerries for routine and critical business and personal functions. For many BlackBerry users (or CrackBerry users as they often are known), this outage was akin to being deprived of oxygen. Instead of the RIM CEO stepping up and immediately accepting responsibility for the problem, the company lamely said that everyone at RIM was busy working full time on a fix. Instead of taking to social media to explain what went wrong, and what was being done to fix the problem and prevent it from occurring again, the company stayed quiet. And when the CEO did finally appear several days into the outage, his apology was widely ridiculed and rejected as too little too late.

Compare RIM's head-in-the-sand mentality with the way Apple managed customer complaints about the flawed antenna placement in its iPhone 4, which was cutting off calls. Steve Jobs addressed the problem directly, although at first haltingly, but Jobs and Apple finally presented and swiftly implemented a comprehensive solution involving the distribution of free iPhone cases that corrected the problem. In the end, the issue became nothing more than a minor speed bump on the iPhone's high-speed race to smartphone dominance.

Moreover, addressing your legal exposure while preserving your capacity to move forward is not mutually incompatible. There are certainly steps that can be taken that protect your legal liability while also ensuring your future viability.

As the press inquiries come pouring in, there is nothing wrong with returning the calls and letting people know that you are cooperating fully in the inquiry, and as soon you are in a position to provide information, you will do so—instead of hiding behind the dreaded "no comment."

When the press or anyone else seeks an explanation, it is perfectly acceptable to say you don't have the answers, but will get back to them when you do. When you don't respond at all, it creates the impression that you're hunkering down in your bunker.

In the abstract, it's accepted that you need to play to win, yet during a crisis, those in the hurricane's eye tend to forget this or suffer from paralysis. To achieve success *you must have the mental toughness and discipline to play to win*.

This commitment to a disciplined approach must be the same whether you are the CEO of a Fortune 500 company that is the subject of a Securities and Exchange Commission investigation or the principal of small-town high school who discovers a cheating scandal.

Discipline demands a commitment to three dictates:

1. Preparation
2. Mental toughness
3. Thinking long term

PREPARATION

Since 2001, no National Football League team—perhaps no major American professional sports franchise—has been more consistently successful than the

New England Patriots. And while the Pats, under Coach Bill Belichick, do a lot things very well, and benefit enormously from one of the sport's all-time greats, quarterback Tom Brady, many believe that the key to their consistent success is their disciplined commitment to *preparation*.

No matter the situation, no matter the variables, no matter the weather, no matter the rules: the Patriots are always prepared. They know the player match-ups they want to exploit; they know the plays they will run to take advantage of imbalances in the match-ups; they know the personnel they need on the field to run the play; the personnel know their assignments; and far more often than not, they deftly execute their assignments. In no small part because of the team's level of preparation, the Patriots have not just won more Super Bowls than any other team since 2000, but especially telling, they have won more games than any other team, with a winning percentage of over 70 percent.

While some may argue it's only a game, like a crisis, football is a full-contact sport, and if you are not prepared, you *will* be hurt.

And while Green Bay Packers coach Vince Lombardi's iconic quote "winning isn't everything—it's the only thing" can certainly be debated in terms of its social merits, the legendary coach was 100 percent right when it comes to damage control: *Damage control is a matter of survival—and the bleak alternative is not surviving.*

Your survival will be directly related to your level of preparation. Therefore, to be in the strongest position to survive you will need the discipline that stems directly from preparation.

The basic crisis preparation steps are the following:

- Know who will be the principal decision makers in your organization.
- Identify the key targeted internal and external audiences with whom you will need to re-establish trust.
- Determine how you will communicate to these targeted audiences.
- Consider what it is that these audiences will care about and want to know.
- And most significantly, get out ahead of a crisis by creating strategic plans to rebuild trust that address possible likely scenarios.

If you are the CEO of a medical products company, assemble plans to address a product defect.

If you are a lawyer, know your response when a State Bar complaint is filed against you.

If you run a professional sports franchise, be ready for what happens when a fight breaks out in the stands and a fan is badly hurt.

If you are an entertainment agent, understand in advance what needs to happen when your top client is caught with a prostitute.

If you are the franchise owner of a fast-food restaurant, think through what you'll do if a patron claims to have found a piece of a rodent in one of your burgers.

If you run a non-profit education program dependent on grants from a local government, be ready to explain embezzlement by an employee.

And if you work for an elected official, be ready to explain your boss being found in bed with a live boy or a dead girl.

Each of the examples above is based on a real case that we had some involvement with (well, almost all—to date we have not dealt with the dead paramour scenario).

And from what we experienced, it did not matter whether an organization was a Fortune 500 company or the new kid on the block—their success in facing a crisis depended on how prepared they were. Thus, when it comes to surviving a crisis and rebuilding trust, *it is not the size of the organization that matters, but the discipline of the organization to commit to a sizable level of preparation.*

To illustrate the above, consider the case of Rachael Solem, the owner of Irving House, a bed and breakfast in Cambridge, Massachusetts, just off of Harvard Square. In August 2010, as reported by *The Boston Globe,* a guest at Irving House claimed that after a stay there, she discovered a number of red welts on her neck: the result of being bitten by bed bugs in her hotel room.

Although not a large hotel or a franchise owner connected to a national chain, Solem was ready. Her B&B had been doing bed bug training for ten years, had a plan, and immediately sprung into action based on a decade's worth of preparation:

- An outside bed bug detection service was swiftly retained and inspected the patron's room and other nearby rooms—and found nothing.
- The report was made available to the guest.
- The owner made clear that the B&B has a standing practice of checking for bed bugs on a daily basis.

- And the B&B made public that the guest making the accusation was also seeking a full refund.

In *The Boston Globe*'s coverage of the bed bug infestation in the Boston region, several much larger hotels, including major chains, did not show the same level of preparation. And, in the story, it was this B&B that came off well—a tribute to the owner's disciplined commitment to preparation.

MENTAL TOUGHNESS

In war, there is the adage that the best of plans are only good until the first shot is fired—at which point the fog of war often leads to confusion and disarray.

Similarly, there is the fog of a crisis. No matter how disciplined you've been in preparing, once in the throes of the crisis, you will also need the discipline to exercise *mental toughness,* so as not to become confused and lose your way.

In particular, during a crisis, confusion followed by a breakdown in discipline tends to manifest itself in one of two specific ways: panic and grasping for straws.

In 1996 the White House faced the dilemma of dealing with the unanticipated appearance of then First Lady Hillary Rodham Clinton's billing records from her time in private practice in Little Rock, Arkansas, when Bill Clinton was governor. By way of background, the billing records had been sought by various investigative entities, including a congressional committee chaired by politically motivated opponents of the president. Ostensibly, the records were sought as evidence that would somehow connect the dots related to the ongoing, highly partisan investigation into the Clintons' investment in a real estate property known as Whitewater. However, the records were not at the Rose Law Firm, where Mrs. Clinton had been a partner, nor were they discovered among the Clinton's personal possessions.

All of that changed on January 4, 1996. As the 1996 presidential re-election campaign was ramping up, and Bill Clinton's opposition was attempting to make ethics a central point in their campaign, an employee of the Clintons stumbled across a file in the White House East Wing. This file turned out to hold the very sought-after, very speculated-about billing records.

Given the nature of the documents and the timing—in a campaign year—there was intense pressure to offer an explanation as to how the records had been discovered in the East Wing, and why they had not previously been turned over. Republicans claimed it was a cover-up. The mystery of the appearance was a major story on the network news (when there was still a large distinction between the network news and cable) and front-page newspaper headlines (when such headlines drove the network coverage). There were even some White House staff pushing for an answer, concerned about the story's impact on the re-election campaign. And almost everyone was demanding access to the records, under the belief that they would contain some sort of a smoking gun.

Rather than panicking under the intense pressure caused by the fog of the crisis, the Clinton White House showed the mental toughness to exercise the discipline to not provide answers to questions for which it did not yet have answers—but rather, the Clinton team simply made the records public (there was nothing of any real note in the documents); explained the chain of custody from the moment they were discovered; and then told the media and investigators that this was all that was known, and the White House was not going to speculate or offer answers it simply did not have.

At the end of the day, while the story stayed in the news for a period and became part of the negative campaign narrative deployed by the president's opposition, it eventually receded from the headlines. And the story never amounted to the kind of game-changing development it could have been had the Clinton team panicked. The White House could have created the far bigger, far more problematic crisis of "it's the cover-up, not the crime" if they had refused to turn over the files or had offered inaccurate responses. In fact, by making the billing records available, explaining to the public and press what was known, and making clear that no one knew how they had moved from Little Rock to the White House—including ensuring that no one from the administration speculated one iota about how they might have found their way into the East Wing—the Clinton White House operated in a way that allowed itself to earn trust in the midst of a potential crisis.

The second way we often see discipline break down is in responding to a third party offering a possible explanation (no matter how outrageous), and the target of the crisis loses their cool and takes the bait. People will always offer up a variety of theories to explain why and how a crisis happened. Sometimes these theories are created or commented upon by bloggers in their sweatpants in the neighborhood Starbucks, with no firsthand knowledge, research, or inside information on the situation. Generally in life, if something sounds too good to be true, it almost always *is* too good to be true. Similarly, in a crisis, an answer that provides a relatively easy way out is nearly always the equivalent of fool's gold.

An example of a large corporation that demonstrated the mental toughness not to panic and grab the bait of an easy answer was seen in the executive offices of Pacific Gas & Electric (PG&E), the giant power utility in Northern California, in its response to a devastating explosion.

In an early September evening in 2010, an explosion ripped through San Bruno, a small city south of San Francisco. Tragically, eight lives were lost and thirty-eight homes destroyed in a gas line explosion. The aerial shots provided by helicopters from local television stations showed a visual scene reminiscent of Dresden, Germany, following its firebombing in World War II. Initial reports from the press suggested that a small plane had crashed and been responsible for the subsequent explosion.

Not only did PG&E find itself in the fog of a crisis, but the actual crisis itself looked like the fog of war.

PG&E had a spotty history of dealing with crises, dating back to a California energy debacle in 2001 where there were large-scale blackouts. But in this case, the company provided a very basic response, indicating it did not know the reason for the explosion but was committed to working with the appropriate authorities to determine what had happened. Subsequent analysis and investigations revealed that root cause of the explosion was caused by a faulty pipe for which PG&E was responsible. The company's minimalist response in the opening moments of the events—and in particular its disciplined ability to exhibit the mental toughness to not impulsively grab on to answers being offered by what would prove to be erroneous news reports—helped the company avoid making a truly bad situation even worse. This put the company in a position to later release accurate information, which was received as a truthful explanation as to what had actually taken place. In the aftermath, PG&E still faced a very challenging situation—but a situation whose difficulties were not compounded by how they addressed the issue at the front end.

THINK LONG TERM

Upon being hit with a crisis, there is an impulse to want to quickly make right what went wrong and somehow swiftly put everything back just the way it was previously. But blunt reality is, the moment you are hit with a crisis, you have to come to grips with the fact that damage control is a long-game endeavor, necessitating that you have the discipline to *think long term.*

It is highly unlikely that with one single quick action you'll be able to return to where you were prior to the crisis. Rather, your comeback story will likely span weeks, months, and maybe even years. Consequently, your mission to restore trust has to be thought of as a long-term strategy.

Your actions going forward—whether related to the crisis or not—will be scrutinized far more closely than they were before the crisis occurred. As a result, you will have a higher burden of proof when it comes to the accuracy of the information you disseminate. Your targeted audiences will be on a hair-trigger, ready to jump on small missteps or seize upon minor inconsistencies or setbacks. Thus, prospectively, you need to be prepared to get well out in front of the information.

To survive a crisis, you must have the discipline to run a marathon and not a sprint.

Few have better shown this discipline than Michael Milken. While at Drexel Burnham Lambert in the 1980s, Milken was known as the junk bond king and seen as a shining example of Wall Street greed. With an apparent scant regard for the law, Milken was charged with ninety-eight counts of racketeering and securities fraud as the result of an insider trading investigation. He pleaded guilty to six charges and was sentenced to ten years in prison (but after cooperating with prosecutors and with good behavior, he only served two years).

As dark as the future appeared for the formerly high-flying Milken, he approached his situation with a long-term plan. After serving his time, he turned his efforts to his charitable works, especially as it related to cancer research. His family foundation sponsors the Milken Scholars, which provides college financial assistance to outstanding high school students, and underwrites the Milken Educator Awards, which has awarded tens of millions of dollars to thousands of high school teachers. And *Fortune* magazine featured Milken on its cover and called him "The Man Who Changed Medicine." Michael Milken made the journey back from his time in prison, and he did it with the discipline of *thinking long-term.*

Another fallen high-profile figure adopted a similar long-term strategy—former New York governor Eliot Spitzer, a crusading former prosecutor who was once considered presidential timber. After resigning from office in the middle of a prostitution scandal, Spitzer took full responsibility for his conduct, blaming no one but himself. He apologized to his family and supporters and commenced a highly disciplined comeback. He initially kept a very low profile, allowing the fire to die out and the media to move on to new stories. Spitzer later stepped into the public arena to speak on carefully selected issues with which he was positively identified, including corruption on Wall Street. He became a columnist for the online magazine *Slate* and appeared in a compelling independent documentary, *Client 9,* which raised persuasive questions about the potential role his corporate adversaries played in exposing his use of high-end prostitutes, which led to his downfall. From such carefully targeted public appearances, Spitzer moved to hosting a cable network talk show, authoring a non-fiction book, and lecturing at the City College of New York.

At every step in his finely tuned comeback, Eliot Spitzer sought to attach himself to issues that cast him in a positive light while simultaneously always being forthright about his accountability and offering apologies for his personal misconduct. Spitzer's disciplined approach has allowed him to reemerge as a respected public figure—after many thought his ability to have a public profile was gone forever. And Spitzer did it by recognizing that he was not running a sprint but a marathon—and thus, had the discipline to *think long term.*

As you seek to control the damage, you must understand the principle of a disciplined approach. While others lose their nerves, you need to stay in control of the three key elements of this principle:

1. Preparation is the name of the game, and it does not matter whether you are big or small.
2. In the fog of a crisis, you need to keep your wits about you by exercising mental toughness.
3. Rehabilitation is not a sprint—it is a marathon: Think long term.

Next, let's consider how we bolster your credibility so you will be in a position to rebuild trust.

FIVE
CREDIBILITY

I want the truth!

—Colonel Nathan Jessep, *A Few Good Men*

IN THE MOVIE A FEW GOOD MEN, LIEUTENANT DANIEL KAFFEE, PLAYED BY TOM CRUISE, PUTS Colonel Nathan Jessep, the commanding officer of the U.S. Guantanamo Bay Naval Base, played by Jack Nicholson, on the witness stand and grills him about an incident on the base that led to the killing of a Marine by fellow soldiers. The colonel, under a withering series of questions designed to elicit the truth, lashes back:

> JESSEP: You want answers?
> KAFFEE: I think I'm entitled to them.
> JESSEP: You want answers?
> KAFFEE: I want the truth!
> JESSEP: You can't handle the truth!

The classic line from the film is Col. Jessep's assertion "you can't handle the truth!" But, for our purposes, it is the line from Kaffee, which precipitated Jessep's oft-quoted response, that constitutes a key damage control principle:

I want the truth.

In a crisis, the commitment to the truth is communicated by whether you are doing everything you can to protect, preserve, and promote your credibility. Every word you utter, every statement you release, every step you take, every action you complete, every tactic you execute must first be evaluated through the prism of how it impacts perceptions of your credibility.

When the crisis hits, before doing anything, make sure you put your response to the test: Does it bolster or degrade your credibility?

The Credibility Principle is a key pillar of damage control, and you bolster your credibility by:

- Understanding that accurate information is the coin of the realm
- Managing expectations
- Controlling the flow of information

THE COIN OF THE REALM

In the Information Age, knowledge is power. In a crisis, when it comes to earning credibility, *accurate information is the coin of the realm.*

You earn credibility by providing trustworthy information, and you earn extra credibility points when the information release is not positive for your side or particularly exculpatory.

You earn credibility by demonstrating openness and transparency when you affirmatively release information—especially in the absence of a legal obligation that the information be released.

You earn credibility by pre-emptively releasing the most damning information—and this has an additional benefit: Since the information, in all likelihood is going to eventually be discovered in some form or fashion, you get the credit for first putting it in the public sphere.

Short of releasing information that could generate the equivalent of a death penalty for your organization (in which case you are probably well beyond help), no matter how bad the information may be, packaging and releasing such negative information is among the most powerful ways to restore trust.

When you are in a deep, dark, unspinnable place (as *New York Times* columnist Maureen Dowd famously said), it's only a matter of time until the underlying information gets out. Given that your mission is to restore trust, you should have a strategy to get in front of the information and earn credibility points for releasing it.

We refer to such situations as the Tylenol moment—and we're not merely referring to the five-alarm headache you will be feeling in such a situation—but to the precedent-setting approach Johnson & Johnson took in September

1982 when seven people died from taking Tylenol pills that had been deliberately laced with cyanide.

As anyone who was a teenager or older at that time will likely remember, with people dying from the poison and a nation paralyzed with fear over whether it was safe to buy pain reliever, Johnson & Johnson's franchise product—indeed the entire company's future—was at stake. Johnson & Johnson responded with a series of actions that to this day define how to manage a crisis.

First, and significant to its credibility, Johnson & Johnson told the public what it knew about the situation—which was not much.

Second, and even more important to the company's credibility, it told the public what it did not know about the situation—which was considerable.

Third, and crucial to the drug manufacturer's credibility, the company told the public of the proactive steps it was taking to ensure that future pills would not be poisoned, including pulling their product from store shelves, destroying all the existing Tylenol bottles and then introducing new tamper-free containers, which were triple safety sealed (the type of containers that are now standard).

And fourth, and most significant of all to Johnson & Johnson's credibility, the company diligently did everything it said it was going to do and continued to be open and transparent about what it did and did not know.

And when all was said and done, Tylenol ultimately regained most of the consumers that it had before the crisis, and today controls over a third of the painkiller market in North America.

While few individuals or organizations will ever face a life and death situation as serious as the Tylenol case, many will face an equivalent Tylenol moment when their very future is at stake. And such a Tylenol moment demands putting in place an approach that understands: *Communicating accurate information is the coin of the realm.*

MANAGE EXPECTATIONS

When confronting a crisis you can bolster your credibility and begin to re-establish trust by earning credibility points when you *manage expectations*.

To successfully manage expectations you will need to:

1. Determine what information you control, how you can release it, and when you will be in a position to release it.

2. Set the expectations with your targeted audiences to what you know you will be able to deliver.
3. Meet or exceed those expectations. To do so you will need to put in place a process that allows you to get ahead of the story as it relates to controlling when information becomes available to your target audiences and how it is released.
4. And while doing the above, avoid over-promising and under-delivering.

When the crisis first hits, know that successfully managing expectations is one of the most important parts of the job of bolstering your credibility:

1. Determine if you are in a place where you can answer specific questions. Explain to the public what you are doing to get those answers, and then go get the answers and report back.
2. If you cannot provide information because you are not in a position to be confident that the information is correct, give the public a timeline for providing additional information—and be sure that you will be able to meet that timeline.
3. If you are concerned that there is limited confidence in your organization's ability to ascertain information, or whether the information will be considered valid, identify an independent, outside, highly respected third party of impeccable credentials who will be trusted, and beyond reproach to investigate the matter and issue a report.

If you manage expectations properly, you will end up *under-promising and over-delivering* when it comes to your credibility.

This was what former Los Angeles mayor Tom Bradley accomplished in 1991. Following the Rodney King beating, he appointed a man of impeccable credentials, the former assistant secretary of state and future secretary of state Warren Christopher, to investigate charges of excessive force by the Los Angeles Police Department. Secretary Christopher's report spurred far-reaching reform in the city's police department, and for Mayor Bradley, and really the entire city, the report and the subsequent actions it brought about far exceeded expectations.

THE PIVOT POINT

In a crisis, information must be deployed to ensure your key audiences will be fair when it comes to evaluating you in terms of what went wrong and why. To be in the best possible position to get a fair shake, you need to consider how to control the flow of information through the use of a *pivot point*, so the information is released at the right time, and in the right way, and to maximum effect when it comes to your credibility. And in turn, that credibility can be deployed to rebuild trust. If you are in a position to control the flow of information, you can establish credibility on key elements of the crisis, and then push off from it to significantly alter the course of a story:

- The *timely release of good information* can kill bad information and, in doing so, simultaneously legitimize your credibility while delegitimizing the credibility of whoever is spreading the bad information.
- The *smart dissemination of quality information* can provide valuable context that bolsters your credibility as well as being an intriguing hook to get key audiences to take a second look at the situation.
- Putting out *facts to which only you have access* can increase your credibility, while providing a basis for the public to reconsider what is being said by whom, and to what end in terms of motives and agendas (especially when your foes release information designed to undermine your organization or company).

Oftentimes, in a crisis, we look for that defining moment when there is the opportunity to exercise a decisive pivot point. We seek the optimum time when important information that we know is sustainable has been assembled and can be put out in a way that will maximize its effectiveness. But this also can require some patience—given that the execution of such a pivot point is generally highly dependent on sustainable information, and the pivot point moment usually does not come in the opening moments of a crisis.

A pivot point is intended to draw a bright line between the past and the future and change the course of the story. The pivot can alter how you are perceived, and how others in the crises are viewed when it comes to credibility.

And a successfully executed pivot point can fundamentally change the course or direction of a story.

In politics, business, entertainment, or sports it is well documented that audiences are generally willing to give second chances to those whose actions precipitated a crisis—as long as the public is given a good reason to take a fresh look at them.

Successfully finding and executing a decisive pivot point will often provide people with the reason to upend previously settled views.

A successful pivot point will promote one's credibility by accomplishing these key objectives:

- Draw a bright, indelible line between the past and future, so that what has happened before is explained in a credible way. This explanation can be the basis for audiences to re-appraise the matter, and now focus on how you are handling the issues going forward.
- Communicate both externally and internally that an organization's leaders have openly and candidly acknowledged the problems that caused the crisis, and fully recognize the need to operate differently in the future.
- Demonstrate a clear determination to close the book on what has not worked, and take advantage of the current opportunity to put things right for future success.

Successful pivots have these important characteristics in common:

- The decision to make the pivot must come from the top.
- The pivot must be embraced by the entire organization.
- The pivot itself must be clear and unambiguous.
- The pivot must consist of more than words. The initial statement must be followed up with genuine, tangible deliverables that are meaningful to the key audiences.

Such effective pivots can be executed any number of ways.

- A comprehensive and self-critical report
- Management changes at the top levels of an organization
- An apology

Let's take a look at the last of these—the apology, which is becoming an important vehicle by which to exercise the decisive pivot. The apology is a direct reflection of the times in which we live, where there is a recognition that when it comes to preserving a politician's image, a celebrity's reputation, or a company's brand, credibility is the key to surviving a crisis—and an apology is a key tool in protecting that credibility.

First, an apology allows audiences to focus on the future. With one apology, you can avoid the drip, drip, drip, drip dynamic that can lead to a slow and painful death by a thousand leaks.

Second, an apology communicates both externally and internally that the organization's leaders have candidly acknowledged the problems with their previous approach and now recognize the need to operate differently in the future, allowing the organization or individual to avoid the "it's the cover-up and not the crime" trap.

And, third, the apology demonstrates a determination to put behind you what has not worked and take advantage of the current opportunity to put things right. This shows you are now able to communicate with an open, honest, and forthright approach.

However, not all apologies are executed equally effectively.

How is it that Mayor Gavin Newsom of San Francisco can apologize for having an affair with his chief of staff's wife and go on to be re-elected with historically high margins, while the dynamic and effective Governor Elliot Spitzer is forced from office?

Some of the effectiveness of an apology is explained by the *what*—*what* is the nature of the underlying misconduct: an inappropriate relationship with a staffer, versus frequenting prostitutions.

Some of the difference is explained by the *how*—*how* authentic were the apologies? Or at least how good was the person at selling the public on their apologies' heartfelt authenticity?

And some of the difference is explained by the *when*—*when* is the apology made: at the front end of a crisis (Mayor Newsom) or only after one has been publically publicly shamed into saying "uncle" (Governor Spitzer).

As mentioned above, the public is often willing to give second chances— as long as they are given a *good reason* to move on from the underlying crisis. And consequently they will take a fresh look at the besieged, thus offering an opportunity to re-establish credibility. An apology can be that good reason, serving as a decisive pivot point.

Notable historic examples of successful apologies include President John F. Kennedy taking responsibility for the Bay of Pigs fiasco; Amazon CEO Jeff Bezos successfully addressing his company's deletion of books from Kindles; David Letterman apologizing on-air to his wife and staff for having affairs; and Alex Rodriguez on ESPN expressing remorse for his use of steroids.

All these successful apologies have the necessary crucial characteristics in common: The decision to apologize came from the top. The apology was supported throughout the organization. The apology itself was clear and unambiguous. Further, the initial apology was followed up with genuine, tangible deliverables that were meaningful to the apologizer's key audiences.

Whether it is on a national stage, or a more discrete community, the public can be very forgiving of mistakes—especially when one apologizes and takes full responsibility. For many, it can be tough to suck it up and say "I'm sorry," but the benefits are enormous. They can help bolster your credibility, put the past in your rear-view mirror, and pave the way to rebuilding trust.

By limiting harm and exercising discipline, you will have the capacity to get on the road to rebuilding trust so long as you abide by the Credibility Principle. To stay on this road, follow the sign posts of the principle:

- Releasing and communicating accurate information is the coin of the realm.
- Manage expectations so that you are able to under-promise and over-deliver.
- Seek out a decisive pivot point, such as an apology, that will allow you to draw a clear line between the past and the future.

And now let's talk about getting operational.

PART III
THE TEN COMMANDMENTS
OF DAMAGE CONTROL

SIX
PLAYING TO WIN

Now I want you to remember that no bastard ever won a war by dying for his country. He won it by making the other poor dumb bastard die for his country.
—General George S. Patton, in the movie *Patton*

THERE'S A POLITICAL CAMPAIGN JOKE: THREE BLOODIED AND DAZED MEN EMERGE FROM THE smoldering wreckage of an airplane that has crashed on a remote and unchartered island, and are set upon by a fierce-looking group of heavily tattooed, knife-wielding cannibals whose animal skin attire is accessorized with shrunken human skulls.

The cannibal chief looks at the three men and turns to the first survivor and poses a choice—"Death or chi-chi?"

The first survivor, assuming that chi-chi must be preferable to death, tentatively answers, "chi-chi." The chief responds by giving a knowing nod to his colleagues, who immediately descend upon the first survivor, breaking all of his bones, flaying his skin, and leaving him a whimpering mess of humanity lying in a heap on the jungle floor with blood oozing from his various orifices.

Turning to the second survivor, the chief, who gravely looks back and forth between the second survivor and what remains of the first survivor, solemnly poses the same question—"Death or chi-chi?"

The second survivor trembles as he considers the choice but concludes that living is still a better option than dying, and in a shaky, barely audible voice whispers, "chi-chi." The chief stoically acknowledges the choice by waving back his warriors, who not only break the second survivor's bones and flay him but also disembowel him, leaving him barely alive, and then cover him in honey and deposit him on top of an ant hill.

Looking to the remaining survivor, the chief puts the question to him—"Death or chi-chi?" The third survivor, now all too aware of what has happened to his fellow travelers, and noting that the damage inflicted on the second survivor was worse than the damage inflicted on the first survivor, decides that some things are, in fact, worse than death, including the now clearly defined "chi-chi." And, with resignation, he mumbles "death," at which point the chief breaks into a wide grin, lets out a loud laugh, claps his hands in glee, picks up the third survivor in a bear hug and says, "A wise choice, my good man!"

Survivor three, thinking that it was always a trick question and he may survive intact after all, lets out a breath of relief.

Setting him down, the chief turns to his warriors, does the equivalent of a cannibal's end-zone victory dance, and proclaims—"Death! But, first, a little chi-chi before death!"

Chi-chi before death is the experience far too many endure when attempting damage control—they endure a great deal of pain and at the end of the process they still spill their guts, and they still do not survive.

In Part II, we focused on the idea that to survive a crisis, you must effectively communicate to the audiences determining your fate that you can be trusted going forward.

In Part III, we will present the specific tactics of damage control on an operational level that, if properly executed, will allow you to succeed in restoring the public trust.

As you consider our step-by-step strategy, you will see that the three crucial principles discussed earlier—Do No Harm, Discipline, and Credibility—comprise the fundamental DNA of damage control. How they interrelate and translate into specific actions are what we call the Ten Commandments of Damage Control.

The Ten Commandments of Damage Control include defensive actions intended to demonstrate to your target audiences that you are responding to the crisis in a proactive way that represents a firm commitment to restoring the public trust.

The Ten Commandments also include a number of offensive strategies. In a crisis, there is often an opposing side fanning the flames and/or seeking to benefit from your demise. Effective damage control means exposing the actions of those with unclean hands.

These Ten Commandments of Damage Control are intended to be a user's manual for all—companies big or small, public or private entities, for-profit businesses or non-profits—by providing a set of universally applicable operational steps to make sure you minimize your blood loss and protect your guts when you find yourself in the midst of knife fight.

As a user's manual, each of the individual commandments build upon one another. While reading this book and considering the individual applicability of each commandment, it is important to understand that they are iterative of one another and should be viewed in their totality and not as individual, stand-alone tactics. And it is also important to understand that at times, if applied in isolation, they will create a tension with one another. On the other hand, if applied in conjunction, they will work in a complimentary manner.

Our overriding mission with this book is to provide leaders in organizations of all types with a how-to manual of damage control in a crisis. This book, and especially the Ten Commandments, is designed to provide you with a step-by-step guide to survival.

Each commandment will be presented in the following way:

1. The stipulation of the commandment;
2. High-profile examples of the commandment being respected and disrespected. (These will illuminate the use of the particular commandment, and the elements of these crises will highlight a particular point. In many of these examples we had either a direct or indirect involvement.);
3. The explanation of the commandment and a specific enumeration of the steps needed to effectively execute the commandment;
4. An example of the commandment being applied to the type of crisis that everyday people will confront in our Information Age, where crisis is a state of nature;
5. A corollary to the commandment to demonstrate how to best apply the commandment—and to make sure the commandment is not misapplied.

General George S. Patton, known as "Old Blood and Guts," didn't achieve fame because he was a character in an Oscar-winning movie—he was one of America's most brilliant military tacticians and one of the finest leaders in the history of the U.S. military. When he spoke, his troops paid rapt attention, and we, too, pay heed to his famous words: *No bastard ever won a war by dying for his country. He won it by making the other poor dumb bastard die for his country.*

In a crisis, by doing all you can to stop the bleeding and protect your own guts—you are playing to win.

SEVEN
COMMANDMENT I
FULL DISCLOSURE

Show me the money.

—Rod Tidwell, *Jerry McGuire*

THE FIRST COMMANDMENT—FULL DISCLOSURE

Everything can and will come out. The issue is not *if* it will come out, but *when* it will come out, *how* long it will take to come out, *who* will put it out, and the greater damage that will be done if the inevitable disclosure is not controlled by putting it out on your terms, with your context, and at the time of your choosing. You *can* control the damage if you exercise the discipline to get ahead of the issue by putting the whole story out to avoid getting completely run over by it. By affirmatively disclosing the matter, you will not only avoid doing greater harm to your current situation, you will also bolster your credibility and, thereby, contribute to the rebuilding of trust.

DISRESPECTING THE FIRST COMMANDMENT—SHARKS VERSUS TIGER

The parenting maxim "nothing good happens after midnight" is particularly relevant when it comes to the intersection of a crisis involving entertainment and sports figures.

Just ask Tiger Woods.

In 2009 he was at the top of the world. The athlete of the decade. The number one sports brand. And then came the morning of November 27, 2009.

At 2:25 A.M. Woods's SUV struck a tree and a fire hydrant. Woods was reportedly found bloodied and dazed by his then wife, Elin, who, it was reported, broke the back window of the SUV with a golf club in an effort to rescue him. Shortly thereafter, the news zoomed around like a supersonic tee shot. Everyone—and we mean everyone—understood that the early morning timing of what seemed like a bizarre series of events was of some interest, and the emerging facts were drops of blood in the water for the sharks now circling Tiger.

Several days passed without any information from Woods. The police, interested in questioning Woods about the events, were turned away on September 27, 28, and 29. Clearly, something was up. The speculation and rumor-mongering intensified, amplified, and multiplied in the absence of any material response from the Woods camp.

Satellite tucks bivouacked outside of the Woods compound as if they were covering a major criminal trial or national political event.

News helicopters hovered overhead like they were chasing O. J. Simpson in the white Bronco.

Breaking news scrolls from across the media universe—from CNN to ESPN—gave constant updates on whether or not there was going to be a meeting with law enforcement.

On September 29, three full days after the incident and following the latest brush back given to the police, Woods issued his first statement via his website:

As you all know, I had a single-car accident earlier this week, and sustained some injuries. I have some cuts, bruising and right now I'm pretty sore.

This situation is my fault, and it's obviously embarrassing to my family and me. I'm human and I'm not perfect. I will certainly make sure this doesn't happen again.

This is a private matter and I want to keep it that way. Although I understand there is curiosity, the many false, unfounded and malicious rumors that are currently circulating about my family and me are irresponsible. The only person responsible for the accident is me. My wife, Elin, acted courageously when she saw I was hurt and in trouble. She was the first person to help me. Any other assertion is absolutely false.

This incident has been stressful and very difficult for Elin, our family and me. I appreciate all the concern and well wishes that we have received.

But, I would also ask for some understanding that my family and I deserve some privacy no matter how intrusive some people can be.

The part of the statement suggesting it was a private matter and Woods' desire to want to keep it that way—turned the drops of blood into a full-out gash gushing blood, and now the circling sharks started biting.

The statement from the world's most celebrated golfer was followed by flurry of media reports that were now able to use the peg of Woods's own words to begin surfacing damaging stories that many in the press were purportedly aware of, but which had not yet made it into the mainstream media.

Social media around the world was suddenly abuzz with rumors, speculation, and innuendo. A Chinese animation company got into the act, producing a video purporting to show what actually happened the night of the crash, which rapidly became a viral sensation.

And the magazine *US Weekly* published a cover story of a Los Angeles cocktail waitress who claimed to have three hundred text messages documenting an affair with Woods that began in 2007.

On December 2, 2009, Woods issued a second statement on his website that continued to push his privacy message:

[F]or me, the virtue of privacy is one that must be protected in matters that are intimate and within one's own family.

That statement was akin to dumping buckets of chum into the bay, bringing about a feeding frenzy with the ravenous sharks.

Soon thereafter reports of numerous affairs with multiple women began to appear. Among those leading the charge were the New York City tabloids, who took Woods to the public woodshed by repeatedly putting the story on the front page (including twenty straight days of *New York Post* cover stories— one more than 9/11). The *Post* (which is famous for headlines such as "Headless Body in Topless Bar") was in rare form:

"CAGEY TIGER, DUCKS POLICE 3RD DAY"

"TIGER'S SEX TEXTS: ANOTHER DAY, ANOTHER BOMBSHELL"

"TIGER'S BIRDIES, TWO MORE SEXY GALS COME OUT OF THE
WOODSWORK WITH THEIR STEAMY TALES"

"TIGER ADMITS: I'M A CHEETAH"

This and more global reports of Woods's infidelities featuring multiple lovers and their lurid texts led to a third website statement from the golfer, posted on December 11, 2009:

> I am deeply aware of the disappointment and hurt that my infidelity has caused so many people, most of all my wife and children . . . After much soul searching, I have decided to take an indefinite break from professional golf.

And while Woods may have hoped that admitting to his transgressions and stepping back from his profession would get himself off the tee at the media driving range, he had no such luck and the press continued to whack away.

Finally, on February 19, 2010, almost *three months* after the precipitating event, Tiger Woods appeared before the public in person and issued a statement where he publicly acknowledged his failings and took full responsibility:

> The issue involved here was my repeated irresponsible behavior. I was unfaithful. I had affairs. I cheated. What I did is not acceptable and I am the only person to blame.

And Woods then felt compelled to step back from the sport that made him an international icon and enroll in a clinic that specialized in treating addictions, including sexual addictions.

When the dust had settled, the value of a multibillion dollar brand was badly degraded with the public and his sponsors and major corporate sponsors such as General Motors, Gatorade, Gillette, and Accenture all ended their relationships with the golfer in one form or another.

The platinum reputation of one of the most respected and admired individuals in the world was severely tarnished.

Woods had gone from an unparalleled superstar athlete who drove the economics a professional sport to a surefire punch line for late-night TV hosts.

And it didn't have to go this way.

UNDERSTANDING THE FIRST COMMANDMENT— FULL DISCLOSURE ALLOWS YOU TO GET AHEAD OF THE STORY

Tiger Woods's attempt to manage his crisis stands as a stark example of the perils of not respecting the edict of the first commandment of damage control:

Full disclosure.

There's a reason why this is our first commandment. It's the first step on the road to recovery. Effective damage control is built on the recognition that everything can and will come out. Thus, get out ahead of the story and reap its benefits with full disclosure:

- Full disclosure allows you to get the news out in one fell swoop, and thus avoid being swamped by the constant drip, drip, drip nature of the story.
- Full disclosure has tangible benefits that bolster your credibility and help you earn back trust.
- Full disclosure allows you to avoid the "cover-up" trap, as it's so often the cover-up aspect of a crisis that does the most severe damage.
- Full disclosure allows you to make clear that while they may have committed inexcusable acts, they are still credible and can earn back the public trust.

HE OR SHE WHO DISCLOSES FIRST, WINS

While Woods undoubtedly now has a deeper appreciation of the maxim that "nothing good happens after midnight," the approach he took should give everyone a deeper appreciation of the need to tell the story on your own terms—by disclosing the story. It was a given that the information was going to come out and that it was going to be bad. The real issue was how bad, as defined by whether Woods could have controlled the damage by containing the sordid nature of the information, and avoiding the inevitable drip, drip, drip syndrome, thus limiting the amount of time that he was going to spend on the front pages. Instead, by not fully disclosing first, Woods ended up not just being a record setting golfer but setting, what is to the best of our knowledge, a modern record for consecutive days on the front page of a New York City tabloid.

It is immutable that when Woods came to his senses in the early morning hours of November 27, 2009, he was in a deep, dark, unspinnable place. While it is understandable that Woods was not prepared to answer questions in the immediate aftermath of the accident, what he should not have done was to do more harm to himself by issuing statements that simply did not add up and making representations that did not pass the straight face test. All of which was further compounded by the fact it took Woods until February to finally confront the situation head-on—only after reports of numerous affairs, the loss of corporate sponsors, and being forced to step back from golf.

For Woods and everyone else facing a crisis, full disclosure limits the harm you will face by affording you the first and most important crack at framing, explaining, and defining an issue on your terms, and not allowing others to do the framing, explaining, and defining—especially those who are adversarial to you or have a self-interest in fanning the flames, such as those publishing tabloids.

He or she who discloses first, wins when it comes to limiting harm. Had Woods provided his story, he would have had a much cleaner shot at limiting, reducing, and containing the story—but, instead, he shanked his disclosure shot.

In comparison, consider Earvin "Magic" Johnson, who, after being diagnosed as HIV positive in 1991 had the courage to stand up before the public and explain his situation, including how he contracted the disease. Now, that took courage. And it served Magic extremely well in the long run, as he limited the damage by speaking about a very difficult matter on his own terms. There was enormous sympathy for Magic and his family, and years later he continues to be popular and respected.

THE WHOLE STORY AND NOTHING BUT THE WHOLE STORY

In a crisis—especially one where there are audiences who will pursue the matter—it is important to appreciate that at the end of the day the whole story is going to find its way out. And the sooner you have the discipline to lead the disclosure parade, the better your position will be with the audiences who are evaluating you. In short, the story is coming—the question is whether you will be run over by the story, or whether you will be able to get in front of it.

Consider Arizona senator John McCain. McCain, along with five other senators, was accused of interfering with a federal investigation into a savings and loan owned by Charles Keating, who had also made hefty campaign contributions to the senators. McCain not only acknowledged his poor judgment but actually led the effort for campaign finance reform. In part, because of his full disclosure and subsequent actions, McCain was later able to make a successful bid for the Republican presidential nomination in 2008.

In the Tiger Woods situation, whether because of concerns about his relationship with his then wife clouded his decision making, or a naive belief that the storm would pass him by, there was a failure to recognize that the moment the crash at 2:25 A.M. on November 27, 2009, became public, he was on the clock. It was only a matter of *when,* not *if,* the story would become public. And for a golfer known for incredible discipline, he exhibited a very undisciplined approach to telling the whole story—instead, telling only parts, telling those parts in drips and drabs, and providing information that was, in fact, not the whole story (or even accurate parts of the story). For full disclosure to be truly effective, it is critical to get out *the whole story and nothing but the story.*

Those in a crisis need to gather themselves, get the real story together, and then tell the story—even if it takes time to do so (so long as they are not putting out inaccurate representations during the interregnum). Ultimately, whether you do it immediately or wait several days, you will still end up effectively being in front of the story if you put the whole story out in one fell swoop. Equally important, when considering the story you will tell, is to make sure you have the discipline not put out information that you know to be false or misleading, as you will find it very difficult, if not impossible, to recover from such a breakdown in discipline.

FULL DISCLOSURE AS A SHIELD AND A SWORD

There is a direct relationship between the ability to protect your credibility and your commitment to full disclosure—they go hand in hand. And, if done well, they can serve as the basis for asserting credibility and rebuilding trust. If you are not committed to an approach based on full disclosure, your capacity to bolster your credibility and use it to rebuild trust will be far more challenging. Moreover, if you shank your shot at full disclosure by a failed disclosure, you will find your ability to rebuild trust greatly compromised.

Full disclosure in the Woods case would have allowed him to address the issues of infidelity on his terms, take responsibility on his terms, and put himself in the strongest position possible to avoid the "women in every port" plotline that emerged. And if he had gotten ahead of the story, conveyed his remorse early on, demonstrated that he was a credible person, and taken responsibility, the ability to limit the degradation of his brand and secure the continued support of his sponsorships would have been far stronger. Finally, Woods would not have endured a months-long scandal saga that ended with him holding a nationally televised press conference followed by a massively covered stint at an addiction treatment center.

Full disclosure can serve as both a shield and a sword when it comes to protecting one's credibility. Disclosure works as a shield in that by affirmatively putting the information out, you avoid the steady chipping away of your credibility that comes from the matter being fully disclosed over an extended time period. Disclosure can serve as a sword in that it allows you to convert the communication of the information into credibility. We have discussed that in a crisis, credibility is crucial, and providing access to accurate information is effectively the money you spend to earn credibility. Therefore, full disclosure is the damage-control equivalent of "show me the money."

To respect the first commandment, follow these three steps:

1. He or she who discloses first, wins.
2. Give the whole story and nothing but the whole story.
3. Use full disclosure as a shield and a sword.

Woods's ability to perform on the golf course will determine how much he can come back from these events. It is possible he will never return to his previous standing. But there is no doubt he would have had the opportunity to come back far more rapidly and to greater heights had he sought to disclose the story on his own terms, with his own context, and with his own timing.

RESPECTING THE FIRST COMMANDMENT— KOBE BRYANT'S ROCKY MOUNTAIN DISCLOSURE

Los Angeles Lakers basketball superstar Kobe Bryant's handling of his crisis offers another lesson in the power of disclosure. Two superstar athletes in crises involving sex, but very different results.

On July 1, 2003, while staying at the Lodge and Spa Cordillera in Eagle County, Colorado, in advance of a scheduled surgical procedure, Bryant was accused of raping a woman who worked at the hotel. The incident exploded into an international news story. And as the media descended on the small town, Bryant cooperated with Eagle County law enforcement and agreed to both a lie detector test and a DNA test.

Immediately after his arrest, Bryant held a public event where, standing beside his wife, he acknowledged his relationship with the woman and apologized to his spouse for the infidelity, but maintained that the sex was consensual.

This immediate public disclosure by Bryant—where he faced the media, admitted to sex with his accuser, and took responsibility for what happened—allowed him to get in front of the story. Bryant established his credibility, which, in turn, served as the decisive pivot point by which to raise questions about the nature of the woman's rape claims.

The disclosure by Bryant showed that he who discloses first, wins, as it allowed him to get the news out in one decisive moment on his own terms. This action put him in a position to minimize the harm that would have come from the death-by-a-thousand-stories dynamic.

By having the discipline to provide the whole story and nothing but the whole story, Bryant's disclosure helped him get ahead of the story. As such, Bryant put himself in a stronger position to be able to distinguish between what he did and did not do.

The disclosure was a shield and a sword: a shield that deflected the version of events being proffered by his accuser and others involved, such as law enforcement, who otherwise would have dominated the discussion; and a sword that allowed him to cut through the noise and build credibility by affirmatively telling the story on his terms. In such a way, Bryant was able to take responsibility for his conduct and also have the credibility to defend himself from the criminal accusations.

At the end of the day, questions were raised about the nature of the accusations, and when his accuser refused to testify, the district attorney dropped the case. Bryant later settled a civil suit with his accuser. And while Kobe Bryant's reputation and brand took a significant hit, his ability to come back further, farther, and faster from the charges reflected well-executed damage control. Since 2003, Bryant has signed endorsement deals with Nike, Mercedes-Benz in China, Turkish Airlines, and others. In 2011, Bryant was ranked by *Forbes* as one of the world's highest-paid athletes. He's cheered enthusiastically on the court, and his jersey is a perennial NBA top seller.

THE FIRST COMMANDMENT APPLIED TO AN EVERYDAY CRISIS— THE REPLY ALL SYNDROME

Virtually everyone has a "reply all" story—that heart-pounding, perspiration-inducing moment when you hit "send" on an email intended for your best friend, your brother or sister, or a trusted colleague—but inadvertently hit "reply all," instantly creating your own self-inflicted crisis. It can be extremely scary, especially in the moments of panic that occurs when you first see the responses that come back and you become aware of what you've just done.

While it is a phenomenon that cuts across all sectors, the "reply all" crisis anecdotally seems to have hit law firms especially hard where, ironically, lawyers are trained to be especially careful about what they put in their electronic correspondence.

At the highly respected major international law firm Morrison & Foerester, in August 2011, a partner sent an email to a fellow partner asking, "Why are we both still at this firm?" But instead of just emailing the intended recipient, the message inadvertently went to more than one thousand fellow partners around the world.

At Skadden, Arps, Slate, Meagher & Flom, another major firm, a partner mistakenly emailed his entire department confidential evaluations of other lawyers at the firm, including who was likely to make partner and who was being asked to leave.

And a summer associate (i.e., a law school intern) at Cadwalader, Wickersham & Taft, a venerable firm since the eighteenth century, sent a private farewell email to his fellow summer associates. The message, which included his belief that the firm was bigoted and that there was widespread drug use in the company offices, found its way to a much larger public audience.

Of course, the "reply all" syndrome is not isolated to the legal profession. There was the infamous 2001 case of Peter Chung, a young, Ivy League–educated aspiring "Master of the Universe" who, while working for the private equity fund The Carlyle Group in South Korea, sent out an email to a group of his friends touting that "CHUNG is KING of his domain," and which provided salacious details of a hard-partying lifestyle. And shortly after Chung hit send, the email excerpted below went viral:

From: Peter Chung

Subject: LIVING LIKE A KING

Date: Tue, 15 May 2001 20:26:21 –0400

So I've been in Korea for about a week and a half now and what can I say, LIFE IS GOOD . . . .

   I've got a spanking brand new 2000 sq. foot 3 bedroom apt. with a 200 sq. foot terrace running the entire length of my apartment with a view overlooking Korea's main river and nightline. Why do I need 3 bedrooms? Good question, the main bedroom is for my queen size bed, where CHUNG is going to fuck every hot chick in Korea over the next 2 years (5 down, 1,000,000,000 left to go) the second bedroom is for my harem of chickies, and the third bedroom is for all of you fuckers when you come out to visit my ass in Korea.

I go out to Korea's finest clubs, bars and lounges pretty much every other night on the weekdays and everyday on the weekends to (I think in about 2 months, after I learn a little bit of the buyside business I'll probably go out every night on the weekdays). I know I was a stud in NYC but I pretty much get about, on average, 5–8 phone numbers a night and at least 3 hot chicks that say that they want to go home with me every night I go out.

What can I say, ... live [*sic*] is good, . . .

CHUNG is KING of his domain here in Seoul

So, all of you fuckers better keep in touch and start making plans to come out and visit my ass ASAP, I'll show you guys an unbelievable time. . . .

Oh, by the way, someone's gotta start fedexing me boxes of domes, I brought out about 40 but I think I'll run out of them by Saturday. . . . .

Laters,
CHUNG

And unfortunately for Chung, it appeared his Seoul-version of *Bonfire of the Vanities* had only this one chapter. Once his email went viral, his tenure at Carlyle was extremely short lived.

ANOTHER WAY

At Skadden, the prestigious law firm mentioned earlier, summer associate Jonas Blank also experienced the nitroglycerine of "reply all." Blank replied to a friend's email—but failed to note that he had included an entire legal department in his response:

I'm busy doing jack shit. Went to a nice 2hr sushi lunch today at Sushi Zen. Nice place. Spent the rest of the day typing emails and bullshitting with people. Unfortunately, I actually have work to do—I'm on some corp finance deal, under the global head of corp finance, which means I should really peruse these materials and not be a fuckup . . .

So yeah, Corporate Love hasn't worn off yet . . . But just give me time . . .

Within minutes—two minutes, according to published reports—Blank, after being alerted to his mishap, set to work on another "reply all," to the lawyers who received his initial email, explaining his mistake and apologizing. Blank forthrightly wrote that he recognized the damage he had done to Skadden and further was concerned with "the implicit reflection such behavior could have on the firm."

And while the "reply all" went viral and soon spread to other law firms, legal blogs, and even found its way into *The New Yorker* magazine—there was a different tone to the stories. Blank's mishap was portrayed as a "teachable moment" for summer associates not only at Skadden Arps but at law firms around the country (another respected Manhattan firm sent a memo to its summer associates featuring Blank's email, stating, "This is a good lesson in what NOT to do"). Yet the real teachable moment is Blank's subsequent actions to address his initial mistake:

- He fully disclosed the mistake and put out the story first and on his terms.
- He got in front of the story by telling the whole story.
- He put himself in a position to take responsibility and earned credibility for doing so, and this allowed him to rebuild trust.

And despite all the attention generated by his "reply all" email, and immediate speculation that he lost any opportunity for a job at the law firm, Blank was reportedly invited back and hired by the firm after he graduated from law school.

Just imagine if there had not been an immediate response. The subsequent story would have been far worse—in the Peter Chung category—and the lawyer would likely have been escorted from the building, never to be invited back.

COROLLARY TO THE FIRST COMMANDMENT— YOU HAVE ONE BITE AT THE DISCLOSURE APPLE

Legendary New York City mayor Fiorello LaGuardia was one of the first modern politicians to understand the need for full disclosure in surviving a crisis, when he acknowledged an error by saying, "When I make a mistake, I make sure it is a really big mistake."

The corollary to the first commandment of full disclosure is that you cannot have a series of public disclosures on the same subject. As a general proposition, you get one bite at the full disclosure apple.

If love means never having to say you are sorry, a crisis means you only get one opportunity to fully disclose and say you are sorry.

Our favorite example illustrating this is former Italian prime minister Silvio Berlusconi. Berlusconi was a bit of a serial apologist.

In 2001, he said he was sorry for his comment that Western civilization was superior to Islam.

In 2003, just as Italy was assuming its position as the rotating head of the European Union, the prime minister had to apologize for saying that a German member of the European Union Parliament would be "perfect in the part of a Nazi camp guard."

Later in 2003, Berlusconi apologized to Italy's Jewish community following his assertion that Italian Fascist dictator Benito Mussolini "never killed anyone."

However, our favorite Berlusconi apology was in response to his then wife Veronica Lario's, public chiding of his penchants for flirting with beautiful women (the prime minister's out-of-the-box political approach included recruiting attractive women to run for office on his La Forza political party ticket). Berlusconi replied with an open public letter, effectively disclosing his flirtations and offering an apology—*the apologia*—like no other:

> Your dignity should not be an issue: I will guard it like a precious material in my heart even when thoughtless jokes come out of my mouth. But marriage proposals, no, believe me, I have never made one to anyone.
>
> Forgive me, however, I beg of you, and take this public testimony of private pride that submits to your anger as an act of love. One among many. A huge kiss. Silvio.

Generally speaking, the public is very forgiving of a mistake—especially when one discloses and accepts ownership over the issue at hand. However, you cannot test the public's patience. Not only must you fully disclose for the disclosure to be effective but the same conduct that precipitated the disclosure cannot become a re-occurring event—something that Berlusconi discovered in 2009.

In 2009, his former wife accused him of not only flirting with beautiful women but also consorting with minors—when it was made public that he had attended the nineteenth birthday party of a friend's daughter. This news led to a series of disclosures, including news that the prime minister infamously participated in lewd and lascivious parties involving minors (among the guests was an aspiring teenage model, Karima el-Mahroug, nicknamed Ruby Rabacuori or "Ruby Heart Stealer"), which according to news reports he called Bunga Bunga parties.

Berlusconi was an enormously powerful man with a fortune worth billions; he controlled a vast swath of the media in Italy and was the country's longest-serving prime minster since World War II. But the totality of the information disclosed about his private life, coming at a time when Italy was struggling with a global economic meltdown, contributed to the loss of his political standing, undermined public confidence in him, and ultimately put the prime minister in a position where his leadership was challenged on multiple fronts.

Berlusconi is a politician who makes the proverbial cat with nine lives look like an amateur. But by 2011, his number ultimately came up and he was finally forced from office. He violated the full disclosure corollary of *one bite at the disclosure apple*—and if his actions had ended with the original *apologia* and not the Bunga Bunga, his leadership may not have gone boom boom.

EIGHT
COMMANDMENT II
SPEAK TO YOUR CORE AUDIENCE

You talkin' to me?

—Travis Bickle, *Taxi Driver*

THE SECOND COMMANDMENT—SPEAK TO YOUR CORE AUDIENCE

By explicitly identifying your core audience, you can best determine what information they want to receive, while avoiding communicating unwanted information that would do more harm than good. Know how your core audiences receive their information and align your communication channels appropriately. Effectively targeting your core audience with the most reliable messenger will also support your efforts to rebuild credibility and trust by keeping you focused on directing the right information to the right people.

DISRESPECTING THE SECOND COMMANDMENT—BLINDSIDED IN HAPPY VALLEY

In early November 2011, people had good reasons to be happy in Happy Valley, Pennsylvania, the name for the community where Penn State University is located.

Penn State's football program, nicknamed the Nittany Lions, was ranked number twelve in the country under the leadership of the late head coach Joe Paterno. Coach Paterno, the winningest college football coach in history, was finishing up his sixty-first year with a team that maintained one of the nation's highest player graduation rates relative to its peers. Coach Paterno, up to this point in time, was beloved in town for his philanthropy, having given and raised enormous amounts of money for the school. And perhaps most impressive for such a competitive, national championship–caliber football program, under Paterno's leadership Penn State as of the fall of 2011 had never been the subject of a major NCAA rules infraction.

The success of the football program under "Jo Pa," as Coach Paterno was known, along with the leadership of university president Graham Spanier, had helped transform the university from a respectable regional school into a nationally recognized research institution. The university was ranked as one of the top fifteen public universities in the country and considered one of the public Ivy universities. Penn State's graduates were renowned for their loyalty and support of the university—with the football program widely acknowledged as the driving force of this tremendous alumni support.

And then, on November 5, the situation turned very grim in Happy Valley. News broke that Pennsylvania attorney general Linda Kelly had filed a forty-count criminal indictment against former Penn State assistant coach Jerry Sandusky for sexually abusing minors. The university was now in the middle of the growing scandal—the alleged incidents involving Sandusky and minors occurred on campus, and there were also disturbing revelations that President Spanier, Coach Paterno, and others on campus had failed to report to law enforcement authorities a 2002 abuse incident that was reportedly witnessed by a graduate assistant and involved Sandusky and a child in the team's locker room showers. The filing also included indictments against Penn State athletic director Timothy Curley and senior vice president Gary Schultz for perjury and failure to report the 2002 incident.

The attorney general's criminal filing ripped Sandusky as a sexual predator "who used his position within the university and community to repeatedly prey on young boys." It was also unsparing in the characterization of the university, and in particular Penn State president Spanier and the two indicted administrators, for failing to take any action beyond banning Sandusky from campus once they were told of the shower incident. The criminal filing also documented:

> Additionally, there is no indication that anyone from the university ever attempted to learn the identity of the child who was sexually assaulted on their campus or made any follow-up effort to obtain more information from the person who witnessed the attack first-hand . . . [T]hey didn't tell law-enforcement officials about the matter . . . Despite this so-called ban, which was reviewed and approved by university President Graham Spanier without any

further inquiry on his part, there was no effective change in Sandusky's status with the school and no limits on his access to the campus.

The news reports generated by the filing on the weekend of November 5 and 6 put Penn State in the middle of a criminal proceeding, and it was the first time that the thirty-one member Penn State Board of Trustees, the institution's governing body, became fully aware of the magnitude and scope of the inquiry. And while the Board was blindsided, it was clear from the criminal filing that Penn State's president Graham Spanier had to have been well aware that the university was going to be in the middle of this appalling story (a suggestion Spanier subsequently disputed, claiming he was not fully informed by the university's lawyers).

In fact, a *New York Times* report based on interviews with thirteen members of the university's Board of Trustees documented that the trustees were "caught completely unaware." The story quoted trustee Mark H. Dambly, acknowledging, "There was a lack of information being provided to us . . . We found out about it when the rest of the world found out about it." Other trustees interviewed for the story openly discussed about how they learned about the incident from news reports. In short, the governing Board of the university was out of the loop.

That weekend, as the news spread and the national media began descending upon Penn State, President Spanier, without any prior Board approval, issued a statement on behalf of the university expressing strong support—"unconditional support"—for Athletic Director Curley and Senior Vice President Schultz. This generated further criticism, as it created the impression that the university was more concerned about the legal exposure of its administrators than the plight of the children. The university president's statement read:

> The allegations about a former coach are troubling, and it is appropriate that they be investigated thoroughly. Protecting children requires the utmost vigilance.
>
> With regard to the other presentments, I wish to say that Tim Curley and Gary Schultz have my unconditional support. I have known and worked daily with Tim and Gary for more than 16 years. I have complete confidence in how they have handled the allegations about a former university employee.

Tim Curley and Gary Schultz operate at the highest levels of honesty, integrity and compassion. I am confident the record will show that these charges are groundless and that they conducted themselves professionally and appropriately.

Graham Spanier

News reports then began to provide still more lurid details about Sandusky's conduct, and specifically the nature of the university's involvement. And as the national attention escalated, the issue of President Spanier's and Coach Paterno's future at the university became an increasingly central issue and questions were raised about why neither man did not do more to stop the abuse, as opposed to doing nothing.

For the most part, the university had very little to say publicly, with President Spanier apparently muzzled by the Board following his "unconditional support" statement for the two indicted administrators, and for a time no one stepped forward from the university leadership to externally represent Penn State. This lack of publicly visible leadership contributed to the impression that no one was in charge.

The university then cancelled Coach Paterno's usual weekly press conference, and amidst intensifying reports that support on the Board of Trustees for keeping him was eroding, the coach, apparently without communicating to, or discussing with the Board, transparently sought to pre-empt any Board actions by announcing his intent to retire at the end of the year. The coach also made a public appearance, leading a fist-pumping "We are Penn State" cheer with students who had gathered on his front lawn to express their support for him, which immediately was played and replayed across local and national television outlets.

That evening, Wednesday, November 9, 2011, the Board announced that President Spanier had "resigned" and Coach Paterno had been fired.

UNDERSTANDING THE SECOND COMMANDMENT—SPEAK TO YOUR CORE AUDIENCE

The Penn State crisis was a terrible, terrible episode where the abused children are truly the only real victims. At every step of the way, the people and institutions that should have been protecting the minors failed to do so. In June 2012, confirming the community's worst fears, Jerry Sandusky was convicted of sexually assaulting ten boys. And further, the next month, an investigation by former FBI director Louis Freeh was released that showed Coach Paterno knew about the incidents as early as 1998 but did nothing to stop the abuse; other top officials at the university were also culpable in failing to protect the victims. In focusing on Penn State's approach to damage control, by no means do we wish in any way to minimize the tragedy of what happened to the children. The university's mishandling of the entire crisis, and especially its failure to protect the children, deserve significant and enduring attention. However, for the purposes of this chapter, we are only going to examine the approximately one hundred hours between when the scandal broke and Joe Paterno and Graham Spanier were sacked. The events of this period document the peril both men faced by failing to abide by the second commandment of damage control:

Speak to your core audience.

Full disclosure is the first step to controlling the damage, and to maximize what it is you are disclosing, it is critical to identify who it is that you are targeting to receive the disclosed information.

Explicitly identify the core audience with whom you need to communicate: Who are they? What information do they want to receive as it relates to the particular situation? Moreover, what information do they not want to hear?

Don't make the mistake of playing to the crowd and irritating the referee, or engaging in a sideshow and forgetting who you need to be focused on.

Once you know who is determining your fate, you need to make sure that you get to them.

Determine how and where your audience receives its information—and then figure out the best ways to make sure you are actually delivering the information they desire.

Whenever and wherever possible, make it as easy as possible for your core audience to get the information—don't make them work for it.

And focus like a laser, directly communicating to this audience with the most effective message possible—and with the best messenger. What they may want to hear may not be what you want to say; who they are looking for to present the information may not be who you are entirely comfortable providing; and what will most impact them may not be what you would like them to know. However, this is not about you—it is about giving your core audience the information they want from the sources they deem credible, all in the service of rebuilding trust.

A brief anecdote makes the point about playing to your audience.

Several years ago we were retained by a major public company that had resolved a dispute with the government that resulted in a financial settlement. The company, in preparing to announce the settlement, had written a lengthy statement—the *War and Peace* of press releases—defending the underlying actions that led to the settlement.

Reading the statement was the equivalent of fingernails on a chalkboard. The company officials responsible for the press release failed to "get" that the core audience the company needed to target was the investment community. Their analysts' report made clear that Wall Street had already baked into the company's share price a settlement they anticipated was coming—and the settlement number the company was going to be announcing was, in fact, significantly lower than what investors, analysts, and pundits had already digested. Therefore, at this point, all the target audience wanted to know was the settlement number—and, because the number was smaller than anticipated, the release was, in a narrow financial sense, going to be perceived as good news by this core audience of investors.

We then helped the company rewrite the ten-plus page document down to three sentences that effectively said, "Today, we have formally resolved our outstanding matter with the government. We have agreed to pay X. The company is pleased to have put this matter behind it once and for all." And once the statement was released, the company saw its stock price immediately move—upward.

HIT THE BULL'S-EYE

In a crisis there is usually a defined core audience that collectively will make up its mind on whether you can or cannot be trusted going forward, and who will, in turn, have an influence on all the other audience circles. Therefore, your communications must be directed at convincing the members of this core audience that you are trustworthy. If you do not begin your communications with a plan to *hit the bull's-eye* of your audience, you risk increasing your harm by not talking to those who will ultimately decide your fate.

The core audience is your primary and most important constituency in a crisis:

- For a public company, it could be the shareholders and analysts.
- For a school principal, it could be the parents and school district superintendent.

- For a restaurant, it could be the paying customers and the critics.

And at Penn State, both President Spanier and Coach Paterno had one core audience that was going to determine their fates: the university's Board of Trustees.

Every communication, every action, every step that they made, needed to be directed at convincing the Board of Trustees that they were credible and could be trusted—if Spanier and Paterno were to have any chance of surviving.

However, neither President Spanier nor Coach Paterno seemed to appreciate to whom they needed to be speaking.

Spanier's initial failure to adequately inform the Board about the ongoing grand jury inquiry reflected a lack of understanding of the steps needed for his survival and for preserving the integrity of the university's reputation. The Board should have received thorough, comprehensive, and ongoing briefings as to the status and scope of the investigation, and the university's response plan ought to have been the product of a collaborative process between the president and the Board. And all of the responses should have centered on the victims.

Further, their most critical audience, the Board, should not have seen breaking news clips of their beleaguered coach engaging in rally cheers with students; rather, the coach needed to be out of the public spotlight and focused on one-on-one direct and personal conversations with the Board.

Instead, there appeared to be no briefings, no advance notice, and no plan.

To mitigate against doing more harm and put yourself in a position to move forward, ask yourself who it is that will decide your fate—who is your core audience? And once you identify the core audience, you need to relentlessly hit the bull's-eye. From there, you can expand out in a series of concentric circles, as necessary from the most important audiences to the less significant. But the single most important thing to know is who will be making the decisions about your future.

FIVE-STAR CONCIERGE SERVICE

In speaking effectively to your core audience, you need to have a mindset that you will *provide five-star concierge service*. In a crisis, your core audience will not only react and respond to what you say and what you do—but *how* you do it, and *how* you say it. Thus, you need to have the discipline to be calm and cool, maintain your professionalism, be responsive, and, even under extreme pressure, demonstrate studied nonchalance as you deliver the goods. Treat your core audience the way you would offer room service in the presidential suite of a five-star hotel—complete concierge service with white linen, silver utensils, and a presentation replete with poise, grace, and a modicum of aplomb.

At Penn State, President Spanier and Coach Paterno needed to have made abundantly clear to the Board that they were there to help. And instead of issuing their own statements and taking their own actions, they should have looked for ways to be helpful and supportive of the Board. As a consequence of their actions, they ended up isolating themselves—so much so that Coach Paterno—a revered coach for over six decades—was fired by the Board over the phone.

In a crisis, more so than at any time, you must have the discipline to make sure your core audience is receiving the five-star concierge service. Return calls promptly. Take questions seriously. Get back to people with the information they request quickly. Don't play favorites. Deal with the facts—the time for spinning is over. Realize the burden of proof is on you to win people over and to provide the information they want—even if, before the crisis, they were trying to win you over.

COMMUNICATIONS BEGIN AT THE TOP

Once you know to whom you need to be speaking, there must also be personal, positively engaged leadership driving the actual communications. It's important to remember that organizations take on the qualities of their leaders. Therefore, to be as effective as possible at re-establishing credibility, it is critical to *understand that communications begin at the top.*

The past success of the organization is usually related to the current leadership team. Leaders typically have a reservoir of credibility and goodwill that can be tapped into during a crisis. The core audience is familiar with the existing leadership team, and this is who they expect to hear from in difficult times. And if the core audience does not hear from the leadership, then the credibility of the leadership team—and by extension the entire organization's credibility—will immediately take a hit, and the hole you find yourself in becomes even deeper.

At Penn State, both Spanier and Paterno needed to have been their own messengers in communicating with the Board. They were the leaders of the university. They were both involved in the matter. And they both had long-standing personal ties to the Board. Yet, both men seemed to go out of their way to avoid personally communicating to the Board. The fact that trustees learned about the situation from the media is clear evidence of an inexcusable breakdown in President Spanier's crisis communications.

President Spanier's decision to issue a statement on behalf of the university in defense of his administrators (especially considering the severity of the charges) without consulting the Board in advance was not only a lost opportunity to build credibility by working with his immediate bosses, but also served to exacerbate the problems with a Board that was quickly losing faith in him.

In determining how the senior leadership of an organization can most effectively communicate, there are a number of factors to consider.

Ideally, you want the person who is in charge to take on a leadership role. However, there are times that such a person may not have the skill set to assume such a role, or they may also be a player in the crisis and constrained in their ability to effectively serve as the face and voice for an organization (e.g., they may face legal exposure and cannot avail themselves). In such situations, identify and elevate the individual who will assume these responsibilities from the beginning of the crisis. An example of this was seen during the aftermath of Hurricane Katrina. The Bush administration suffered from the inability to find a capable public leader for the administration's dreadful disaster response—as symbolized by the repeated failings of the then head of FEMA, Mike "Brownie" Brown—until Lt. Gen. Russell Honore showed up on the scene, earning the moniker the "Black John Wayne."

You want someone capable of being able to perform in terms of what they say, the emotions they reflect, and how they comport themselves. If you have a senior leader who simply is not an effective communicator, you will need to consider who else from the organization has the standing and stature with the core audience to assume this duty. During the BP Gulf Coast spill, BP ultimately replaced British Tony Haywood with Mississippi native Robert Dudley, who was far better than Haywood at connecting with the people of the Gulf Coast.

Often the initial test of the credibility of an organization's leadership is whether their leaders communicate the crisis responses and damage control actions first and directly to its core audiences. In a crisis, when possible, every important constituency should learn important news from the leadership first—well before they hear about it from the news media, a competitor, or the rumor mill.

In diagramming the plays you intend to execute in responding to a crisis, remember that before you even put the ball in the air, it is critical to consider how you are going to inform your core audience about your actions going forward—so they hear it first from you.

Organizations, big and small, often do not realize that their core audience is usually defined and limited in nature—even in a major crisis—and that with a disciplined approach, they can effectively pursue hands-on, personal communications from their leadership that will be especially credible.

To produce the most strategic hands-on communications from its most credible messengers, organizations should catalog the varying ways its leadership can most personally and directly communicate. In our work, we have seen leaders communicate effectively through the use of a number of effective hands-on tools.

In the midst of an impending National Hockey League lockout, NHL commissioner Gary Bettman held town halls in Canada with rabid hockey fans to explain the league's position.

In the 2008 presidential election, candidate Senator Barack Obama had nearly twenty-five times the number or Twitter followers as his opponent Senator John McCain, enabling the future president to inform and galvanize his supporters.

And at Stanford University, where Bill Guttentag teaches, there is an alert system where email, texts, and phone messages rapidly go out campus-wide in the event of a crisis, so that students, faculty, administrators, and staff all hear from the school first—whether it is an assault on campus or an earthquake.

All of these hands-on communication approaches help ensure that the leadership of an organization is taking steps to communicate directly and personally with their core audiences.

To respect the second commandment, follow these three steps:

1. Identify the bull's-eye.
2. Provide five-star concierge service.
3. Understand that communications begin at the top.

RESPECTING THE SECOND COMMANDMENT—NEW VISION TELEVISION'S USE OF NEW MEDIA

New Vision Television, like many media companies, was hit hard when the economy collapsed in 2008. As a company that owned and operated fourteen major network-affiliated television stations across the United States, it was facing the challenge of significant advertising cutbacks on local television from auto companies, banks, and other consumer-oriented businesses who had slashed their advertising budgets.

The company's senior leadership team had a well-established success record when it came to leading consortiums of local television affiliates—but no one in the TV business had experienced such a downturn in the economy.

In the summer of 2009, as the recession continued to wreak havoc on the U.S. economy, the company chose to restructure its finances through the Chapter 11 bankruptcy process. In making this decision, New Vision immediately realized it needed to communicate effectively to its core audiences—employees, customers, investors, and local opinion leaders—in order to emerge from the restructuring process in as strong a position as possible.

On July 13, 2009, as New Vision was preparing to announce its restructuring plan with the release of a public statement, executives were first dispatched around the country in the form of "task forces" to personally communicate the company's strategy in one-on-one meetings with employees, partners, and clients—before the news became public.

Then, like the military executing the D-Day plan, New Vision commenced a well-organized, vertically and horizontally integrated crisis communications R-Day plan ("R" for restructuring):

- The CEO publicly issued a prepared statement that went on Business Wire.
- A custom-designed website went live that provided information about the bankruptcy process and had a section with frequently asked questions related explicitly to questions the company anticipated from its investors, employees, and advertising customers.
- The company opened a dedicated phone line to answer questions.
- New Vision launched a social media program featuring the company's senior leadership answering media questions and other inquiries.
- The communications team monitored the online reactions to the news and responded appropriately and quickly to reports that were inaccurate or incomplete.
- Executives reported back from their meetings to ensure that all inquiries were being handled appropriately and in a consistent manner, so that questions were answered in real time.

- Moving forward from the restructuring day, the company
  communicated regularly about the process when there were
  developments—such as the scheduling of hearings, the approval
  of the reorganization plan, and the completion of the bankruptcy
  process.

Within days, New Vision was generating and distributing news about positive developments on the restructuring—and by September was able to successfully wrap up the restructuring.

Most damage control situations do not require you to deliver your message to the entire world—or even the entire country or state. Rather, in most cases, success can be achieved by delivering the message in a precisely targeted way to narrowly defined core audiences.

The restructuring of New Vision Television exemplifies the fundamental importance of speaking to your core audience—the company really did hit the bull's-eye.

New Vision recognized that in restructuring its communications, the company needed to start with its core audiences, and then expand out from there, in a series of concentric audience circles.

Therefore, the company targeted the following:

- Employees: The company needed to retain its employees, who were
  crucial to its success, and address their uncertainty, and thus keep
  them from being recruited away.
- Customers: In order to maintain its current prospective advertising
  revenue, the company needed to make sure their customers
  understood that they would not be adversely impacted.
- Investors and lenders: The company needed to show them that there
  was a well-conceived plan in place.
- Business and local media: Most crises, such as New Vision's, will not
  be national news; therefore, the focus needed to be squarely be on the
  trade press that reports on the industry and the local media that was
  likely to impact the company, its employees, and customers.

Beyond knowing to whom they needed to speak, New Vision was all about having the discipline to provide five-star concierge service. The company realized its success would be determined less by the national media and more by how individual stations dealt with the issue in their local marketplaces—with their media, employees, customers, and the blogger rumor mills.

Given that the company's core audience included the relatively defined universe of its investors, employees, lenders, and key clients—and coupled with the fact that typically in a restructuring, interested parties have to either wade through complex legal and financial filings or rely on analysts and financial reports—New Vision's Twitter feed proved to be extremely successful. Here are some samples of the Tweets:

NewVisionTV Lisa Cohen

New Vision reached an agreement with its debt holders on a financial restructuring tonight, news release here: http://tinyurl.com/m5ckuo

NewVisionTV Lisa Cohen

The restructuring is powerful news for New Vision. Here is a message from Chairman and CEO Jason Elkin: http://tinyurl.com/knn5td

NewVisionTV Lisa Cohen

Good sign that New Vision's restructuring will move swiftly through the court process. Hearing already scheduled for Wednesday at 11am/ET

NewVisionTV Lisa Cohen

For employees of NV: the restructuring process will not result in any employee layoffs or furloughs and benefits will remain intact.

The tweets worked, the meetings worked, the communications all worked, and with strategy, forthrightness, and the support of all its constituencies New Vision Television began to right the ship.

For all of these audiences, New Vision's communications were credible, as they were communications that came from the top. The company's shareholders respected the fact that the leadership team had historically proven themselves as deft managers. And since their core audiences understood the importance of the leadership team and considered them highly credible, the company needed to assure their constituencies that the situation would be managed personally by the company's leadership. Which it did by having the leadership deliver messages in the most personal and direct ways possible. Every important constituency learned important news from the leadership—well before they heard about it from competitors or the news media. And they were assisted by the company's lawyers, who explained the restructuring process as precisely as possible and reported progress at every key step of the way.

THE SECOND COMMANDMENT APPLIED TO AN EVERYDAY CRISIS—TRAVEL ADVICE

In our day and age of empowering consumer choice through crowdsourcing, hotels have increasingly taken to monitoring online activity regarding their guests. A negative online review, a bad tweet, or a low TripAdvisor rating are all real crises for a hotel—whether it is a small family-owned operation or a major chain.

In fact, a significant percentage of travelers make their decisions based on online reviews. News reports confirm what hotels have known for years to be the case: Over 40 percent of leisure travelers and 50 percent of business travelers rely upon reviews when making travel decisions.

In response, hotels have replied to negative reviews or comments with their own individually crafted responses; they have actively encouraged guests to post positive reviews on sites like TripAdvisor and engaged in proactive online strategies, such as running search engine optimization campaigns, to help impact what is seen in an online search.

And seizing upon this, some hotels have approached the issue with a sophisticated understanding of the value of not just monitoring social media in order to identify a crisis—but hitting the bull's-eye when it comes to responding to the crisis by identifying and communicating to their core audience.

There have been numerous reports of hotel managers responding immediately online to customer complaints or observations—and in real time. A June 2010 *Wall Street Journal* story documented how hotel managers actively monitor and engage past, future, and current hotel guests via social media platforms such as Twitter, Facebook, and Foursquare in order to be able to quickly engage in damage control before the issue becomes a permanent online black mark that could impact the decisions of future travelers.

The story detailed how one guest complained that his room overlooked air conditioning ducts, and just how quickly the hotel's management responded:

Horan, a 47-year-old who works in sales at a software company, tweeted, "At the Orlando Marriott World Center for RIM WES 2010 [a technology conference]. But I have the crappiest room in the hotel." Front-desk employee Zachary Long saw Horan's comments while searching Twitter and went into damage-control mode. Long had a note of apology for the "current room situation" slipped under Horan's door and offered to move him to a pool-view room the next day.

"It was on Twitter, so it could spread," Long says.

"It was a complete shock" that Marriott saw the message and reacted, Horan says.

Consider the social media company Revinate (for their political counterpart, PolitEar, Chris Lehane is on the board of advisors), which has designed a capacity for hotels to monitor the social media in and around their hotels and guests, in order for the hotels to be able to speak directly to their customers. And smart hotels, using the Revinate platform, have used the technology as a valuable crisis communications tool—allowing them to effectively speak to their core audiences.

There is also the example of the Holiday Inn St. Louis sales manager Lauren Berry, who wanted to drive up the hotel's online ranking score. In pursuit of this, she took to responding directly to 100 percent of the online reviews for the hotel, and also put in place a variety of other online tools to help her communicate directly with guests. The result was that her hotel climbed twenty spots in its online rankings.

And then there is the case of Kristin Spitz, the electronic sales and marketing manager at the Grand Hyatt in San Diego. Spitz was monitoring Twitter references to her hotel and noticed a guest complaining that the Wi-Fi wasn't working. By watching the stream of tweets during meetings, she was able to maintain a real-time view of how the hotel was handling their guests' needs. And when she was saw the Wi-Fi problem, she instantly responded, and within minutes a technician was at the guest's room. Spitz later reflected, "The guests were floored at how responsive and on-the-ball we were."

All of these anecdotes have a common denominator: The hotels addressed a crisis by identifying their core audience and their needs.

The communications back to the guests were from the "leaders" at the hotel—the night manager, the front desk, a sales manager, etc. The guests heard the information from the hotel first—and it was delivered in a very hands-on way. You can't get more hands-on than a tweet back to you.

COROLLARY TO THE SECOND COMMANDMENT—NO PANDERING

There can often be a fine line between speaking to your core audience and pandering to your core audience. But like Supreme Court Justice Potter Stewart's legendary remark on what constitutes pornography, you know pandering when you see it.

We knew it was pandering when to try to minimize their share of the blame after the cruise ship *Costa Concordia* went aground and partially sank in January 2012, the CEO of Costa Cruises (the Italian subsidiary of Carnival Cruise Lines who owned the luxury liner) sought to pile on to news reports about the captain of the ship who reportedly sailed too close to shore and then was said to have rushed ahead of some passengers to get off the boat. The company's statement immediately following the accident included:

> While the investigation is ongoing, preliminary indications are that there may have been significant human error on the part of the ship's master, Captain Francesco Schettino, which resulted in these grave consequences.

And the Penn State trustees (and many others) saw it as hollow pandering when, in announcing his intent to retire at the conclusion of the season, Coach Paterno released a public statement suggesting he was merely trying to act in support of the Board. In fact, his very action was clearly designed to attempt an end run around the Board. Coach Paterno wrote:

> I am absolutely devastated by the developments in this case. I grieve for the children and their families, and I pray for their comfort and relief.
>
> I have come to work every day for the last 61 years with one clear goal in mind: To serve the best interests of this university and the young men who have been entrusted to my care. I have the same goal today.
>
> That's why I have decided to announce my retirement effective at the end of this season. At this moment the Board of Trustees should not spend a single minute discussing my status. They have far more important matters to address. I want to make this as easy for them as I possibly can. This is a

tragedy. It is one of the great sorrows of my life. With the benefit of hindsight, I wish I had done more.

My goals now are to keep my commitments to my players and staff and finish the season with dignity and determination. And then I will spend the rest of my life doing everything I can to help this University.

To avoid pandering, don't put lipstick on the proverbial pig. Just give people the facts and do not try to pretend the situation is something other than what it appears to be. Costa Cruise's immediate focus on blaming the captain came off as an effort to sidestep their own accountability—when the company's entire focus should have been on doing all it could to help those who had been on the ship. Pointing fingers creates a circular firing squad. And, of course, if the captain was indeed at fault, Costa Cruise should have allowed others to tell that story, or told the story in a way where their company accepted its share of the responsibility.

Furthermore, crises have storylines, so do not drown your credibility trying to fight the current. Penn State president Spanier's statement of standing behind the officials named in the attorney general's filing served no real purpose—other than to squander his credibility with the Board of Trustees and the broader public. To the extent Spanier and the university said anything, it should have been focused on the health, safety, welfare, and justice for the abused children.

And, finally, don't stick your finger in the eye of the authorities. If someone holds your fate in their hands, but has yet to make a decision, do not engage in conduct that is likely to force them to take actions detrimental to your interest. Coach Paterno's announcement that he would be retiring at the end of the season left the Board of Trustees little recourse but to fire him—or they would only have reinforced the negative storyline coming out of the criminal filing: that Penn State was a school so lacking in institutional controls that the football coach ran the entire show.

In all of these situations, and many more, a tragedy was made still worse by insensitive, ham-fisted responses that failed to recognize that you need to always keep your focus on speaking to your core audience.

NINE
COMMANDMENT III
DON'T FEED THE FIRE

What we've got here is a failure to communicate.
— Prison Warden Strother Martin, *Cool Hand Luke*

THE THIRD COMMANDMENT—DON'T FEED THE FIRE

Do not allow the pressure of the situation to result in taking actions that feed the fire and increase the harm. Instead, exercise the discipline to determine what it is you should do, and what it is you should *not* do, to stop the fire from spreading. Extinguish the fire by using good facts to promote your credibility and smother bad facts, which, in turn, will facilitate the rebuilding of trust.

DISRESPECTING THE THIRD COMMANDMENT—
TOYOTA'S UNINTENDED CRASHING OF ITS BRAND

In January 2009, Toyota officially surpassed GM to become the world's number one auto company.

Toyota's success was decades in the making and directly attributable to the commitment of the Toyoda family (the company's founders) to building one of the world's most trusted consumer brands.

A number of surveys over the years documented that the carmaker's brand was among the best in the world, and this was grounded in consumer perceptions of Toyota vehicles as safe, high-quality automobiles. Consumers trusted the Toyota brand so much that the company had developed a significant competitive advantage on the basis of its customer loyalty. If you bought one Toyota, there was a good chance you would have a long-term relationship with the carmaker.

In late August 2009—the same year the company became the world's number one auto brand—an off-duty California policeman was driving a Toyota Lexus that accelerated in excess of one hundred miles per hour and crashed, killing the officer and his family. The incident received news coverage that featured a recorded cell phone call to 911 documenting that the acceleration was uncontrolled, and the driver had no part in the sudden acceleration. In part because of the novel, TV-friendly existence of the 911 cell phone recording, this became a story in the electronic media and spiked existing concerns about whether Toyota vehicles suffered from an electronic defect that caused uncontrolled acceleration—in turn putting pressure on federal safety regulators responsible for protecting the public.

The subsequent events provide key lessons in damage control careening out of control.

At the time of the fatal accident, Toyota was well aware of quality and safety questions about unintended accelerations. The trail of evidence included data from the NHTSA (the National Highway Traffic Safety Administration—the government agency empowered to ensure automotive safety) from 2004 indicating that Toyota vehicles accounted for 20 percent of all uncontrolled acceleration accidents (compared to 4 percent in 2000); the company's own 2009 analysis into these accidents, which suggested that the cause of the uncontrolled acceleration was due to floor mats obstructing gas pedals; and an early October 2009 recall of 3.8 million cars to address concerns that the floor mats could be obstructing the gas pedal.

However, the story ratcheted up even further when in October 2009, the *Los Angeles Times* launched an investigative series examining Toyota's safety and quality practices.

Over the course of several months, the paper reported that:

- Toyota's acceleration issues dated back to 2002, when the company began installing drive-by-wire systems in its vehicles.
- The company had received 1,200 complaints of unintended accelerations, and the uncontrolled accelerations continued even when the floor mats in question were removed.
- Toyota sought to prevent making available the data collected by onboard recorders of vehicles that had experienced uncontrolled acceleration.

- And more people had died from uncontrolled accelerations involving Toyota cars than from all the other car companies put together.

In the face of these articles and other media coverage, Toyota continued to insist that there was no defect and that the floor mats were the root cause of the uncontrolled accelerations. The company even sent a letter to its customers at the end of October 2009 explicitly stating, "no defect exists."

A few days later, the NHTSA took the highly unusual action of issuing an especially harsh response to Toyota's "no defect" letter, calling it "inaccurate" and "misleading," and adding that the recall of the floor mats "does not correct the underlying defect."

The rebuke by the feds turned what was a big story into an even bigger story.

The controversy continued to escalate and Toyota issued a press release denying media reports about the defects. However, by late November, Toyota dealers were being instructed to remove and replace gas pedals and update the onboard computers on some vehicle models.

But the accidents continued.

On the day after Christmas 2009, a Toyota Avalon carrying four passengers accelerated and crashed into a Texas lake, killing everybody on board.

By December 31, 2009, Toyota had accounted for 33 percent of all uncontrolled acceleration complaints that year.

On January 16, 2010, Toyota stated that a supplier was responsible for the gas pedals that may have had a dangerous "sticking" defect.

Then five days later Toyota announced a recall for 2.3 million cars to fix sticky pedals.

And the problems for Toyota grew still worse.

On January 26, 2010, the company suspended the sale of eight models and announced that beginning the following week it would temporarily shut down five North American assembly plants. The company did not make public that it took these steps at the direction of the federal government, but the next day, Department of Transportation secretary Ray LaHood effectively called Toyota on the carpet by publicly stating that his agency had directed Toyota to suspend its operations—a statement that Toyota had to confirm.

On February 5, Toyota president Akio Toyoda finally appeared at a press conference. Facing the media, he apologized and announced a task force involving outside experts. But by now—after multiple explanations—the damage had been done.

Toyota temporarily shut down its manufacturing plants at a cost of $54 million a day; monthly car sales dropped below 100,000 for the first time in more than a decade; Toyota's U.S. market share fell to its lowest level since January 2006; the company's stock dropped 16 percent; *Consumer Reports* removed its "buy recommendation" on eight Toyota models; the Department of Justice and the Securities and Exchange Commission initiated investigations; and Congress opened up its own inquiry, complete with public hearings.

By 2011, two years after ascending to the top, Toyota was passed by GM as the number one carmaker in the world.

And even though a subsequent NHTSA study came out generally supporting Toyota's claim that there were no defects in the technical sense, and Toyota has since worked to claw its way back to its previous position in the public eye, Toyoda acknowledged that Toyota's crisis response, like the warden and prisoners in *Cool Hand Luke,* suffered from a failure to communicate:

"We came to realize the problem was rather with communications."

UNDERSTANDING THE THIRD COMMANDMENT—DON'T FEED THE FIRE

The chief defect in Toyota's response was the company's failure to respect the third commandment of damage control:

Don't feed the fire.

Once you are in the throes of a crisis, you cannot duck, dodge, or bob and weave. Disclosure to your core audience is most effective when you admit your mistakes quickly.

The more time it takes to admit your mistakes, the more harm you will do.

The longer it takes you to get to the bottom line, the longer you will be in crisis.

And the harder you push back against those empowered by the public to review your actions, the harder it will be to establish the credibility you will need to rebuild trust with your target audiences.

IF THE MISTAKE FITS, BE QUICK TO ADMIT IT

A company's decision to either contest an issue or to acknowledge that "mistakes were made" is often a defining moment in a crisis.

If you are going to insist you are right and others are wrong, like Toyota did, you have to be 110 percent sure that you are right, which Toyota was not.

If you are going to continue to persist that you are right, like Toyota did, you have to be 110 percent sure that you will be able to communicate to your key audiences that you are, in fact, right, which Toyota was unable to do.

If you are going to assert your claims of righteousness in the face of contradictory information, like Toyota did, you have to be 110 percent confident in the plan you have to communicate your righteousness, which Toyota eventually acknowledged they were not.

And if you are going to stand and fight, like Toyota did, if you are not 110 percent sure of your ability to win such a fight, the quicker you move to communicate your awareness of a problem and the need to address the problem, the more likely your organization will be able to limit the harm caused by the problem.

It's essential to ensure you're not feeding a destructive fire, but rather initiating a process to address the issues—and to put out the fire.

In the Toyota recall crisis, the company knew it needed to communicate to its customers, government regulators, and the press. And what these audiences wanted to know was if Toyota honestly recognized there was a problem, and how the company was going to fix the problem and guarantee it would not happen again. But Toyota not only failed to fully disclose its problem (thereby violating the first commandment—full disclosure), Toyota did not follow the third commandment's edict of don't feed the fire. Instead, the company actively avoided disclosing the pertinent information to its audiences, which threw fuel on the fire and led to the company's brand being badly burned.

In other words, *if the mistake fits, be quick to admit it.* The admission will mitigate the harm you are facing.

In admitting a mistake, the sooner you express regret, say you are sorry, or give an apology, the more effective the admission. To underscore this point, consider an October 2011 *Wall Street Journal* online analysis of the recent trend of high-profile CEOs battling crises who take to YouTube to explain their situations. The *Journal* specifically focused on the evolving art form of the YouTube apology, including examining the time in each video it took the CEOs to actually utter the word "sorry." The *Journal*'s review leads to the conclusion that the sooner in the video a CEO apologizes, the more effective the YouTube apology.

Throughout the entire acute period of the Toyota crisis, from September to February, the company struggled with acknowledging the magnitude of the problem. The company's target audiences believed that whatever the precise cause (whether it was technically a "defect" or not), the indisputable fact was that vehicles were self-accelerating—and in some instances killing passengers. Toyota needed to address this reality, as opposed to insisting that there was not a technical defect, or trying to parse the specific reasons as to why the accidents were occurring to avoid the dreaded word "defect."

Do not deny the undeniable, try to explain away the unexplainable, or stay silent on the immutable—such actions will only conflict with reality. By aggressively denying there was a serious problem with their cars' braking systems in the face of a rising flood of evidence that there was indeed some kind of a problem, Toyota's response only served to create conflict—and it's that very conflict that generates additional coverage and controversy. In short, by fighting the story, Toyota was fanning the flames of the fire.

KNOW YOUR BOTTOM LINE, AND AVOID DRAWING HARD AND FAST LINES

To follow the third commandment's prohibition of don't feed the fire, you need to be exceptionally disciplined when it comes to *knowing your bottom line and avoid drawing hard and fast lines* when communicating to your target audiences. Your effort to control the damage by saying all the right things, cooperating, and being transparent will come off as crisis communications window dressing if you are taking positions that simply do not get purchase with your key audiences.

Toyota wandered into the Gary Hart trap: When you draw hard and fast lines, you are effectively daring others to challenge your position when you are in fact vulnerable.

As background, Colorado senator Gary Hart was the leading Democratic presidential contender in 1987. As he was planning his White House run, rumors were circulating about the senator having extramarital affairs. In response, he told *The New York Times,* "Follow me around. I don't care. I'm serious. If anybody wants to put a tail on me, go ahead. They'll be very bored." Anybody who has spent even the smallest amount of time around the media knows this was waving the proverbial red flag in front of the bull. Unfortunately for Hart, *The Miami Herald* had already taken him up on his offer. More unfortunately for Hart, he was having an affair. And most unfortunately for Hart, the paper secured photos of an attractive twenty-nine-year-old model, Donna Rice, sitting on Hart's lap on a dock as the two enjoyed a cruise to Bimini on a yacht named *Monkey Business,* while the senator was wearing a

T-shirt emblazoned with "Monkey Business Crew" (no, you cannot make this stuff up).

To fight the damage and protect your bottom line, you need to avoid locking yourself into a position that may evolve or shift over time. In a crisis, even the slightest shift will stoke the fire. For Toyota, shifting between the "no defects," to the it's "the floor mats" explanation, to subsequently pointing to the stickiness of the pedals—represented a series of red flags that the company was not being straight about what it knew and what it did not know. And it certainly did nothing to give the public confidence that Toyota had an adequate plan to even determine the base cause of the problem.

Toyota's insistence that there was no defect (even if at the end of the day elements of that answer were technically accurate) simply did not resonate with the public and reflected a serious tone-deafness to the severity of the situation—namely the tragic accidents and mountain of evidence against the car manufacturer.

Above and beyond whether Toyota's "no defect" position was tenable, the fact that the company adopted this position while investigations were under way virtually guaranteed that their representation would be aggressively challenged—which is precisely what happened, and it made an already bad situation far worse.

Toyota's "no defect" position, subsequent multiple recalls, and shifting explanations introduced an accelerant to a fire the company desperately wanted to extinguish.

When hit with a crisis, you need to determine What is the bottom line? What is it that I can say that will not implode, explode, evolve, shift, or be effectively challenged over time? Even a minimalist statement that appears substantive by using the right words without any real substance is a better approach than an explanation that will not hold, or that appears to be tone deaf. A minimal and effective approach might have been, "We are aware of the issues and are cooperating fully with authorities. Our first priority is the safety of our customers. Once we learn more we will make that information public."

OPERATE TO COOPERATE

In many crises, especially those implicating the public interest, there will some sort of entity responsible for reviewing the situation—from federal oversight agencies, to local government authorities, to professional boards. In addition to acknowledging a problem or admitting to a mistake, there must also be a commitment to fully cooperating—*operate to cooperate* with any entity that is empowered or responsible for reviewing or investigating the matter. Such a commitment to cooperation will reassure your key audiences by signifying that you recognize an issue exists and you have a sincere desire to get to the bottom of it, so that the problem can be swiftly corrected.

In considering the importance of cooperating, we want to distinguish between cooperating with agencies responsible for protecting the public good, and litigation where you may face legal exposure and will need to mount a robust defense. We recognize that cooperating with an entity responsible for public safety could produce information impacting your legal exposure. Each legal situation is, of course, idiosyncratic, and it's important you consult your own attorney on legal matters. We also know that too often entities point to legal exposure as a basis for not cooperating when, in fact, it is often possible to work with the lawyers to find a way to cooperate that protects your credibility as well as your legal flank. Ultimately, you could face a balancing test between cooperating with the responsible agencies to protect the public and your credibility versus protecting your legal exposure. Our experience is that when all is said and done, to survive you must protect your credibility above all else.

Moreover, as a practical matter of human nature, in a typical situation an investigating authority will nearly always respond much more aggressively if you appear to be contesting or stonewalling on an issue. Therefore, before making any decision to poke the oversight entity, be damn sure that that you are in a position to win that fight in the court of public opinion. Whether it is the Department of Justice or the local building-code inspector, the old adage that "you can't beat City Hall" still stands. Even in this era of distrust, government entities are still perceived as representing the public; consequently, do not begin any such fight unless you have a significant advantage. And the actions of public institutions (even if taken without any basis) can undermine your credibility and, in the long run, inflict additional harm to your brand.

To this point, Toyota's posture appeared to be adversarial to the NHTSA. When the federal agency chastised Toyota for its "no defect" letter, combined with news reports that the company was resisting disclosing information obtained from vehicle recording devices, this communicated to the public that Toyota was putting its interest in profits before the public's interest in safety. This is a highly damning perception for any company selling consumer products, but especially so for a corporation whose very brand was built on quality and safety, and which operates in a business space where trust and consumer loyalty go hand in hand.

Now, to be very clear (and we will explore this further in later chapters), there are times—and we have been in our fair share of these—when the judge, jury, and executioner are demonstrably biased or unfair. In such cases, you really have no choice: You absolutely need to communicate the unfair nature of such an investigation and fight back aggressively. However, in these situations, fighting back aggressively also means fighting back smart. And your ability to raise questions about the conduct of the investigating authority will be directly connected to whether you made an honest and good-faith effort to cooperate fully, and can demonstrate the opposing party had a specific bias or agenda that blocked them from recognizing the truth.

Rather than fight the proverbial City Hall, operate to cooperate with the responsible investigating entity in order to demonstrate a commitment to securing the facts, protecting the public, and taking responsibility. Such a tactic will protect your credibility and communicate to your key audiences that you are an organization with a true commitment to the public good, and thus deserving of the public trust.

Such a good-faith effort was used to expose the various congressional investigations of the Clinton White House as nothing more than partisan prosecutions—and, in doing so, protected the credibility of the administration. After Republicans gained control of Congress in the 1994 midterm elections, a White House SWAT team was created and given responsibility for helping the Clinton administration respond to a series of planned Senate and House investigations.

Justifiably believing the congressional activity to be highly partisan in nature, the Clinton White House's initial instinct was to fight the Republicans every step of the way, whether it came to turning over documents or administration officials agreeing to testify before the committees.

However, the White House became convinced that document fights were only going to play into the opposition's hands, as the disputes would create the perception that the administration was trying to hide something from the public, thus undermining its credibility. During White House strategy sessions, the Clinton team concluded they would be better off making it clear that the White House was bending over backward to be cooperative. They then used this commitment to cooperation (including publicly releasing the very documents being sought by the Republicans the moment they were made available) as the basis to demonstrate that the administration's opponents were far more interested in abusing the oversight process to inflict partisan political damage than in conducting a truth-seeking exercise that served the best interests of the country.

Consequently, between 1995 and the Clinton re-election campaign of 1996, the White House managed to flip perceptions about the Republican investigations—from being legitimate exercises of congressional oversight, into Republicans abusing their powers for political gain.

To respect the third commandment, follow these three steps:

1. If the mistake fits, be quick to admit it.
2. Know your bottom line and avoid drawing hard and fast lines.
3. Operate to cooperate.

RESPECTING THE THIRD COMMANDMENT—MAPLE LEAF FOODS

In August 2008, one of Canada's largest food manufacturers, Maple Leaf Foods, faced the worst nightmare for any company—across Canada people were dying from listeria, a bacteria that can cause severe food poisoning, and it was connected to contaminated meat produced and sold by Maple Leaf Foods.

As the initial reports came in, Maple Leaf Foods almost immediately issued a voluntary recall of twenty-three lines of ready-to-eat meat, shut down a plant, and made clear that they were issuing a broader recall than their testing indicated was necessary. Within days, it became apparent that the contamination was far bigger than they initially realized, and the voluntary recall was expanded several times until all of the company's meat products produced in the previous three months were recalled.

Concurrent with the voluntary recalls, the company pursued an aggressive crisis communications approach, including: the CEO, Michael McCain, issuing a YouTube video; holding press conferences; posting updated information online; the release of advertising designed to inform the public about the food contamination; and engaging in a number of other proactive activities.

On each of the communications platforms, all of which prominently featured the CEO, Maple Leaf Foods apologized, made clear it was cooperating with the government investigating authorities, vowed transparency, and explained that the company was developing plans to make sure its food was safe going forward.

In their many statements and releases, McCain had a core bottom line on which he continually focused: putting the safety of the public first.

- August 20: "We believe it is important to take these broader preventive actions to respond to this situation promptly, comprehensively, and in the best interest of our consumers."
- August 23: "We know this has shaken consumer confidence in us. Our actions will continue to be guided by putting their interest first."
- August 24: "Our actions are guided by putting public health first."
- August 25: "We remain steadfast in our belief that our actions must continue to be guided by what is in the best interests of public health."

In one of the company's television ads, which featured McCain: "We have an unwavering commitment to keeping your food safe with standards well beyond regulatory requirements, but this week our best efforts failed and we are deeply sorry."

On the Maple Leaf Foods website: "Our management of the Listeria outbreak will be motivated by one thing only—the best public health interests of Canadians and specifically, our customers."

And even in a question-and-answer section in a newspaper several months later, McCain responded to positive praise from a reader about the handling of the issue by sticking to the bottom line:

> Thanks for your kind words . . . although we have made it quite clear that we aren't allowing ourselves any luxury or opportunity for "back patting" in such a terrible situation. We have just tried to handle it in the most responsible way we knew how, by putting the consumers' interests and public health first.

Let there be no mistake: Maple Leaf Foods was seriously impacted by the crisis. Sales dropped by 35 percent, the company's stock plummeted from $13.99 a share in January 2008 to $8.27 in October that year, and it was reported the company lost between $25 and $30 million. But—and this is the true test of successful damage control—the company limited the harm that could have been inflicted by protecting its credibility. By the fall of 2008, Maple Leaf Foods meat was back in stores, sales were climbing, and the stock rebounded to over $11 in December. McCain not only remained the CEO but was named Canada's Business Newsmaker of the Year, as chosen by editors and broadcasters. And, most indicative of the company's success in restoring trust with its customers, by December consumers again embraced buying Maple Leaf Food products.

McCain understood from the get-go that he was facing a raging fire—and his mission was to do all he could to make sure that he was not throwing any additional fuel on the flames, but rather, looking for ways to quell the fire.

His steps should be part of any business school curriculum:

First, almost immediately Maple Leaf limited the harm they faced by acknowledging a mistake, as shown with their voluntary meat recall. The CEO "got it," recognizing that if the mistake fits, be quick to admit it. And even though they needed to go back several times to expand the recall, the fact that it was "voluntary" spoke to the company's true desire to admit their failings.

Second, the company had the discipline to resist offering hard and fast explanations as to what led to the contamination—and rather got to its bottom line (putting the public safety first). Maple Leaf Foods understood that this is what the public cared most about. Simply put, they understood that it was critical to know your bottom line and avoid drawing hard and fast lines.

And, third, the company protected its credibility by cooperating with the regulators. There was a commitment of operate to cooperate. In fact, not only did Maple Leaf Foods cooperate, it lavished praise on the beleaguered regulators for their efforts. And in a fascinating twist to the story, the combination of the speed, openness, and voluntary nature in which Maple Leaf Foods executed its recalls shifted public scrutiny from the company to the adequacy of the existing food safety regulations in Canada—aided by a series of bone-headed quotes from the regulators themselves, including the suggestion by the agriculture minister on the political impact of the crisis that "this is like a death by a thousand cuts. Or should I say cold cuts."

Maple Leaf Foods, under the direction of McCain, put the fire into the freezer, shut the door, and threw away the key.

THE SECOND COMMANDMENT APPLIED TO AN EVERYDAY CRISIS— DON'T TURN A BAD YELP REVIEW INTO A MOUNTAIN OF A STORY

In our era of crowdsourcing—where consumers leverage the power of social media to make decisions about the restaurant where they will eat (or even the entrees they will order), the hotel where they will sleep (down to the room number), the movie they will see (and at which theater), or the barbershop where they will get their hair cut (and by whom)—a crisis is only a bad social media review away.

An embarrassing YouTube video of what is going on in a restaurant's kitchen can badly tarnish a fast food chain's reputation. A bad TripAdvisor comment can ruin an innkeeper's sleep. A 140-character negative trending Twitter line can ruin a movie studio's opening weekend box office. And a bad Yelp review can cause a barber to lose his hair.

The power of social media levels the playing field for all—and it does not matter whether you are big or small. What does matter is how you handle your social media crisis. And with the level playing field, the don't feed the fire commandment is more relevant than ever.

Consider these two telling examples involving Yelp that underscore the imperative of the don't feed the fire commandment. On one hand there is the New York dental office of Dr. Stacy Makhnevich, and on the other is the Los Angeles–based Bolt Barbershops.

Dr. Makhnevich, responding to a negative Yelp review and other critical online reviews, demanded that the social media sites take down the comments, which they predictably refused to do. She then attempted to hold a patient financially accountable for a bad review. The end result of her actions was that the incident ended up generating coverage by a number of major news organizations, including ABC News and the *New York Daily News* who portrayed the dentist in a less than flattering light.

In the aftermath, anyone who did a Google, Yahoo, or Bing search for "Stacy Makhnevich" found a one-star rating from Yelp and a number of links to news stories about her efforts to sue a patient for writing a negative review, all of which resulted in far more additional negative online material than she would have had otherwise.

Rather than attempting to address the substance of the complaints in the spirit of a don't feed the fire approach, the dentist gave herself a public relations root canal.

In contrast, consider the approach pursued by the Bolt Barbershop. Billed as a "guy's sanctuary," Bolt has large plasma televisions and a PlayStation, serves beer, and even has a shuffleboard table. And this being Los Angeles, perhaps the hair capital of the world, Bolt generates considerable attention with the reviews it receives on social media platforms such as Yelp, most of which are flattering, but some which are not so flattering.

Bolt takes the don't feed the fire commandment to an entirely new level—essentially fighting fire with fire by seeking to proactively and affirmatively address any negative complaints it gets by directly reaching out to their customers to better understand the nature of the complaints so that they can be addressed. Bolt even posts some of the unflattering comments on its walls in the barbershop in order to make clear how the issue was addressed.

While it is not unusual for a small business to feature positive comments such as restaurant reviews on their walls and in other advertising, it is extraordinary to see a business highlight unflattering comments (including a complaint about the quality of the barbershop's shuffleboard table). Bolt is quick to admit its shortcomings. It gets to the bottom line (i.e., seeks to fix the problems). And it works with its customers, as opposed to fighting its customers.

Today, while Bolt may not have the city's highest-rated shuffleboard table with its five-star Yelp reviews, it is one of the highest-rated barbershops in Los Angeles.

COROLLARY TO THE THIRD COMMANDMENT— THE PREVENT DEFENSE CAN PREVENT YOU FROM WINNING

The prevent defense is the football strategy where the team holding a lead toward the end of the game gives up large chunks of the field to prevent the other team from being able to score a touchdown. However, this strategy often results in the losing team moving down the field in short order, positioning itself for an easy score, and changing the dynamics of the game. For this reason, the prevent defense was famously criticized by former National Football League television analyst and Super Bowl–winning coach John Madden as "the only thing the prevent defense does is prevents you from winning."

In a crisis, refusing to communicate at all is guaranteed to create a "failure to communicate" and can prevent you from exercising damage control.

In particular, we've often seen an organization so concerned about its legal liability or financial exposure that it simply goes into a crisis prevent defense mode, where it narrowly focuses on litigation mitigation—and, in doing so, digs itself a deeper hole, further degrades its credibility, and loses the trust of its key audiences altogether.

This bunker approach can result in winning legal battle in court—but at the cost of losing the war to survive as a viable entity in the court of public opinion.

Recognizing that winning the war to survive can be far more important than winning the legal battle is a distinction that was not lost on Maple Leaf Foods. At one point during the crisis, the CEO shrewdly publicly acknowledged that there were two types of advisors he was not listening to: his lawyers and his accountants. This statement reflected the fact that the company was free to pursue an aggressive damage control approach. Moreover, the comment also communicated to the key audiences that the company was truly most concerned with the public's safety.

The late, great accounting firm Arthur Andersen represents a cautionary tale of the perils of a bunker mentality. In using Arthur Andersen as an example of this, we want to be clear that most of the lawyers we have worked with are exceptionally talented (Chris and Mark are both recovering lawyers) and "get it" when it comes to lawyers balancing issues related to legal exposure with the need to make sure the organization protects its credibility (though we are not sure if the same can be said of accountants).

When the Enron scandal exploded in October 2001, many entities were caught up in the maelstrom of malfeasance—banks that had been closely involved with Enron, pension funds that invested in the company and lost billions in health and retirement funds, law firms that represented Enron, and Arthur Andersen, one of the nation's five largest accounting firms, which was responsible for reviewing Enron's books.

The Enron debacle led to Department of Justice and Securities and Exchange Commission investigations and prosecutions. Congress held hearings and pursued legislative reforms. State attorneys general embarked on their own inquiries. The press was all over the story. Executives later went to prison. And Arthur Andersen, as Enron's auditor, was in the middle.

Given that an accounting firm cannot function if it is convicted of a crime, the strategic direction Arthur Andersen chose to pursue became the defining moment for the firm.

Rather than acknowledging mistakes had been made and seeking to cooperate with the government in hopes of avoiding a prosecution of the firm itself, Arthur Andersen went into a prevent defense. The result was that in 2002, the Justice Department charged and convicted the accounting firm with obstruction of justice over the fact that a small number of employees had destroyed documents and erased emails. At which point Arthur Andersen appealed the ruling, which ultimately went all the way up to the Supreme Court. And three years later, in August 2005, the court ruled in the accounting firm's favor.

An Arthur Andersen press release on the news stated:

We are very pleased with the Supreme Court's decision, which acknowledges the fundamental injustices that has been done to Arthur Andersen and its former personnel and retirees. We pursued an appeal of this case not because we believed Arthur Andersen could be restored to its previous position, but because we had an obligation to set the record straight and clear the good name of the 28,000 innocent people who lost their jobs at the time of the indictment and tens of thousands of Andersen alumni, as well as help secure a fair resolution of the civil litigation facing the firm. The decision represents an important step in removing an unjustified cloud over the professionalism and integrity of the people of Arthur Andersen. As we have stated, this decision has far-reaching implications for businesses and individuals across the country in the way routine business decisions are implemented.

Of course, almost three years earlier, Arthur Andersen was forced to relinquish its CPA license and 85,000 people lost their jobs. The press release was issued by a company that was no longer in the public accounting business.

When the dust settled, Andersen won the legal battle, but had lost the war to survive. We can never know if the firm had approached the issue differently whether they would have had a better result, but what we do know is that a well-conceived approach would have given them a far better opportunity to remain a viable company.

Arthur Andersen needed to have fully cooperated with the investigations, built back its credibility, and respected our third commandment—don't feed the fire.

TEN
COMMANDMENT IV
DETAILS MATTER

All right, Mr. DeMille, I'm ready for my close-up.

—Norma Desmond, *Sunset Boulevard*

THE FOURTH COMMANDMENT—DETAILS MATTER

In a crisis, whether or not you have a grasp on the details can be the difference between losing or gaining control of a story. You must have the discipline to have fully considered the situation, anticipated the likely questions, and be prepared to address the details—because the failure to master the details can create discrepancies between the answers provided and the actual facts—and the smallest discrepancy will be magnified into a major inconsistency and expose you to more harm. Demonstrating a complete handle on the details will promote your credibility and convey that you are trustworthy.

DISRESPECTING THE FOURTH COMMANDMENT—MEG WHITMAN NOT HAVING "WHAT IT TAKES"

On September 22, 2009, Meg Whitman threw her hat into the political ring when she announced her candidacy for the governorship of California. Whitman had achieved great success as the president of the highly regarded Internet company eBay. She had been hired by eBay's founders early in the company's history and helped run it in a period of explosive growth. The company was frequently in the public spotlight, and since Whitman had amassed an estimated $1.3 billion fortune, an expectation was created that she was ready for prime time and her transition into politics would be easy and smooth.

In a heavily Democratic state, many believed Whitman—because of her talent, skills, and ability to pour massive amounts of personal wealth into the race—was the one Republican candidate who could give the presumptive Democratic nominee, former governor Jerry Brown, a real run for his money.

California political strategists and the punditocracy considered the combination of Whitman's ability to spend money, her status as a prominent woman, and the fact Brown had not been at the top of the ballot for a very long time meant she could make a play for the state's critical Latino vote and have special appeal to women voters. It was well understood by both Democrats and Republicans that to win a statewide election in California Whitman would have to shave the margins that Democrats typically captured from the growing Latino vote and from women voters.

However, as her campaign played out, these expectations proved to be inaccurate. Whitman indeed spent a lot of money—more than $160 million (which translated into approximately $50 for every vote she received in an election where she was badly beaten)—but it was not enough for one very simple reason: *She was not ready for her close-up.*

Almost immediately upon announcing her candidacy, Whitman faced questions about her personal history of political and civic participation, especially her voting record. Questions about a candidate's past record of voting are common, completely predictable, and typically asked and answered in advance of a formal announcement; and if there are any issues that need to be pre-empted, they are normally addressed before the campaign gets underway. Candidates coming from business backgrounds often have spotty voting records. Whitman, as a first-time candidate, *had* to know that her decision to enter the political ring was going to trigger a scrutiny of her voting record—and, if she did not know, her army of consultants and staff, many of whom were the best in the business, surely knew (leaving one to conclude Whitman ignored their counsel).

Therefore, it should have come as no great surprise when *The Sacramento Bee*, the respected and influential paper of record in the state capital, pursued and subsequently published a comprehensive analysis of the Whitman voting record on September 24, days after she announced her run for governor. The paper determined that, as with many other business leaders transitioning into politics, Whitman had a less-than-stellar record in showing up to the voting booth.

However, what *was* surprising were reports indicating that Whitman had not even bothered to register in the counties where she lived in both Ohio (her previous residence) and California until 2002—an assertion that the campaign did not vigorously dispute or contest.

This report of her failure to even register, coming almost immediately after she announced her candidacy, swiftly became a major issue in the California political press, and stepped all over her political launch at precisely the time when she was seeking to make a favorable first impression with the voters.

Whitman then was forced to publicly acknowledge that her voting record was "unacceptable."

However, a few weeks *after* the story ran (and weeks represent a lifetime in a hot political race), her campaign finally had a response to the charges. A spokesperson for the Whitman campaign stated in a letter to *The Sacramento Bee*'s political editor that while Whitman did not have a particularly good voting record, there were also questions on the paper's reporting of the issue. Here are some excerpts from that letter:

Dear Amy:

Thank you for our conversations in recent days regarding *The Sacramento Bee*'s September 24th story on Meg's voting history. As we discussed, the campaign has been in the process of reconciling its information and Meg's recollections with *The Bee*'s coverage. So far, we have found a number of disturbing discrepancies that raise serious questions about the quality of *The Bee*'s reporting and the integrity of your newspaper.

After your story ran, we went back to the San Francisco registrar and asked them to confirm your assertion that Meg had not registered or voted in San Francisco between 1981 and 1989. They could not. The registrar's office again confirmed in writing that it no longer has records for voters prior to 1992. Records from that period were never transferred and they simply don't have them.

In an attempt to confirm our findings, we then asked the registrar to provide voting information for several prominent San Franciscans, including Dianne Feinstein and Nancy Pelosi. (Dianne Feinstein was Mayor of San Francisco from 1978 to 1988. Nancy Pelosi has lived in San Francisco since 1969 and was elected to Congress in 1987.) The registrar's office came back in writing with the same result. There are no records in any system of Dianne Feinstein or Nancy Pelosi voting in San Francisco prior to 1992.

Clearly, Nancy Pelosi and Dianne Feinstein voted in San Francisco during the 1980s, and so did Meg Whitman. Based solely on a mysterious unnamed source at the registrar's office, *The Bee* conveniently asserts that Meg never voted in San Francisco. This flies in the face of any information actually available at the San Francisco registrar's office.

And the list of errors in your September 24th story goes on and on.

In an interview with *The Washington Post* following this letter, Whitman admitted knowing that her voting record was likely to be an issue, but explained away the delayed response—which occurred only "once the story broke"—as a product of her directing the campaign team to develop a "'deliberate' and 'thoughtful' response."

In fact, the slow-motion nature of her response raised serious questions about her credibility and also began to generate concerns about whether she had what it takes to be a candidate who could win. She had to demonstrate that she was trustworthy in what was guaranteed to be a race where she was going to receive significant public scrutiny.

The next major hit to Whitman's trustworthiness was another instance of failing to handle the details and involved an incident at eBay. On June 14, 2010, *The New York Times* published a story reporting that as CEO of eBay, Whitman had engaged in some sort of physical confrontation with an employee that had resulted in a legal settlement. Whitman did not respond to the story, which included the following reporting:

> According to one of the eBay employees knowledgeable about Ms. Whitman's version of the incident, Ms. Whitman said she had *physically guided* Ms. Kim out of the conference room. [emphasis added]

More than a week after the initial story broke, a time in which interest in the story grew more and more intense, due in large measure to Whitman's silence, the candidate finally chose to finally address the issue. Whitman granted a radio interview, during which she offered her version of events:

> We had a misunderstanding . . . It was *a verbal dispute*, and that kind of thing can happen in a high-pressure work environment and we put it behind us a long time ago. [emphasis added]

Given that these were Whitman's first real comments on the story, the California and national press, the political community, her opponents, and the pundits were all on a hair-trigger when it came to scrutinizing the details of her statement. And, not surprisingly, all of these groups seized on the discrepancy between her characterization of the dispute as "verbal" in nature, compared to *The New York Times* reporting that the incident had a "physical" component.

This discrepancy further elevated the story, heightened interest in the press, and increased the story's profile with the public. And by June 25, 2010, eleven days after the story first appeared, Whitman was once again forced to address the issue, this time admitting that the incident *had,* indeed, become physical. Whitman's approach resulted in yet another round of damning coverage and contributed to a growing storyline that she was incapable of providing credible answers (especially when it came to the details on her challenging personal issues) and was not a trustworthy person deserving of holding public office.

And then the next hit to her credibility—and it's quite a list here—came in late September of 2010. With polls showing a competitive race, and Whitman having spent tens of millions in paid advertising targeting Latinos, and additional substantial resources spent appealing to women, a new hit demonstrated she had *still* not learned the lesson that details indeed matter.

In a September 28 gubernatorial debate on the campus of the University of California, Davis, Whitman was asked about the hot-button issue of employers hiring undocumented workers. She said, "We do have to hold employers accountable for hiring only documented workers, and we do have to enforce that law."

The day after the debate, on September 29, Whitman's long-time former nanny, Nicandra Diaz Santillan, held a press conference where she went public with the accusation that Whitman had employed her for years and knew for much of that time that she was an undocumented worker. Diaz Santillan went on to say she was fired in 2009, only after Whitman decided to run for governor and became concerned that the nanny could be a campaign liability. In her press conference, Diaz Santillan said that Whitman and her husband, Dr. Griff Hersh, became aware of her status when letters arrived from the Social Security Administration indicating that her Social Security number did not match her name. At the press conference, Diaz Santillan did not provide the actual letters or other documentation.

The Whitman campaign categorically denied the charge, characterizing it as a smear campaign, and released a statement from Whitman stating that Diaz Santillan had been terminated in 2009 immediately upon the discovery of her citizenship status:

> Nicky told me that she was admitting her deception now because she was aware that her lie might come out during the campaign. Nicky said she was concerned about hurting my family and me. As required by law, once we learned she was an illegal worker, I immediately terminated Nicky's employment. It was one of the hardest things I've ever done. I considered Nicky a friend and a part of our extended family.

The next day, on September 30, appearing on ABC's *Good Morning America,* Whitman offered an "absolute unequivocal denial" of the nanny's assertion that she and her husband received documentation that would have suggested issues with Diaz Santillan's citizenship, disputing that the couple received any documents from the Social Security Administration pertaining to their nanny's citizenship:

> We never received those letters ... When we hired Nicky we used an employment agency. Nicky provided her social security card, a California driver's license, she filled out a 1099—because we told the employment agency, we have to hire people only who are documented to work here. So we had no idea that she was not here legally.

Following Whitman's categorical statements on *Good Morning America,* Diaz Santillan's legal representative made public the actual Social Security letters, which included on them a handwritten note purportedly from Whitman's husband, Dr. Hersh, saying: "Nicky, please check this, thanks."

By the end of the day, Whitman, her spouse, and the campaign were in full retreat mode—and acknowledging it was possible they had received the documents. Whitman's husband stated:

> While I honestly do not recall receiving this letter, as it was sent to me seven years ago, I can say it is possible that I would've scratched a follow up note on a letter like this, which is a request for information to make certain Nicky received her Social Security benefits and W-2 tax refund for withheld wages.

The admission, coming after unequivocal denials, demolished Whitman's credibility on the issue, while bolstering Santillan Diaz's version of events.

Within days, what had been a competitive race broke wide open for Jerry Brown, who went on to cruise to a landslide win. And no matter how much money Meg Whitman spent blanketing the state with paid television ads, the fact that she did not have a grasp of the details doomed her candidacy, because it led to voters—especially Latino voters, her core audience—questioning her credibility and regarding her with a fundamental level of distrust.

By the time the votes were counted, Whitman had alienated Latino voters (who represented a record 22 percent of the vote) by a margin of over 60 percent, and had connected so poorly with women voters that she was booed on stage at a women's forum, attended by 14,000 women, which took place late in the campaign.

UNDERSTANDING THE FOURTH COMMANDMENT— HAVE WHAT IT TAKES TO HANDLE THE DETAILS

For the two years that Whitman was a candidate for governor, and despite spending in excess of $160 million, Whitman and her campaign failed time and time again to heed the lessons of the fourth commandment of damage control:

Details matter.

A crisis is a close-up.

You and your organization will be under a microscope.

Every action will be rigorously examined.

Every part of the available record will be closely scrutinized.

Every statement will be carefully reviewed.

When you provide answers, you must be prepared for how you will respond to detailed questions.

And everyone involved will be demanding not only answers, but detailed answers that withstand the scrutiny.

Thus, while it is important to disclose fully and quickly to your core audiences, you cannot rush the disclosures until you have adequate answers as to the details.

DEPLOY GOOD FACTS TO BEAT BAD FACTS

In a crisis, it is often the case that there is an awful lot of bad information out there that can be interpreted differently if put in the proper context; can be trumped with additional information; or is simply wrong. And, if the response to these "bad facts" is managed correctly, you can diminish the magnitude of the problem and shorten its life span. But the best way to disabuse people of incomplete or inaccurate information is to counter it with detailed information of your own. Bad facts will only be trumped by good facts—and the good facts have to be accurate. Thus, to limit the harm, you must *deploy good facts to beat bad facts.*

In the Whitman campaign's first crisis out of the box, her voting record, Whitman was caught flat-footed when it came to deploying good facts to beat bad facts.

In Whitman's situation, the failure to be prepared was inexcusable given that she knew well in advance of announcing her candidacy that her voting record was likely to be an issue.

And while Whitman's voting record was problematic, had she deployed the fact that she was indeed a registered voter, the story would have been more limited and far less damaging.

The most "newsworthy" item of the voting record story, the suggestion that she had not even bothered to register to vote, was the most damaging aspect of the story. In some regards, voters have become conditioned to people with poor voting records running for office, but in this case, not even registering to vote and then running for office was a relatively new phenomenon— and therefore more troubling to voters. And the impression that Whitman did not even bother to register was created by the initial news story—an impression that was left unanswered by Whitman and her campaign. An impression, as it turned out, that was wrong.

At the end of the day, the Whitman campaign assembled a good response that relied on accurate details to address bad facts. But the time it took to get the details out was far too long and reflects how critical it is to make sure you are prepared to handle the details if you hope to control the story.

DO YOUR HOMEWORK

In a crisis, to be in the strongest position possible to control the damage, you need to actually have the facts. Once you have the facts, they need to be 110 percent accurate. And once they are authenticated, you need to make sure you do not create any discrepancies.

Be sensitive to the fact that the smallest discrepancies, even ones that may not appear to be material to the underlying issue, will be highly magnified and reflect on your credibility. Your core audiences and the media will be ultra-sensitive when it comes to any inconsistencies. A discrepancy will be seized upon and flung back at you; the story will be made bigger and your credibility impacted—and the hole you are in will become much deeper. Any inconsistencies, differences, or discrepancies compared to the existing record will appear much larger than they otherwise would.

Mark Twain noted that the difference between a lightning bug and lightning is a big one that comes down to one word. Well, in a crisis, the difference between damage control and losing control can come down to a discrepancy over a detail. When Whitman found herself in a very challenging position with the information that came to light in *The New York Times* regarding her interaction with the eBay employee, she did not understand the importance of taking the time to get her story and the facts nailed down—she did not show the discipline to *do your homework*.

Instead, Whitman appeared to go into a candidate's version of a witness protection program, and when she finally emerged to address the issue, she simply characterized it as a "verbal" disagreement—without providing any real details to disabuse people of the fact that that it indeed had a physical element.

Whitman had a week to prepare a response on the nature of her "confrontation" with the eBay employee. In her first media appearance, she knew this was going to be the news of the interview—in fact, it is likely she and her campaign picked the specific radio outlet because it was a favorable venue for her to address the issue. Despite all of this, Whitman answered the question in such a way that it created a significant discrepancy. Therefore, not only did Whitman fail to adequately control the damage, she made the situation far worse by reigniting the story and damaging her credibility in the process.

As a result, what objectively appeared to have been a minor physical interaction (walking the employee out by the arm) was elevated into a story that was bigger, longer, and more damaging—the exact opposite of what one is seeking to accomplish in such a situation.

Throughout her campaign, Whitman simply did not do her homework.

In *The Washington Post* story following the voting records blow-up, she acknowledged directing her campaign to develop an answer *after* the story appeared, despite knowing that her voting record was going to be an issue long *before* the story ever broke.

And in her nanny-gate scandal, where the hiring of undocumented workers was sure to be a significant public policy issue in the campaign—and an issue where Whitman had adopted the position that employers should be held accountable for employing such workers—Whitman not only did not hold herself accountable, but she did not hold herself accountable to doing her homework on the topic. If she had done her homework, she would have been in a position to respond if and when the matter became public.

Upon finding yourself in a crisis, before seeking to address the underlying issue—whether it is to an internal audience such as your Board, your clients, or your employees or to an external audience such as your shareholders, your customers, or your voters—assiduously do your homework, and make sure that you have nailed down the details. If you take the "dog ate my homework" approach reflected in the Whitman campaign, you will be throwing your credibility like a raw piece of red meat to a pack of wild and hungry dogs.

Tough questions are going to be asked, and those asking them will expect you to address the details or, at least, provide a credible explanation as to why you cannot provide detailed answers to their questions (a specific approach we will discuss later).

When you know there is going to be a challenging issue, take time in advance to think the issue through and nail down the details. Getting them nailed will help you limit the damage by best positioning you to accurately address the issue—and not allow it to become bigger or worse than it ought to be. Getting the details nailed will help protect your credibility by alerting you to what you can and cannot answer. And getting the details nailed will enable you to begin to rebuild trust, because you will now be capable of correctly providing information to questions that your core audiences will have for you and want answered.

Approach a crisis like it's a final examination: Think through all the likely questions in advance and *practice* your answers. With such a disciplined approach, you won't find yourself in a position where you will be asked a question to which you do not have a prepared response—even if that response is an explanation about why you cannot address the issue.

Here are some tricks of the trade:

- Spend time writing out the questions you are likely to be asked and carefully consider and rehearse your answers.
- If you are going before your core audiences—be it an internal or external audience—have your team take you through a rigorous "murder board" of exceedingly tough questions so you are completely prepared.

- Create a document of frequently asked questions and then use it with internal and external audiences.
- Always think in your seat and never be in a position where you have to think on your feet. And if you find yourself in a position where, in fact, you are answering questions to which you have not already rehearsed the answers, you are on dangerous ground.
- Consider whether your answers square with what is in the public record. Where possible, and when your answer is generally consistent with what is public, frame your answers so that they are in accord with what currently exists—for the shelf life of the crisis will certainly be extended if there are any discrepancies between what actually happened.
- If your answer *is* in conflict with what is public, determine whether your version of events will materially alter the course of the crisis— and, if so, determine how best to explain this so that your answer prevails (keeping in mind that the burden of proof to buttress the explanation will rest with you).
- If your version of events will not materially alter the crisis, consider whether injecting such information is worth it, given it will only serve to elevate and/or extend the crisis.
- Fight the urge to issue a categorical statement or adopt a categorical position. Take a big step back and consider the worst-case scenario of how such a statement could be challenged, and whether the categorical statement you are considering could withstand this worst-case challenge.
- And finally, avoid words that can serve as handcuffs, such as "absolutely," "never," "beyond a doubt," "I can for sure," etc.

MEET THE BURDEN OF PROOF

In a crisis, you are usually on the defensive. Something bad has happened for which you appear responsible. Someone has accused you of misconduct. Some negative information has come to light portraying you in a problematic way. As by definition you will be on the defensive, you will need to be able to *meet the burden of proof*. And you can satisfy this burden by providing the details.

In nanny-gate, if Whitman was going to dispute the story—or an element within the story, such as the reason she terminated Diaz Santillan—the burden was on her to provide details to buttress her position. The Whitman campaign's attack on her former nanny for engaging in a "smear," followed by Whitman's appearances on *Good Morning America,* where she categorically denied her nanny's allegations, was a classic example of someone seemingly making it up as she went along, and not meeting the requisite burden required to effectively address the issue—which, predictably, turned out to be the exact wrong way to handle the crisis.

In a crisis, you have to meet the burden of proof by having a grasp of the details that will support the version of events you are presenting.

Are there primary documents backing your version of the events that can be made available? Was there a formal inquiry with findings?

Are there eyewitnesses who can validate your story? Were other people in the room, so the story is not *she said vs. she said,* but rather, *they all said vs. she said.*

Are there memorialized communications that can be provided? Did people have conversations that were recorded electronically or otherwise?

Was there subsequent conduct by the participants in the matter that would support your version of the events? In an issue involving an employee and CEO, did the employee continue to work at the company, and in the same position?

In short, determine what information is available that can be deployed to back up your position—and crucially, consider whether your proof points will, in fact, meet the burden of proof you need before publicly relying on these details.

To respect the fourth commandment, follow these three steps:

1. Deploy good facts to beat bad facts.
2. Do your homework.
3. Meet the burden of proof.

RESPECTING THE FOURTH COMMANDMENT—BE READY FOR A HARD CHECK

On September 16, 2004, the National Hockey League, following months of protracted and challenging negotiations with their players over the league's collective bargaining agreement, took steps to formally lock out the players, a move that eventually led to cancelling the league's eighty-eighth season.

The headline in *Sports Illustrated*, similar to headlines all over the United States and Canada, said it all—making it clear to the fans that the season was imperiled:

"NO DEAL IN SIGHT; OWNERS LOCK OUT PLAYERS"

At the core of the lockout was a battle over the state of the league's financial health.

The owners argued that they were paying over 70 percent of the sport's gross revenues to player salaries, the highest percentage in professional sports, and consequently they were losing hundreds of millions of dollars. They claimed this loss threatened the long-term economic strength of the league to the detriment of the owners (who did not want to lose money), the players (who wanted to have a successful North American professional hockey league), and the fans (who wanted a sport where all the teams could be financially sound so as to be competitive on the ice). This, in turn, led to franchises being sold at prices that the owners felt were too low to justify their investments.

On the other hand, the players vigorously disputed the owners' position, contending that the sport was doing far better financially than the owners claimed; the high salaries were a product of the owners paying too much to unproven players; and competition issues between big-market and mid-sized-market teams.

The stakes for fans, players, and owners could not have been higher—the very future of the league was at stake.

For the owners, cancelling the season would make it very difficult to win the fans back, and as those taking this action (in the belief that it was in the best long-term interest of the sport), it was highly likely that the owners were going to bear the brunt of the backlash from the fans, the media, and others.

For the players, they were risking time from their careers and salaries in a sport where the longevity of players was limited.

For the fans, they wanted to do as they always had: attend the games with their friends and families or watch on television hockey played by the world's top players.

For league commissioner Gary Bettman and player association head Bob Goodenow, how these negotiations played out was going to shape the way their core audiences—the owners and the players—viewed their leadership.

And for all, the issue was going to turn on the details—as the details would dictate who had the best argument when it came to what kind of financial system would best serve the sport.

In advance of announcing the formal lockout, the league determined it needed to address the issue head on. Thus, in July 2004, the league publicly released a report on the state of the league finances by Arthur Levitt, the well-respected former head of the Securities and Exchange Commission. *The Levitt Report,* as it became known, for the first time offered real details and provided a comprehensive analysis of the number.

The Levitt Report, which was released in its entirety, had this to say about the NHL's economics, "The results are as catastrophic as I've seen in any enterprise of this size . . . They are on a treadmill to obscurity, that's the way the league is going. So, something's got to change . . . I would not underwrite as a banker any of these ventures, nor would I invest a dollar of my own personal money in what appears, to me, a business that's heading south." The report also included the following details:

- The league had $1.996 billion in revenues and $2.269 billion in player and other costs. About 75 percent of revenues—$1.494 billion—went to player costs, which included salaries, bonuses, and benefits.
- Factoring in below-the-line costs such as interest and depreciation, losses increased to $374 million.
- Twenty-six of the thirty teams were audited. Buffalo and Ottawa were not because they were in bankruptcy proceedings, and two unidentified teams could not be audited because accountants concluded they were not viable ongoing concerns.
- Nineteen teams lost money, while eleven made a combined profit of $69.8 million. The largest team loss was $40.9 million. The largest profit was $14.6 million.

As most observers in the media and the sport expected, the league locked out the players on September 15, 2004.

Passions ran high.

Said one fan in Manitoba, "Put it this way: They took away my religion."

Fans naturally wanted their games, they wanted to see their heroes on the ice, and wanted to share the excitement as their fathers and grandfathers had done. And a great many, as reflected in numerous media reports, were upset that the lockout was denying them the enjoyment of what was an important part of their lives.

The owners, armed with *The Levitt Report*—which was deemed credible due to the reputation of the author and the candor of its financial details—mounted an aggressive public campaign over the 310 days of the lockout:

- The commissioner held town hall meetings with fans to explain the league's position.
- League officials met with important advertising partners, vendors, and other key members of the broader NHL community impacted by the lockout to explain the League's financial challenges.
- In addition to making *The Levitt Report* public, the league disseminated extensive fact sheets and related materials to further explain the details in the report.
- The league maintained an ongoing dialogue with the press.

And, over the course of the lockout, a curious thing happened—it was becoming clear that public opinion was shifting back to the league, as more and more people understood why the league was doing what it was doing, and the pressure on the players began to intensify.

On July 13, 2005, the league's owners and the players reached an agreement that put in place the "cost certainty" approach (which tied player salaries to league revenues) favored by the owners, which they believed was crucial to the future of the sport.

And toward the end of the lockout, a public opinion poll reported that fans were blaming the lockout on the players far more than on the owners, by a ratio of 52 to 21—a remarkable validation of the league's approach.

Much of the NHL's effective public strategy in the lockout was predicated on understanding that in a crisis details matter.

As the lockout loomed, the league appreciated that they needed to be prepared for their close-up—and they had to have a handle on the details. They understood that their financial claims were going to be scrutinized, and they had to beat bad facts with good facts.

The league did their homework by using primary documents and solid facts and figures to back up their call for a financial system that would secure the league's future.

When the commissioner and other league officials conducted town halls and media interviews, they had the details down—they were not skating by on the facts or making it up as they went along. They deployed good facts to beat bad facts.

And throughout the entire lockout, the league was highly disciplined about staying on top of any discrepancies that could undermine the owners' credibility (in fact, this was never an issue). Beginning with the commissioner and extending throughout the league's offices and individual teams, the NHL appreciated the importance of doing your homework.

The league communicated to their core audience—the fans—recognizing that they needed to meet the burden of proof when it came to providing the details on the league's finances, and they did so in a forthright and credible way, through *The Levitt Report.*

As a result, when it came to winning, the NHL understood the key to being able to take a hard check to the boards was in the fourth commandment: details matter.

THE FOURTH COMMANDMENT APPLIED TO AN EVERYDAY CRISIS—PLAYING THE RIGHT TUNE

On January 23, 2006, three violinists and one cellist representing the San Francisco Symphony gathered in the historic City Hall of San Francisco. Attired in their concert best, they played under the golden dome of the soaring rotunda during the lunch hour as city workers, staff, supervisors, and representatives from the mayor's office enjoyed the music. As the musicians played, their audience had only one question: Why were these musicians wearing Cleveland Indians baseball caps?

The musicians, who were members of the Musicians Union Local 6, had been playing without a contract since November 2005. They played City Hall in an effort to bring the issue to the attention of the city's elected officials, the press, and, by extension, the management and the Board of the San Francisco Symphony. These world-class musicians had donned the Indians hats to deliver a message: The musicians of the renowned San Francisco Symphony were being paid less than what orchestra members were earning in other parts of the country—where the cost of living was far less—such as in the Cleveland Symphony.

Several years earlier, the San Francisco Symphony workers had engaged in a round of contract discussions and felt that their message on fair compensation did not break through because the symphony management had focused purely on the salary numbers, which on paper looked good compared to what an average American earns, but, compared to what their peers made, was demonstrably not competitive.

The local media covered the "string quartet press conference," and because of the Indians hat gimmick, the reporting included detailed explanations of how the San Francisco musicians' compensation matched up with other leading symphonies across the country. This was the story reported by KGO, the local ABC affiliate:

> The three violinists and one cellist comprising the quartet wore Cleveland Indians baseball hats along with formal attire to symbolize the similarity between their wages and those of the Cleveland Orchestra musicians. San Francisco Symphony musicians make $2,195 a week in base salary and seniority wages while Cleveland's musicians make $2,230.

And after finishing the concert to enthusiastic applause from the crowd who had assembled for the impromptu performance, the musicians met with elected officials and provided comprehensive material comparing their compensation packages with those of other cities—and making clear that the San Francisco Symphony, with a $175 million endowment, was clearly in a position to pay a fair compensation to their orchestra members.

And shortly after the halls of San Francisco City Hall were graced with Cleveland Indians hat–wearing violinists and a cellist playing Mozart's *Dissonance Quartet*, the symphony's management sat down with the musicians, and all agreed to a new contract.

Despite being a small union of a few hundred symphony members, Local 6's approach reflected an understanding of the fourth commandment—details matter.

The musicians knew from their past experience that they were going to be scrutinized—and, thus, they were prepared for their close-ups. To this end, they were determined to deploy good facts to beat bad facts.

The musicians understood the importance of needing to do their homework. Before engaging in the negotiation and interacting with officials, they carefully assembled their facts and marshaled their arguments—and effectively took their case to the public.

And the union was aware, based on its prior experience, that they had to meet the burden of proof when it came to the compensation issue, and they were able to utilize specific details comparing San Francisco to Cleveland to address that burden.

COROLLARY TO THE FOURTH COMMANDMENT—YOU ARE NOT IN A CONFESSIONAL

In Washington, D.C., a political gaffe is often characterized as someone unintentionally telling the truth. If there were to be a gaffe hall of fame, featuring Washington politicians "unintentionally telling the truth," former Idaho senator Larry Craig would have his own wing.

Senator Craig gained national notoriety for his actions in a Minneapolis airport men's room, where when he was accused of seeking sex with an undercover police officer, Craig attributed his actions with the officer to a "wide stance." However, in 1982, early in his political career, and years before the concept of a "wide stance" pierced the American consciousness, Craig was already gaining fame for his actions.

On June 30, 1982, CBS News broadcast an investigative story featuring Leroy Williams, a congressional page, who alleged that, "he had sex with three House members when he was 17." The story did not name any specific members of Congress, and Williams did not provide any names.

The next day one member of Congress—and only one member of Congress—issued an on-the-record statement denying that he was one of the Leroy Williams Three. That member: Larry Craig.

In his statement to the nation, Craig claimed that he was affirmatively denying that he was one of the three members of Congress because he believed various media outlets were going to name him, attributing this to "part of a concerted effort at character assassination."

He went on to state, "I have done nothing that I need to be either publicly or privately ashamed of. I am guilty of no crime or impropriety, and I am convinced that this is an effort to damage my personal character and destroy my political career." And the congressman added, "Persons who are unmarried as I am, by choice or by circumstance, have always been the subject of innuendos, gossip and false accusations. I think this is despicable."

As the only member of Congress to offer a statement on Williams's charges, Craig found himself in the middle of a big national story over that July 4 weekend. Network news helicopters trailed him, he was besieged with media calls, and he found himself as the one and only star actor in the follow-up coverage.

Craig pointed to media outlets such as the *New York Post* as being among those who were going to report his name in conjunction with the congressional underage-page sex scandal. However, according to a subsequent story in the *Idaho Statesman*, the *New York Post* reporter on the story asserted that the paper never claimed it was going to cite Congressman Craig, stating:

> No, no—it wasn't "are you under investigation?" It was simply an inquiry: "Have you heard anything? Who have you heard about? Have you heard any names mentioned? What's your reaction to this news?" The next thing I know, Larry Craig has issued a press release: "This isn't me." Which I just thought was a bizarre and ultimately very foolish thing to do. He was the only person going on the record anywhere . . . And of course, when you do that, it's like raw meat. He's saying, "Nobody's actually accusing, but it wasn't me!" It's no wonder it's dogged him. *He denied something that no one had accused him of.* [emphasis added]

Four weeks after the CBS News report, and Craig's public commentary, Leroy Williams recanted his charges. And six months later a congressional ethics committee dismissed the matter, chastising CBS for the network's reporting.

Years later, and in the context of the 2007 "wide stance" scandal, Craig explained his 1982 reaction to the *Idaho Statesman*, "I was scared, plain and simple scared . . . When you have somebody walk into your office and make that kind of allegation and tells me he's gonna go to print—and I'm a freshman congressman and go, 'Oh my God!'"

The Craig story is an especially explicit reminder of the confessional corollary.

It is important to be ready for your close-up by mastering the details— and it is equally important to recognize that you are *not in a confessional* and not under an obligation to affirmatively put out information that is detrimental to your cause.

Don't deny having done something when no one has accused you of having done it in the first place!

No matter how intense the heat, only release information that serves a strategic purpose. Don't panic. A self-inflicted crisis often stems from putting out information in a vacuum; and that act places you in the middle of a problem. The on-the-record denial, the-on-the-record attack on a source to a story, the non-denial denial—all of these can serve as the basis for you or your organization to be injected into the crisis. Before deciding on a response, first determine whether the mere act of responding will do more harm than good.

In a crisis you will have all sorts of information being put forth like bait in the water by those on a fishing expedition And you are the swordfish they are trying to hook. Don't become a trophy on someone's wall by taking a bite. Be sensitive to whether or not the release of your information will serve a purpose. Don't fall for the bait and let your adversaries fool you into thinking you need to release the information.

Finally, consider your body language. If you are not guilty, don't act guilty (and even if you are guilty at some level, try not to show it). When contacted about an issue, maintain a posture of studied nonchalance. Those soliciting information often try to read your body language to get a sense of whether you may—or may not—be a player in the crisis.

In any crisis—like it or not—you will get your close-up. There will be a swirl of activity—some of it not very pleasant—but you will have a goal of establishing that you are trustworthy. And the way to reach that goal is to keep your discipline, do your homework, show the world you can be trusted, and *always nail the details*. They really matter—and how you handle the details can make all the difference.

ELEVEN
COMMANDMENT V
HOLD YOUR HEAD HIGH

No-one said anything to me about the full monty!

—Horse, *The Full Monty*

THE FIFTH COMMANDMENT—HOLD YOUR HEAD HIGH

A crisis will almost inevitably involve negative information that will be highly unflattering, but don't be so embarrassed that you do yourself even more harm by disclosing the fundamental basis of the crisis while withholding specific unflattering information. The unflattering information will inevitably become public and will take on more importance than it might otherwise warrant. Having the discipline to put out even the most embarrassing information, and then leveraging the act of putting out the unflattering information to bolster your credibility bona fides, puts you in a position to move on and re-establish trust.

DISRESPECTING THE FIFTH COMMANDMENT—SENATOR CHRIS DODD ON THE HOT SEAT

U.S. Senator Chris Dodd was on the hot seat.

It was March 2009, and a controversy had erupted over a provision in the Wall Street congressional bailout legislation that allowed the financial giant AIG to pay its executives highly lucrative taxpayer-funded bonuses.

Dodd, who had been a senator from Connecticut for nearly three decades, was chairman of the Senate Banking Committee, which had overseen much of the U.S. bank bailout legislation known as the Toxic Asset Relief Program (TARP), including the specific amendment that barred the bailout banks from paying bonuses to their highest-paid employees, but included this specific AIG loophole language. The language wasn't noticed until after the legislation was passed, but when it was flagged, it had a profound effect on Senator Dodd's future.

At the time the amendment banning these bonuses was being developed, Senator Dodd was being whipsawed between an angry public who did not think his legislation was tough enough on Wall Street, and by those, primarily in the business community, who claimed the amendment would hurt the ability of banks to regain their financial footing. All of this activity took place in the context of the senator facing a very difficult 2010 re-election challenge. And, to top it all off, Senator Dodd had received substantial campaign contributions over the years from AIG.

Senator Dodd, as chair of the Senate Banking Committee, had authored the amendment. Therefore, as news of the AIG bonus provision spread and generated a significant public outcry, CNN interviewed the senator on March 18 and, predictably, asked him whether he was responsible for the AIG bonus provision.

Here is the exchange:

> CNN: There is the suggestion being made that you received more money from AIG than any other senator, and that you were responsible for the February 11, 2009 date . . . So—you know again, I just want to get at . . .
> SEN. DODD: No.
> CNN: You're saying you had nothing to do with that date.
> SEN. DODD: Absolutely not.

By the next day, sources had told CNN and other news organizations that contrary to what the senator had represented in his interview, he had, in fact, been directly responsible for the controversial language. But it was language that had been insisted upon by the Treasury Department given their specific concerns related to AIG, and Dodd had simply inserted it into the legislation.

Senator Dodd once again went on CNN and answered the question very differently:

> SEN. DODD: I agreed to a modification in the legislation, reluctantly . . . I wasn't negotiating with myself here. I wasn't changing my own amendment. I was changing the amendment others were insisting upon it.

CNN: You were very adamant yesterday, very adamant that you didn't know
    how this change got in there . . . and now you are saying that your staff
    did work with the administration?

SEN. DODD: Going back and looking—obviously, I apologize.

At a subsequent press conference, the senator discussed how he was,
in fact, the person who was responsible for prohibiting the bonuses in general, and that he had inserted the AIG language at the behest of the Treasury
Department, saying, "I'm angry about it, and angry in a sense I've been held
up as sort of responsible for all this when in fact I responded to what I thought
was a reasonable request at the time . . . I went through six weeks of a lot of
criticism from the financial press, Wall Street and others that my amendment
was too restrictive, that it was unfair, that there would be a brain drain, that
people would leave right and left."

However, by then the damage had been done. Not only was the public upset by the AIG loophole, but Wall Street was upset too, and Senator Dodd was
the one taking the heat. The media was all over him, as exemplified by the *New
Haven Register,* where an editorial called him a "lying weasel." The senator's
ability to defend himself and provide an explanation was limited because he
had undermined his own credibility. And his re-election effort was badly hurt
by the perception, however inaccurate, of the intersection of the AIG campaign donations and the insertion of the AIG loophole.

In short, Dodd went from being on the hot seat to being on the stake with
a raging fire—all of his own doing.

In January 2010, the senator announced that he was not going to run for
re-election, ending a long and distinguished career.

UNDERSTANDING THE FIFTH COMMANDMENT—
HOLDING YOUR HEAD HIGH ALLOWS YOU TO MOVE ON

Looking back, the senator's second response on CNN was a completely appropriate, indeed smart, crisis response—had it been offered in the *first* interview
he did with the CNN.

The real problem was his first answer, which, by not affirmatively revealing the unflattering information related to the AIG bonus, violated the fifth
commandment of damage control:

Hold your head high.

When it comes to controlling the damage, and for disclosure to be as effective as possible, you have to be prepared to put it all out there.

In a scandal, no element of the story can be too embarrassing.

In a crisis, no material information can be too unflattering.

Understand that you are going from being on regular TV to HDTV—and every blemish, every imperfection will stand out more—and that if you try to cover it up, when it does get exposed, it will take on an outsized importance.

In the movie *The Full Monty* six unemployed men in Northern England perform a striptease, putting it all out there for the world to see—and this is the strategy here.

Hold your head high, state all the facts, and let people conclude what they are going to conclude—while you move on.

DON'T TURN A MOUNTAIN OF A CRISIS INTO A MOUNT EVEREST OF CRISES

As Senator Dodd's experience demonstrates, the embarrassment you may feel about putting out a specific piece of information will translate into far greater shame when the damaging information is finally revealed—and will do you still more harm. In short, *don't turn a mountain of a crisis into a Mount Everest of crises.* When you do not get ahead of the issue and put out the details of the situation, but rather are forced to release the information, or it comes out another way, the information will get greater scrutiny, will receive far more attention, and will become a bigger and more permanent part of the story going forward.

Thus, rather than avoiding the embarrassment, you have created *more* embarrassment. Rather than moving beyond the crisis, you have extended the life of the crisis. And rather than minimizing the harm, you have increased the harm.

Senator Dodd's decision not to fess up to his role in the AIG bonus matter, which in fact was relatively limited, made this a much bigger issue than it needed to have been. First, the senator's original answer left it unclear who was truly responsible for the provision, and various audiences began pounding away to determine who the source was—as there is nothing better than a mystery to generate interest in a subject. Second, the failure to address his involvement led the public to believe, once his role was revealed, that the senator must have had something to hide, and this led to a specific focus on the prior campaign contributions he had received from AIG—thus putting him in an even worse position than the one he had hoped to avoid by initially ducking the issue. And, third, the refusal by the senior senator from Connecticut to own up at the outset created a "gotcha moment" whereby he rolled the dice with his credibility .

While you should disclose the most embarrassing of information, you are not under an obligation to put it out in a way guaranteed to get the most attention. Quite the opposite. One of the benefits of controlling the disclosure is that often you can manage the time, place, and venue for the information to be released, which can allow you to limit the number of people who are exposed to the information, in turn limiting the damage.

In other words, disclosing embarrassing facts does not mean you are required to let it all out in the middle of the day, on the most crowded street, and in front of the largest audience.

Far from it.

In fact, with regards to disclosure, the hold your head high commandment affords you the benefit of putting out even the most embarrassing information in a way designed to significantly modulate the embarrassment.

If you put the information out, you can often pick the time to put it out. For example:

- At the end of the day, after the markets have closed, which is what many publicly traded companies do.
- During the middle of a bigger news story, as Google did in releasing a change in position in its privacy policy on the day President Obama was to deliver his 2012 State of the Union address, thereby minimizing the amount of attention the story would otherwise have garnered.
- On a Friday afternoon before a three-day weekend in the summer. This has become a classic time in politics for what is known as a "document dump." The theory is, the media's leading reporters (and in fact, most reporters) have already gone home Friday afternoon for the weekend (especially on long weekends). And many reporters aren't particularly eager to return to their offices or television studios to report on a fresh story. Thus, those covering the late-afternoon Friday story will likely be the lower-profile second team. Further, the news will break on the electronic news outlets on Friday night, when TV ratings are low, and in the papers on Saturday morning, which is the week's lowest impact news time. The hope is, by Monday,

the media will be chasing newer, shinier things. This strategy was used to great effect in 2008 by then presidential candidate Senator John McCain. Senator McCain had been under pressure for months to release his medical records, and when he finally acquiesced, he released them on the Friday before Memorial Day weekend. And when later the pressure turned to Cindy McCain to release her tax returns, following her husband's lead, the release was done on a Friday night.

Leveraging the timing of a release of negative information comes with a key caveat—in putting it out there, you need to make sure that the information is disseminated in such a way that the information is fully revealed, and the targeted audiences with whom you are communicating feel they have received what they need. And further, they have to feel there has not been an effort to dupe them or bury the information; these are the audiences with whom you must build or rebuild trust, and they have to be respected accordingly.

Therefore, if you are a publicly traded company releasing information after the market closes before a three-day weekend in the summer, or a politician putting out their tax returns as a Friday afternoon document dump, work with the reporters who most often cover the company or the candidate in advance on an embargoed basis (meaning there is a pre-agreed time for the publication of the story). Present the story to them over the course of the day, so when the information appears they have the whole story and they understand it, and in turn your key audiences who will read the news—whether it is shareholders, analysts, political pundits, or voters—will have their questions answered. The reporters will then not feel compelled to write follow-ups or pursue the story, as they will believe the Friday night release was not an attempt to avoid revealing the entire story, but rather what it really is—an effort to control the timing of the release of the story.

You can leverage the timing of the story's release to minimize the amount of coverage, the number of eyeballs that will follow the event, and the duration of the event—so long as you actively communicate to those audiences with whom you need to build trust. This will ensure survival over the long-haul.

You may not always have the flexibility to time the release of the information to your maximum benefit—but, if you do, take full advantage of it.

ONCE ANSWERED, DO NOT DEVIATE FROM YOUR ANSWER

When you abide by the hold your head high commandment—regardless of when and how you put the unflattering information out—it is imperative that you have the discipline to make sure, *once answered, do not deviate from your answer* about how you characterized or explained the unflattering information (of course, this assumes that all the information is out there and your explanation is accurate). If you want to be able to move on effectively, it is critical to stop talking about it. And, in a crisis, the way you stop talking about it is to make sure that when you do talk about it, you talk about it the same way every time.

While Senator Dodd eventually did get his answer right, consider what Netflix did with its apology, non-apology in September 2011. The high-flying company was built on a foundation of charging consumers $9.99 a month for a plan that included DVD-rental by mail plus streaming video. But in July 2011, Netflix announced that it was splitting up the plan, and consumers would have to pay $7.99 for each plan separately—a move that generated an enormous consumer backlash and led to the company losing half of its market share in a matter of weeks. In the face of this, Netflix sought to explain the business rationale to its shareholders, and the consumer reasons to its customers. By September, as the company was hemorrhaging customers, an email was sent to all subscribers from Reed Hastings, Netflix's chief executive, stating:

> I messed up. I owe you an explanation. It is clear from the feedback over the past two months that many members felt we lacked respect and humility in the way we announced the separation of DVD and streaming and the price changes. That was certainly not our intent, and I offer my sincere apology. Let me explain what we are doing.

The CEO also issued a YouTube apology, but announced Netflix was nonetheless staying the course, and, further, that he was going to formally split the two services into different companies.

Consumers were confused. Investors puzzled. Reporters baffled. If there was nothing to apologize for, there should not have been an apology. If there was something to apologize for, it should have been fixed. But an apology without a fix did not seem to add up.

Writing in his *New York Times* blog, David Pogue, the paper's influential technology correspondent, wrote,

> Mr. Hastings thinks it helps to say "I messed up" without actually making things right. That's one of the hollowest apologies I've ever heard. It's lip service. It's like the politician who says, "I'm sorry you feel that way." You're not sorry—in fact, you're still insisting that you're right.

Once you engage in the full monty of the hold your head high commandment—zip it up going forward when it comes to adding in details or injecting extraneous information. Nothing can be regained by revisiting the issue. If asked about a matter that has already receded from the headlines, and for which you have already taken responsibility, resist going back and revisiting it, regardless of whether you were, in fact, responsible or culpable.

Once the wound has scarred over, there is no reason to re-open it unless you enjoy bloodletting.

POP THE BALLOON TO INFLATE YOUR CREDIBILITY

Putting the information out, especially the most unflattering, most embarrassing, or most negative facts, allows you to *pop the balloon to inflate your credibility.* The mere act of putting out bad information communicates to your key audiences that you are dealing with the matter in a credible way, and further demonstrates that there is unlikely to be more information being held back or covered up. While your core audiences may not like what you are admitting, you are nonetheless conveying your commitment to, and interest in, restoring the public trust by being upfront, straightforward, and honest.

Though his career was filled with great accomplishments, and he was considered one of the Senate's most credible and honored members, popping the balloon is a lesson that seems to have been lost on Chris Dodd when he went on CNN. Once the AIG bonus legislation became a public issue, the senator's role in the allowing the provision to be included was *going* to become public. After all, how could it not, given he was the bill's author? If the information about his role in the AIG provision had come from Senator Dodd when the issue first surfaced, he would have had a much better chance at explaining the situation, being perceived as credible, and placing himself in a stronger position to move on. Instead, the news of his role came out after he had missed his opportunity to put it out, which caused the issue to loom much larger (it always looks larger if it appears like you were trying to hide it); consequently, the story was far worse.

In a crisis, you have to seek that moment when you can move on from the story. And you can only effectively move on when all of the material information related to the specific crisis has been presented—you then need to pop the balloon.

To effectively pop the balloon and earn your credibility points, consider working with a respected outlet for a comprehensive foundation story—with all the warts reported on—as your core audience will see this as a level of due diligence to make sure all the information was released. And to fully deflate the balloon, when releasing the information make sure that those who are reviewing it are made aware of the important and relevant points, and that you don't somehow camouflage them.

At the Clinton White House, during various investigations, the administration would often release thousands of pages of documents, and specifically identified the "hot docs"—those documents that it knew would be of the greatest interest. The president's team did this because of the awareness that even if the reporters did not initially locate the information, eventually they or one of the president's political opponents would identify the information and blow it up. If the Clinton White House pointed it out, the administration would be in the best position to explain it. And, finally, the president's advisors pointed to the hot documents because in the long run, a chief objective in releasing the information was to establish credibility—and the focus was on wanting to prove the Clinton White House was deserving of the public trust.

Finally, with online tools there are ways to just put the information out on your own platforms, and when people eventually get around to asking about it, you can point to the fact that it was proactively and affirmatively disclosed. We had one nonprofit client that, due to its own diligence, became aware of an issue regarding the efficacy of one of its programs, and they self-reported the issue in a document that was put right on the organization's website. Predictably, several months later a reporter called because they had been "tipped" to an incipient scandal. We pointed them to the website, noting that the organization itself had made the issue public on its own, and that it was posted and available for all to read. We never heard back from the reporter and the story never ran.

To respect the fifth commandment, follow these three steps:

1. Don't turn a mountain of a crisis into a Mount Everest of crises.
2. Once answered, do not deviate from your answer.
3. Pop the balloon to inflate your credibility.

RESPECTING THE FIFTH COMMANDMENT— "EVERYTHING YOU'VE READ IS TRUE"

San Francisco mayor Gavin Newsom was on the stake of his very own doing.

The front-page headline on the *San Francisco Chronicle*'s website on February 1, 2007, said it all:

AIDE QUITS AS NEWSOM'S AFFAIR WITH HIS WIFE IS REVEALED

Campaign manager confronts mayor, who is "in shock"

Not only was the mayor caught having an affair. Not only was the affair with a staff member. Not only was the staff member married. But the staff member was married to the mayor's current campaign manager, his former deputy chief of staff—*and* one of his best friends.

In short, the mayor had broken the "man code"—an act guaranteed to inflame an enormous portion of his constituency—and he broke the man code nine months from election day.

Asked at City Hall about his actions as the news first broke, the mayor stated, "I'm not making any public comment. I'm just not."

Then, the following day, stepping to the podium to address the story for the first time, his political career hanging in the balance, the mayor looked out on to the press corps in a fever pitch assembled before him in San Francisco's historic City Hall.

Would the mayor follow the path of South Carolina governor Mark Sanford, who, after being caught lying about hiking the Appalachian Trail when he was actually in South America having an affair, spoke about having met the love of his life?

Would he adopt the approach of New Jersey governor Jim McGreevey, who was caught having an affair with a man, and resign?

The mayor looked over the crowd, stepped to the podium, and simply stated:

I want to make it clear that everything you've read is true and I'm deeply sorry about that . . . I hurt someone I care deeply about . . . and his family and friends, and that is something I'm deeply sad about and sorry for.

The mayor did not attempt to parse the facts. No excuses or half-truths were offered. He did not attempt to explain the inexplicable, defend the indefensible, or justify the unjustifiable. Gavin Newsom may have violated the man code—but like the men in the movie who revealed it all, he executed the full monty.

Holding his head high, the mayor acknowledged every embarrassing detail of the affair—and did not flinch from even the most unflattering elements. In doing so, he limited the harm and controlled the damage by not turning a mountain of a crisis into a Mount Everest of crises.

The mayor then had the discipline to shut up. Once he answered the issues honestly and accurately, he did not deviate from those answers, offering the same basic response—virtually to the word—every time he was asked about the incident for days, weeks, months, and even years afterward.

Finally, Newsom both protected and bolstered his credibility by putting out all of the relevant information—he popped the balloon to inflate his own credibility.

In the first few days of the story breaking, the local press had a predictable field day examining, re-examining, and re-re-examining every aspect of the story. The political punditocracy offered numerous predictions as to how the incident would derail the mayor's political career.

But, because of the mayor's respect for the fifth commandment's edict of hold your head high, the story had a limited shelf life—there was no additional news to report, no question of whether the mayor had engaged in a cover-up, and no chance to pick apart his public comments for not being forthcoming.

The mayor's handling of a career-threatening issue was textbook, and showed him to be Picasso-like when it came to the art of damage control:

Nine months later, he was re-elected mayor of San Francisco with a historic margin.

In 2010, he was elected statewide as the lieutenant governor of California.

Today, he is considered one of the state's most influential elected officials, and is among the nation's most promising next generation of political leaders.

THE FIFTH COMMANDMENT APPLIED TO AN EVERYDAY CRISIS—
GETTING CAUGHT WITH RESUME PUFFERY

In November 2011, *The New York Times* featured a story in its sports pages about a Yale football quarterback who was going to have to forfeit his opportunity to pursue a Rhodes Scholarship because his scheduled Rhodes interview conflicted with the Harvard-Yale football game. The article noted that Yale's coach, Tom Williams, had also applied for a Rhodes nearly twenty years earlier while playing for Stanford. The only problem: Coach Williams had not.

The coach, by perpetuating the story in the nation's paper of record, practically begged for significant scrutiny. Consequently, when it was revealed that not only had he not applied for a Rhodes Scholarship, but an additional claim that he had been on the practice squad of the San Francisco 49ers also did not check out, Williams was forced to resign from Yale.

In both instances, the truth was not very far off—Williams apparently had been encouraged to apply for a Rhodes in light of his impressive achievements on and off the field at Stanford, and he had participated as an unsigned free agent in a 49ers training camp.

Coach Williams was part of a series of high-profile individuals caught in resume lies. The CEO of Yahoo resigned following reports of an embellished college degree; the dean of admissions at MIT made inaccurate claims regarding her degrees, and she too resigned; and Connecticut governor Richard Blumenthal engaged in puffery regarding the nature of his military service in Vietnam.

A common denominator in many of these situations is that people early in their careers, faced with securing a job, seek ways to enhance their resumes—and then, as they ascend the professional ladder, are too embarrassed to correct the record, even when correcting the record at a relatively lower level may not have impacted their career trajectory in a material way.

While most people submitting a resume or filling out a job application are unlikely to claim that they pursued a Rhodes Scholarship, or have false representations of college degrees, many in the workforce struggle with more mundane resume problems. They may attempt to compensate for gaps in their work history or time at a company that went under, to combine base salary and bonuses to represent a higher level of pay, to fudge job titles, or change their birthdates to appear younger.

However, in tough economic times, when too many people are facing a real crisis regarding their employment prospects, and they are unemployed, underemployed, or underpaid, such resume "puffery" is a temptation many cannot resist to help secure a new position. Paradoxically, in part because the job market is so tight, we are now in an era where resumes are getting especially close scrutiny. Employers are aggressively looking for work history gaps, checking on salaries, and calling references—and in this atmosphere, you *will* get called out on the puffery and need to be ready.

Presuming one has not provided an outlandish lie, but simply sought to fudge the facts a little, when confronted, it is critical to be prepared to answer the question truthfully when called out on it—or to affirmatively address the issue in an interview.

If there are gaps between jobs, be prepared to give details and explain the reasons. Don't turn a gap into a deep chasm that does you even more harm by not being straight about it.

If you sought to make your salary appear higher, detail the amounts of both your base salary and your bonus. Make sure you have your answer down. And once you provide the answer, if you are asked again, make sure you do not deviate from the position you have provided.

If you expanded your title, be ready to acknowledge it, and provide information that details how your responsibilities were commensurate with the title you put down. Pop the balloon and you will have a better shot at providing a credible explanation as to why you used the title on your resume.

In other words, do not be so embarrassed by something that is unflattering or negative, that you compound the damage by turning the fudge into a lie. Approach the issue ready and prepared, and hold your head high.

COROLLARY TO THE FIFTH COMMANDMENT— WHEN IT COMES TO THE FULL MONTY, THERE ARE NO SECOND ACTS

At the defining moment when you put out your explanation, it becomes *the* explanation, and you will have to live with going forward. Forever. The full monty is the *entire show*. If you are putting it all out there in all of its glory, *there is no second act.*

Senator Dodd had a great second act, and had it been his first act, he might still be a highly influential senator. But unfortunately, it was not his first act.

Mayor Newsom had no need for a second act, because his first act accomplished what he needed to do.

In this regard, consider how former Massachusetts governor Mitt Romney handled disclosure issues related to his taxes in the heat of the 2012 Republican presidential primary.

Romney knew full well that his financial background was going to result in repeated demands that his tax returns be made public, a dynamic reinforced by the standard practice of serious presidential candidates typically releasing their tax returns. The demands were further contextualized by the fact that his father, the former governor of Michigan, when he was running for president, established the bar when he released a full twelve years of tax returns. But his son Mitt did nothing to pre-empt the story and get ahead of it.

As the campaign commenced in the summer of 2011, when few outside of possible caucus goers in Iowa and a limited number of reporters were paying attention, he resisted for months the call to release his tax returns.

Late in 2011, heading into the intensity of the Iowa caucuses, when asked about whether he was going to release his returns, Romney said, "I doubt it."

In a later response to criticism over his refusal to release his tax returns, he opened the window slightly, saying he would "consider" disclosure.

This then shifted to saying he would "probably" release his tax returns.

Next, he offered to release the tax returns in April—a clear effort to avoid releasing the information during the most hotly contested part of the primary season.

Then, during a critical Republican debate on the eve of the important South Carolina primary, he offered a muddled answer when questioned on the issue by a CNN moderator, seemingly (and shockingly) unprepared to answer whether he would do as his dad had done and release multiple years of his returns, or just release one year.

The pressure continued to increase on Romney and came from across the political spectrum. Even one of Mitt Romney's top supporters, New Jersey governor Chris Christie, weighed in on the side of disclosure, saying on NBC's *Today Show,* "What I would say to Governor Romney is if you have tax returns to put out, you should put them out. And you put them out sooner rather than later because it's always better in my view to have full disclosure, especially when you're the front-runner."

Following a beat-down in the South Carolina debate at the hands of former House speaker Newt Gingrich, the Romney campaign finally announced it would release the returns. Romney went on Fox News and said:

> Given all the attention that's been focused on tax returns, given the distraction I think they became in these last couple of weeks, look, I'm going to make it very clear to you right now Chris, I'm going to release my tax returns for 2010, which is the last returns that were completed. I'll do them on Tuesday of this week. I'm also at the same time going to release an estimate for 2011 tax returns. So you'll have two years, people can take a good look at it.

In time period between when he said he would not disclose his taxes, and the release of the taxes, Romney had to combat stories about off-shore investments in tax havens such as the Cayman Islands, a Swiss bank account, his low marginal tax rate, how much he made annually from investment income, and more—all of which directly drove the negative storyline that he was the Wall Street candidate, at the very moment when Romney was trying desperately to appeal to Main Street.

And by the time he released his tax returns (and even then, only his tax returns covering a limited time period, ensuring the issue would live on), this second act was definitely not playing in Peoria—the damage had been done.

If Romney's plan had been to minimize the attack that he was the Wall Street candidate by not disclosing his tax returns, his hide-the-salami approach had the opposite effect—it became *the* issue. And by the time he finally released the tax returns, the harm was done.

If the art of damage control is limiting the crisis and allowing you to move on as quickly possible, Governor Romney showed he had difficulty painting by numbers on this one.

Romney had numerous swings with the bat, and he missed a beach-ball-sized target each time. The key for him, and all others, when releasing information, is our fifth commandment—hold your head high.

TWELVE
COMMANDMENT VI
BE STRAIGHT ABOUT WHAT YOU KNOW, WHAT YOU DON'T KNOW, AND WHAT YOU ARE GOING TO DO TO FIX THE PROBLEM

Say hello to my little friend.

—Tony Montana, *Scarface*

THE SIXTH COMMANDMENT—BE STRAIGHT ABOUT WHAT YOU KNOW, WHAT YOU DON'T KNOW, AND WHAT YOU ARE GOING TO DO TO FIX THE PROBLEM

To limit the harm caused by a problem, provide only accurate information at the time the information is secured and avoid speculation, guesswork, or unproven hypotheses. Maintain discipline and be clear in distinguishing between what you know and what you do not know. Most importantly, when the answers are not known, establish credibility by explaining what you will do to make sure the problem is fixed, and then execute that plan.

DISRESPECTING THE SIXTH COMMANDMENT— MINE CEO BLASTS EVERYONE IN HIS PATH

On Monday, August 6, 2007, news broke that there had been an early dawn collapse of the Crandall Canyon Mine in Crandall Canyon, Utah, trapping six miners 1,500 feet below ground. At about the time of the collapse, geological monitoring stations in Utah recorded a seismic event measuring 3.9 in magnitude.

As the local and national news media scrambled to cover the event, Robert Murray, the head of Murray Energy Corp, which owned and operated the mine, immediately flew in on a private jet from Montana to personally take control of the company's response, including providing updates to the media, families of the miners, regulators, and the broader public. Reportedly, Murray's company had over $800 million a year in sales and was one of the largest privately owned coal companies in the country.

Over the course of several days, and, in particular, during an August 7 nationally televised conference, Murray sought to "brief" the public. With the miners still trapped and unaccounted for, Murray declared that the mine collapsed as the result of an earthquake—and not because of any structural failings, which presumably would have exposed his company to liability. He stated:

> This was caused by an earthquake, not something that Murray Energy . . . did or our employees did or our management did . . . It was a natural disaster. An earthquake. And I'm going to prove it to you.

Almost immediately, Murray's earthquake defense was challenged by geologists, mine-safety experts, and the National Earthquake Information Center—in turn giving fuel to those who thought it unseemly that Murray was evading responsibility at a time when everyone needed to be solely focused on one mission: rescuing the trapped mine workers.

Walter Arabasz of the University of Utah's seismographic station had a different view, saying that the data indicated the seismic event was "consistent with the idea that the mine collapse caused the earthquake," and not the other way around, as Murray maintained.

The U.S. Geological Survey stated, "Seismologists have not yet determined how the earthquake of August 6 might be related to the occurrence of a collapse at the nearby Crandall Canyon coal mine that, as of midday August 6, had left six miners unaccounted for."

Numerous other news stories had documented that in prior mine collapses, seismic recording devices had picked up seismic events as a consequence of the collapses—and not as the predicate for the collapses. Undeterred, Murray continued to drill his point, vigorously contesting the scientific experts and the data disseminated by the federal government.

And in response, even more governmental authorities, scientists, and experts pointed out that seismic events similar to what occurred in Utah are often the consequence of a collapse. As reporters and others began to familiarize themselves with Murray and his company, they reviewed the mine's safety record. Some reports raised the issue of whether Murray Energy was engaged in retreat mining—a particularly dangerous form of coal extraction where miners pull down mine pillars behind them when they have completed their work in a particular section of a mine, allowing that area of the mine to collapse. Murray vehemently denied this, stating:

> The damage in the mine was totally unrelated to any retreat mining. The pillars were not being removed here at the time of the accident. There are eight solid pillars around where the men are right now.

As was the case with Murray's earthquake defense, this position was also disputed. The U.S. Mine Safety and Health Administration noted that the company was indeed engaged in retreat mining, which the company had applied and received permission for in 2006.

The result was that quickly, the focus turned to the conduct of the company—the very focus it seemed Murray had being seeking to sidestep in the first place.

The headline in the Associated Press story said it all: "Mine Exec Blames Utah Cave-In on an Earthquake, Denies 'Retreat Mining.'"

Predictably, reporters started looking at the company's history of violations. *USA Today* reported on 325 safety violations since 2004 but sought to contextualize the record with a modulated comment by J. Davitt McAteer, the well-respected former head of the Mine Safety and Health Administration, who observed of the safety record, "It's not perfect but it's certainly not bad . . . It would be in the medium range."

Murray's responses to a review of the company's records were anything but modulated. He went out of his way to extol the virtues of the mine industry and attacked such former regulators who, in fact, had provided relatively positive comments:

> Number one, I wish you would take the word retreat mining out of your vocabulary. Those were words invented by Davitt McAteer, Oppegard, who are lackies for the United Mine Workers, and officials at the United Mine Workers, who would like to organize this coal mine.

Murray went on to challenge the news media, in particular, Fox News (not generally considered sympathetic to labor unions or environmentalists) and the Associated Press, for their reporting on the Crandall Canyon Mine's safety record. Murray's attacks on the Fourth Estate were widely reported.

And all this time, there were six miners trapped underground while their families, friends, and coworkers were in despair on the surface, and the nation was anxiously following the trapped miners' fates.

There was a general sentiment that in a mine collapse crisis such as this, the entire focus needed to be on expressing concern for the workers, whose lives were hanging in the balance, and for the rescue crews fighting to reach them.

And while Murray did express his sympathies for the trapped miners, he nonetheless often came off as seeking to avoid responsibility, and he employed language that was not especially comforting.

> If they're dead, the shock of the earthquake, the concussion killed them, and they died instantly, that's the one scenario . . . The other scenario is that they're very much alive and we're going to rescue them . . . The Lord has already decided whether they're alive or dead.

The result of the press briefings, and, in particular, the August 7 press conference, was captured by the commentary in the coverage.

The CNN anchor called it "one of the most bizarre press conferences I have ever seen."

NPR described the press conference as "rambling" and pointed out the twisting of the facts: "In other words, the seismic data was the result of the mine itself collapsing, not a triggering earthquake."

ABC News said of Murray's performance: "Even if they're still alive, the six miners trapped 1,500 feet below ground wouldn't have heard the boss, but he was intent on making sure everyone else did."

And California congressman George Miller, who at the time chaired the House Labor Committee (which had oversight over such mining-worker-safety issues), commented, "The families of the six trapped miners are deeply worried about the welfare of their loved ones. They need and have a right to the most credible, objective, and up-to-date information available about the status of the rescue effort."

The rescue effort was ultimately abandoned with the six miners presumed dead, and there was an additional tragedy of three courageous rescue workers who tried to save them also dying in the mine.

Pursuant to Murray's performance, Congress announced hearings, regulators opened up an investigation, and family members of the miners sued the company.

And, as for Murray, after presenting himself as the man in charge, he was replaced by other company representatives shortly after his August 7 press conference.

UNDERSTANDING THE SIXTH COMMANDMENT— BE STRAIGHT ABOUT WHAT YOU KNOW, WHAT YOU DON'T KNOW, AND WHAT YOU ARE GOING TO DO TO FIX THE PROBLEM

Robert Murray's August 7 appearance before the local and national media was the press conference equivalent of the scene in the move *Scarface* when Al Pacino's character, Tony Montana, blasts away indiscriminately with his machine gun at a door to a house—and anything and everything behind the door—yelling, "Say hello to my little friend!" In going Scarface at the press briefing, Murray and, by association, Murray Energy did enormous harm to their credibility by violating the sixth commandment of damage control:

Be straight about what you know, what you don't know, and what you are going to do to fix the problem.

The commitment to full disclosure, the targeting of your core audience, not feeding the fire, and presenting the details, can all be for naught if in a crisis there isn't the capacity to distinguish between what is known and what is not known.

Damage control is not like pulling up to the bar in a saloon and spinning out theories like the local gadfly; rather it is a focused execution of specific action steps with the objective of restoring trust.

Therefore, to succeed, it is imperative to make clear what you know and what you do not know—and, most importantly to your core audience, show that you are serious when it comes to fixing the problem.

FEED THE BEAST

In the opening moments of a crisis, your core audience is going to be looking for information. They are like a ravenous beast eating up everything that comes their way. And, frequently, in this moment, you simply are not in a place where you can get your hands around the issue and provide the information in a way that you are confident will stand the test of time, given the coming scrutiny. At such a moment there are good ways to *feed the beast* and there are bad ways to feed the beast.

Murray most definitely picked the wrong way to feed the beast. And the beast bit back. Hard.

The claim that the collapse was the result of an earthquake was gobbled up by the company's core audiences (the family members of the trapped miners, the press, and government officials) and then spat back—at a great cost to both Murray and his company's credibility. Murray should have had exactly one message: sympathy for the miners and explaining what was being done to rescue them. Instead, Murray came off as callous, uncaring, and trying to avoid accountability.

In a crisis, rather than trying to feed the beast by pushing out information that is speculative at best and intentionally misleading at worse, provide information that you know to be accurate. One effective way to guarantee that you are not engaging in the sort of speculation that Murray did is to deploy information that is in the form of primary documents. By putting out the actual documents, you bolster the case you are making in providing accurate information, while avoiding the dissemination of what is inaccurate.

In the aftermath of the mine collapse, Murray could have simply produced documents detailing the company's safety inspections or safety record.

And in a dynamic where it is likely that there will be questions posed to which answers do not currently exist, there is nothing wrong with preemptively making clear that given the nature of the situation, the focus of what can be discussed is going to be limited. To this point, it would have been completely acceptable and understandable for Murray to state that the company's first priority was the fate of the miners, and that he and the company did not yet have all the answers and were not in a place to speculate about what may have triggered the disaster.

AVOID TRYING TO BE THE SMARTEST PERSON IN THE ROOM

In litigation, trial lawyers understand that you should never ask a question to a witness where you do not already know the answer that will be given. In a crisis, never provide a substantive answer to a question unless the answer is already confirmed. Human nature is such that there is a desire to provide information in the face of a challenging situation. Some people seek ways to shirk being held accountable. Others feel compelled to offer explanations. There are even those who want to take full responsibility—even if the facts are not yet known. And then there are those who believe they are back in school and need to provide an answer to every question. In a crisis, have the discipline to *avoid trying to be the smartest person in the room.* A passing grade in damage control does not go to the person who answers the most questions but to the person who provides answers only to those questions to which they know the answer.

Murray Energy, during the August 7 press briefing and beyond, provided answers to questions they were not in a position to answer. By not having the discipline to stick to a simple message, and instead attacking the press and well-respected outside independent experts, Murray demonstrated a lack of discipline. The insistence that the incident was precipitated by an earthquake, and the denials about the type of mining in which the company was engaged despite documentary evidence to the contrary, both contributed to the impression that this was a guy who was either making it up as he was on stage— or someone willfully seeking to misrepresent the facts.

Keep your focus and avoid trying to prove that you are the smartest person in the room. The more you drill down into facts and technical information, the more likely you are to make a mistake. You have to show the discipline to resist answering questions when you do not know with a 110 percent certitude that your responses will be accurate. At the end of the day, the smartest guy is the one who protects his organization and preserves his position by sticking to what is known and being clear about what is not known.

When you're before an audience—whether it's the press, shareholders, voters, or employees—act as if you are dealing with live ammo. Keep the safety on. And only fire after you have aimed and are sure of your target. In the August 7 press conference, Murray adopted a "ready, fire, aim" approach.

A better plan would have been to:

- *Refer* to experts to provide the specific details, saying, "There are geologists who can discuss the seismic event data, our focus right now is on saving our people."
- *Defer* to others who were better positioned to answer the questions, offering, "I am not a structural engineer. I defer to those who have a better understanding of such issues. Our focus at this moment is on the trapped miners."

- *Make clear* the company was working with the relevant authorities as a way to not reply to questions for which they did not yet have answers, while also keeping the focus on the miners, "We will cooperate fully with the investigation in order to get a complete understanding as to why the mine collapsed. Currently, all of our company's efforts are on saving our employees."

Murray should have been echoing the exact statement issued by the district director of the Mine and Safety Administration, who was on site to oversee the process for the U.S. government: "I'll not get into any conjecture about cause and effect of this mine accident. That's not my purpose here. My purpose here right now is entirely focused on the rescue of these trapped miners."

Rather than engaging in conjecture, it is far better to affirmatively and proactively tell your core audiences what you do know—even if it's very little, and nothing more than letting them know you do not yet have the answers.

IDENTIFY A PROCESS TO SERVE AS A SAFE HAVEN

In a crisis where you simply do not have the answers—and are being clear that you do not have the answers—you must identify how you plan to secure the answers.

Your core audience will understand the challenges of getting accurate information, but their appetite will need to be satiated with details of the process you are using to obtain the information.

Therefore, when the answers are not available, identify a process to serve as a safe haven while you get the information and fix the problem.

DEMONSTRATE A SERIOUSNESS OF PURPOSE

There are tried and true ways to show a commitment to ascertaining the facts and establishing credibility by *demonstrating a seriousness of purpose,* which Murray could have employed. As noted, he could have offered full cooperation with federal investigators. He could have announced the retention of an outside expert. He could have asked a third party to come in and review the matter.

And whatever process is chosen to obtain the needed information, your core audiences must "buy in" to the particular process as being legitimate, and one that will produce credible results.

In a crisis, your core audience especially wants to see that you understand the gravity of the situation and are committed to fixing the problem.

Murray Energy, by insisting from the very beginning that the company did not play a role in the disaster, communicated that not only were they not going to fix the problem, but moreover, they created an impression that the company did not think there was even a problem to be fixed. This rang especially hollow and disingenuous in light of the fact that something was demonstrably wrong, as a mine had collapsed and people were trapped.

When making clear that you recognize there is indeed a problem, and you have established a process to fix the problem—you must demonstrate a seriousness of purpose. Your core audiences will be looking for tangible proof that you are taking action to address the issue. It cannot be a whitewash. You can't just check the box. Don't think people will just forget about it.

Steps to demonstrate such a seriousness of purpose that we, and others, have employed over the years to build up credibility include:

- An appointment of a blue-ribbon commission that issues findings, which are then implemented;
- An internal review followed by the public release of substantive recommendations;
- The organization announcing a new approach to the way it conducts business;
- The retention of a man or woman of impeccable credentials to oversee a particular department within an organization and take responsibility for fixing the problem.

To respect the sixth commandment, follow these three steps:

1. Feed the beast.
2. Don't try to be the smartest person in the room.
3. Demonstrate a seriousness of purpose.

RESPECTING THE SIXTH COMMANDMENT— LOS ANGELES MAYOR TOM BRADLEY'S GREATEST CHALLENGE

Tom Bradley, the path-breaking African American mayor of Los Angeles from 1973 until his retirement in 1993, faced his greatest challenge when Los Angeles police officers beat Rodney King in March 1991.

Demands for swift justice for the officers involved in the beating collided head-on with the historically strong support in many neighborhoods for the Los Angeles Police Department, and race relations in Los Angeles deteriorated at an alarming rate.

There were concerns that at any moment the city of angels could explode.

Bradley, who was once an LAPD lieutenant, strongly suspected that racism and the use of undue force were endemic to segments of the LAPD. As mayor, his attempts to reform the LAPD had run up against a succession of police chiefs who were given enormous power by the city charter. And the chief at the time of the King beatings, Daryl Gates, was a bitter opponent of Bradley and his attempts to change the LAPD.

As cries for justice became louder and community divisions became deeper, Mayor Bradley seemed stymied. The public wanted answers that the mayor just did not have, and a broad swath of Los Angeles wanted action that Bradley simply did not have the power to take.

The mayor's solution: Persuade Warren Christopher, the renowned international diplomat and Los Angeles legal titan, to bring together a small group to study the LAPD and to recommend solutions. At the outset, this group, which became known as the Christopher Commission, was derided by many as a meaningless exercise that would lead nowhere, and Bradley was criticized for not acting more forcefully.

But Mayor Bradley knew what he was doing. The mayor understood that in a crisis, the best course of action is to tell the public straight up what you know, be forthright about what you do not know, and be clear about what you are doing to get the answers and create the changes that the public demands.

In the end, the Christopher Commission delivered exactly what Mayor Bradley and the city of Los Angeles most needed: The commission's findings demonstrated, beyond any doubt, a pattern of misconduct and failed discipline within the LAPD. Under Christopher's leadership, and with Mayor Bradley's support and fundraising, a ballot measure to reform the LAPD was passed by city voters. And as a result of the pressure created by Christopher's findings, the seemingly invincible Daryl Gates was forced to resign after thirteen years as chief. And today, the LAPD is widely heralded for a community policing style that has helped reduce crime in Los Angeles to historic lows.

From this crisis Mayor Bradley was able to truly create an opportunity that had eluded Los Angeles for decades—reforming the police department and addressing race relations. And, in a large part, he did so by respecting the sixth commandment—be straight about what you know, what you don't know, and what you are going to do to fix the problem.

From the beginning, the mayor told his core audiences—the African American community and the people of Los Angeles as a whole, civil rights leaders, the press, and the business community—what he knew (that he would do all he could within his limited powers to address the situation), what he did not know (how he was going to specifically do it, given the city's charter), and what he was going to do to fix the problem (a task force led by a man of impeccable credentials, empowered to identify specific recommendations).

The mayor then pursued a process that adhered to the precepts of the sixth commandment:

- The Christopher Commission fed the beast by putting out respected, credible information in the form of a comprehensive report.
- The mayor did not try to be the smartest person in the room at the beginning of the process. By maintaining a disciplined approach, the mayor avoided putting out information that would have been subject to challenges.
- By announcing the task force, the mayor pre-emptively made clear that he did not yet have the answers. However, by giving the task force a mandate and naming a highly-respected eminence gris to head it, Mayor Bradley established a credible vehicle by which to identify the answers and offer a specific path forward. And, when coupled with the political capital expended on it by the mayor, this communicated to his core audiences a seriousness of purpose when it came to fixing the problem.

From the moment of the Rodney King beating to the passage of the reform initiative, Bradley went from being defined as the man who was leading the city during one of Los Angeles' lowest moments, to the mayor whose legacy healed a city and enacted reforms that have made it safer for all its people.

THE SIXTH COMMANDMENT APPLIED TO AN EVERYDAY CRISIS— STUCK ON THE RUNWAY

In the fall of 2001, Clayton Parker, a Silicon Valley–based, technology executive, was on a long United Airlines flight back to the United States from Asia.

Clayton had made this same trip for years on numerous occasions and by now knew the routine.

As the flight neared its destination, San Francisco International Airport, he began to notice that the flight attendants seemed unusually stressed and harried. When he tried to engage them in a conversation, they were atypically curt and brusque (Clayton was in first class, where the attendants still tended to treat passengers with a modicum of courtesy). He could see several intense conversations taking place among the flight crew, who were huddling in the galley.

Clayton turned to the in-flight map to determine the location of the plane and to see if he could gather any information that could explain why the crew was on edge. But the in-flight map was not operational, though it had been working earlier in the flight.

Shortly before the planned arrival time, the pilot came on over the intercom system, and—unlike the typical announcement that provided a local weather report, a welcome to San Francisco, and a "thank you for traveling with us today"—the passengers received a brusque statement that the plane was beginning its final descendent and were asked to remain in their seats.

As the plane descended, Clayton looked out his widow and did not see the familiar marker of the Farallon Islands, which he usually saw on the landing approach for flights originating in Asia. Instead, there were islands that he did not recognize.

As the plane reached land, it was clear to Clayton that they were not flying over the Bay Area. Other passengers went through a similar analysis, and an audible murmur was heard that soon picked up intensity as it swept through the plane. Questions to the flight attendants were met with vague or elusive answers or no responses. Not surprisingly, unease and concern began to spread.

What was going on? Why were they not in San Francisco? Where were they landing?

And why couldn't the airline officials provide any answers—or even explain why they couldn't provide any answers?

As the plan hit the runway, Clayton and other passengers saw a large red-and-white maple leaf on the side of a building, suggesting that they were in Canada; other passengers recognized that they had just landed in Vancouver. By this point, the passengers were in a near revolt, yelling questions to the flight attendants, who continued to provide no information.

As the plane taxied to the terminal, and with passengers throughout the aircraft demanding information, the captain's disembodied voice came over the intercom, and with no additional information, tersely stated:

Ladies and Gentlemen, we have landed at the Vancouver International Airport because the United States of America is under attack.

This was the morning of September 11, 2001.

The passengers began scrambling for cell phones, but whether because their phones were not programmed for international calls from Canada, or due to the huge volume of calls overwhelming the available spectrum, they were not able to get through to friends or family.

Throughout all of this, the airplane sat on the runway for an extended period, as did other inbound planes. And still no updates from the captain or crew.

Eventually, some passengers were able to get through to their families on their cell phones—and you can imagine how the news of 9/11 spread throughout the airplane.

Some passengers began crying; others shouted to be let off the plane. Many sat in a daze.

September 11, 2001, was a terrible, tragic, and hopefully isolated event in U.S. history. It was clearly not a typical day. And, thus, it may not be fair to hold the airline or captain responsible for their failure to tell their passengers what they knew, what they did not know, and how they were going to fix the problem. That said, it's an extreme example of an experience airline passengers have on a regular basis when it comes to receiving information from pilots, flight crews, and airlines when stuck on a plane, whether at the gate, on the tarmac, or in the air.

There was a Northwest flight in 1999 where passengers were trapped on the tarmac in Detroit during a snow storm for eight hours—the bathrooms stopped working, water and food ran out, and on top of it all the passengers endured a dearth of information on their situation.

There was a JetBlue incident in 2007, where passengers boarded JetBlue flight 751 from New York's John F. Kennedy Airport en route to Cancun, Mexico, with a scheduled on-time departure of 8:15 A.M. and found themselves still on the tarmac at JFK after 4 P.M. Reportedly, "passengers waited for hours with no information," prompting one passenger to call CNN on her cell phone and say, "One of the pilots should get out here and have a mini–press conference . . . The longer they wait, the more people are going to get upset. It's Psychology 101."

Whether on a plane stuck on the tarmac, at a restaurant waiting for a meal that has yet to come out despite being ordered an hour ago, in the doctor's office waiting room where you have memorized the two-year-old *People* magazine, or tearing your hair out as you deal with an endless overseas call trying to fix your computer—time and time again, those in the consumer business do not tell their customers what they know, what they don't know, how they will get the information, and how the problem is going to be fixed.

And, in a consumer world where there are lots of other options, one bad flight, one bad meal, one bad doctor's appointment and you can lose someone's business, just because you were unable to explain a flight still on the ground, a cold meal, or a delayed doctor.

In fairness, and perhaps as a function of the sort of airline horror stories above (and government regulations passed in response to such stories), some airlines are becoming better at communicating to their customers, reflecting what appears to be a new found level of respect for the sixth commandment— at least on some flights. (But, sadly, we cannot personally attest to the same level of respect for the sixth commandment from computer call centers.)

There was the story recounted by a passenger and confirmed by The Consumerist (a website in partnership with *Consumer Reports*) of a June 2007 Continental flight from Newark to Boston that left the gate on time for the scheduled forty-seven-minute flight, only to be diverted to a remote airstrip because of a storm. While awaiting further instructions on the ground, the aircraft nearly ran out of fuel. Then the flight waited for more than two hours to refuel. However, the passengers were provided with constant updates as to why the plane had been diverted, and later received what was undoubtedly the pleasant surprise of a flight attendant coming over the intercom to announce that the pilot, out of his own pocket, had ordered pizzas for the entire plane. The communications provided the passengers with an understanding of the situation—and the pilot providing the pizzas showed that he understood there was a problem and had a commitment to addressing it.

It appears that the pizza approach is catching on.

The *New York Times* travel reporter Joe Sharkey wrote in his "On the Road" column in August 2007 about similar stories of delayed flights where the flight crews provided both information and hot pizza. One was a Delta flight from Phoenix to New York City that was diverted to Syracuse because New York's

JFK had been closed due to thunderstorms. While on the ground in Syracuse, the pilot announced that he was going to let everyone off—instead of the usual practice of keeping them imprisoned on the tarmac—so the passengers could eat and stretch, but they would have to be ready to re-board quickly if a departure slot opened. According to Sharkey's reporting, the captain stated:

> I'm not going to keep you on the plane. I'm going to pull up to a gate where you can get off, as long as you wait there in case we have to leave. I know you've only had cheese and crackers. So I called the Sbarro in the terminal and asked them to keep sending pizzas out until the whole plane gets fed.

The passengers remarked about how well treated they felt by the captain and flight attendants, which was really a function of effectively telling people what the crew knew (why they were being diverted), what the crew did not know (how long it was going to take for a slot to open up), what they were going to do about it (bring the passengers to the gate), and how committed the crew was to fixing the problem (they would feed passengers and keep them close to the gate so the plane could leave quickly).

In each of these pizza-on-the-plane stories, the airline crews respected the sixth commandment.

The flight crews, literally and figuratively, fed the beast—their passengers—starting with providing regular updates as to the nature of the delay.

The pilots did not try to be the smartest people on the plane and offer speculation as to when their airplanes would arrive. The crews made clear that they were not in a position to be able to answer questions that pertained to bad weather and airports being shut down—which the passengers respected and understood.

The pilots demonstrated a seriousness of purpose when it came to getting the information that everyone on the plane wanted to know—when are we going to arrive? And the pizza served as both a symbolic and material signifier that the crews recognized that there was a serious issue and were committed to fixing the problem.

COROLLARY TO THE SIXTH COMMANDMENT— DON'T PICK A FIGHT WITH THE PRESS

The lyrics from the great Jim Croce song "You Don't Mess Around with Jim," counsels "You don't tug on Superman's cape/you don't spit into the wind."

When you are in damage control mode, you need to add to Croce's admonition, "you don't pick a fight with the press." And with the rise of social media, you could also add "you don't pick a fight on Twitter."

Unless you are engaged in a fight with a clearly biased media outlet or a news report where you can prove beyond a shadow of a doubt the reporting is inaccurate, picking a fight with the mainstream media or new media is not merely a recognition of the old adage that you shouldn't pick a fight with someone who buys ink by the barrel, but also dangerous because starting a fight with the press has a high probability of undermining your credibility and, in turn, degrading your ability to rebuild trust.

When you are in a crisis, you want to be extremely careful about with whom you are creating conflict (an issue we spend more time on in a subsequent chapter), because this is a moment when you are engaging from a position of weakness. However, a special point of emphasis needs to be put on being sensitive to the dynamics of picking a fight with those who are reporting on you (be it a political journalist, an analyst writing about a public company, or an entertainment reporter). Directly challenging the media's coverage of your crisis is likely to play to your core audiences as an effort to avoid being straight about what you know and what you do not know, while also communicating that you do not believe there is a problem that needs to be fixed.

Moreover, in picking this sort of fight, you are effectively pitting you and your organization's credibility against the credibility of the press. And, even in this day and age where trust is at an all-time low across most sectors, the media is typically is perceived as more trustworthy than business, government, and many other institutions. The Edelman Trust Barometer referred to earlier, specifically found that while trust has declined in many sectors including government and business has declined sharply, the public's trust in the media is on the rise. This was especially true for online media, which recently had a single-year trust increase of a whopping 75 percent. Thus, in picking a fight with media, whether they be new or old, you are pitting your trustworthiness directly against an institution that the public perceives as trustworthy, exactly at your greatest moment of weakness.

When Robert Murray of Murray Energy attacked the media for their reporting on his mining company, he was doing so at a time when the public really wanted to hear what was being done to rescue the workers—and attacking the press served as a tremendous blow to his credibility, and to the company's capacity to demonstrate that their singular focus was on fixing a problem that was a matter of life and death.

One of the very definitions of damage control is to limit the time period in which you are the focal point of the issue. Stories thrive on conflict. Sticking your thumb in the eye of the Fourth Estate—whether their stories appear on dead trees or in 140 electronic characters—is most assuredly a way to lengthen the time in which you are in the bull's-eye.

Additionally, attacking the press is a sign to your core audiences that the problem is even larger than what has been reported—otherwise you would be dealing with the issue head on.

Picking a fight with reporters is the damage-control equivalent of the old line about the lawyer who does not have a case to stand on: When the facts are on your side, argue the facts. When the law is on your side, argue the law. When neither is on your side, pound the table.

To avoid picking a fight with the press, consider these simple actions:

- Return reporters' calls. It sounds simple, but many calls in a crisis go unreturned. Return as many calls as possible, as promptly as possible. Reporters are often under a deadline; they are professionals, and getting back to them in a civil and professional manner will only help your cause.
- Be calm, cool, and collected in your dealings with the media. Reporters are often looking to gauge your concern by your body language. Adopt a posture of being the consummate professional.
- Build up good will. Over the course of a crisis, reporters will evaluate you based on how you treat them. Engaging with them in a constructive and forthright manner will help establish good will.

Mark Twain memorably said, "When in doubt, tell the truth." This admonition dovetails beautifully into the sixth commandment. In the fog of a crisis, there will be frequent and persistent calls for information. But maintain your focus, maintain your discipline, and remember—be straight about what you know, what you don't know, and what you are going to do to fix the problem.

THIRTEEN
COMMANDMENT VII
RESPOND WITH OVERWHELMING FORCE

I'm mad as hell and I'm not going to take this anymore!
—Anchorman Howard Beale, *Network*

THE SEVENTH COMMANDMENT—RESPOND WITH OVERWHELMING FORCE

Identify and stick to one bottom-line message in order to avoid doing more harm by confusing your core audiences with different, multiple, or inconsistent communications. Be highly disciplined in reinforcing and repeating the bottom line in every way possible, at every moment possible, through everybody possible, and everywhere possible. An organization-wide commitment to delivering a bottom-line message will enhance credibility over the long term by consistently communicating to the core audience accurate information and, in turn, contribute to the building of trust.

DISRESPECTING THE SEVENTH COMMANDMENT—SEVEN DAYS IN MARCH

Bear Stearns was a venerable Wall Street firm nearly a century old. The company employed over 15,000, had offices throughout the world, and served governments, leading corporations, and individual investors. *Fortune* magazine recognized Bear Stearns as the "most admired" securities firm in the nation from 2005 to 2007. The company had survived market upturns and downturns, and took pride in the fact that during the Great Depression of the 1920s, the firm did not lay off a single employee. But the twenty-first century was to be different from the twentieth.

Between March 10 and March 16, 2008, Bear Stearns experienced a Wall Street version of the Ides of March—going from being a Wall Street Caesar to dying a death by a thousand cuts in the form of a run of rumors concerning the company's financial standing, which precipitated a run on the firm's cash reserves.

The trajectory of Bear Stearns's death throes over the course of that fateful week can be seen in the de-evolution of statements over the course of seven days from the firm's CEO, Alan Schwartz:

On Monday, March 10, 2008 responding to rumors circulating about the firm's liquidity, a company statement was released that read:

> Bear Stearns's balance sheet, liquidity and capital remain strong.
> —Alan Schwartz, CEO of Bear Stearns

(Share price at time of the statement $62.30; liquidity pool $18.1 billion)

By Friday, March 14, 2008, Schwartz, responding to a run on the Wall Street giant's cash reserves as clients and lenders took flight in response to the rumors (despite an announced rescue plan), acknowledged:

> Our liquidity position in the last 24 hours has significantly deteriorated. We took this important step to restore confidence in us in the marketplace, strengthen our liquidity and allow us to continue normal operations.
> —Alan Schwartz, March 14, 2008, in a statement on the
> company receiving an emergency Federal Reserve loan

(Share price $30.00; liquidity pool $2 billion, as of March 13)

And by Sunday, March 16, 2008, the Ides of March had come, and Schwartz announced the demise of Bear Stearns in the form of JP Morgan acquiring the company at a garage sale price:

> The past week has been an incredibly difficult time for Bear Stearns. This transaction represents the best outcome for all of our constituencies based upon the current circumstances. I am incredibly proud of our employees and believe they will continue to add tremendous value to the new enterprise.
> —Alan Schwartz, on the company being acquired by JP Morgan

(Share price paid by JP Morgan: $2)

What caused the collapse of this eighty-five-year-old firm in less than a week's time? There are varying theories on what was substantively behind the collapse—from a skittish market that panicked to an orchestrated effort by a shadowy network of short sellers. But what is clear is that Bear Stearns was run over not because it suffered from a liquidity issue, at least when the rumors of such took hold, but because of the *perception* that it suffered from a liquidity crisis.

On Monday, March 10, 2008, as rumors began circulating about the firm's liquidity position, Wall Street was already on pins and needles as a result of growing concerns about the health of a number of Wall Street banks related to exposure from toxic subprime mortgages. Despite the prevailing atmosphere (or maybe because of the atmosphere), Bear Stearns resisted providing a formal response, purportedly concerned that such a response, even in the form of a denial, would lend legitimacy to the rumors.

However, in a seeming response to the intense pressures being created by the swirling rumors and lack of a company position, Bear Stearns's former CEO Allan "Ace" Greenberg offered his own comments. Greenberg, a Wall Street legend who had famously helped lead Bear through the 1987 crash, called the rumors of a liquidity crunch "totally ridiculous," a statement that was reported by the highly influential financial cable outlet CNBC on March 10.

The fact that it was a former CEO (especially one who had been at the helm in a prior period of great market distress) and not the current CEO offering a statement proved confusing internally and externally.

Was Greenberg speaking on behalf of the company?

Was the fact that a former CEO, but not the current CEO, was speaking evidence that something was amiss?

Why wasn't the company providing normal guidance?

What Greenberg's response did in fact accomplish was exactly what the company had hoped to avoid in not providing a formal comment—the public surfacing of the liquidity issue, which gave reporters, pundits, analysts, and others on Wall Street the license to openly talk about the rumors. As a result, by the end of the day, with the rumors now "legitimized," Bear Stearns felt compelled to issue a formal denial in the form of a press release, where the company stated, "There is absolutely no truth to the rumors of liquidity problems that circulated today in the market."

However, the comments did not do enough to extinguish the fuse that was now lit.

Over the course of Monday evening and throughout Tuesday, business reporters, analysts, investors, clients, competitors, lenders, and government regulators were picking up rumors that only served to heighten the panic as they ping-ponged off one another—with no effective response from Bear Stearns.

On the morning of Wednesday, March 12, 2008, Schwartz attempted to staunch the bleeding by appearing on CNBC from Florida, where he was attending a conference with several of the firm's major clients. But an interview that was intended to answer questions about the liquidity crisis early in the day and put the rumors to rest, only added to the growing confusion.

First, right out of the box the Bear Stearns CEO was dealt an aggressive question that established that the "rumors" of a liquidity crisis had transitioned into the "reality" of a liquidity crisis, so no matter what Schwartz said, he was already playing defense.

Schwartz responded by repeating the rumor before attempting to discredit it, saying, "Some people could speculate that Bear Stearns might have some problems . . . since we're a significant player in the mortgage business. None of those speculations are true."

His response was interrupted by breaking news involving a crisis of another kind, a political scandal with Wall Street ramifications—the announcement that New York governor Elliot Spitzer was resigning as the result of the disclosure that he frequented high-priced prostitutes.

CNBC eventually came back to Schwartz, and he gamely marched through his talking points. When he actually got around to the message he needed to deliver on the fiscal strength of Bear Stearns, it was so late in the segment that it was buried.

And even his location, in Florida, created additional issues. Bear faced a "damned if you do, damned if you don't" dynamic. Schwartz was reluctant to return to New York because he feared leaving would only lend credence to the rumors, especially since he was in Florida with significant clients who could have viewed an unplanned departure as a sign that something *was* amiss. However, for others, his not being in Manhattan at the corporate headquarters in these critical hours sent the wrong signal about who was at the helm of this ship.

Why was the CEO not at the corporate headquarters?

Who was in charge?

In short, the interview created more questions than answers—not a good development in an environment where rumors were running out of control.

And while the firm's stock momentarily recovered a bit on the morning of March 12 following the CNBC interview, behind the scenes, Bear Stearns was now hemorrhaging as clients and lenders withdrew their money.

As subsequently reported by *The Wall Street Journal*, on the morning of March 13, Schwartz met with Bear's top executives in the firm's twelfth-floor, wood-paneled dining room and attempted to allay internal concerns by asserting that the rumors of a liquidity crisis was merely "a whole lot of noise," which struck some of those executives as inconsistent with what was actually happening: Cash was leaving, clients were deserting, and lenders were seeking payment.

And by the evening of Thursday, March 13, the firm had a cash crunch, with its reserves plummeting from $17 billion to $2 billion.

Though Bear Stearns had begun the week on Monday, March 10, like a March lion, in a strong financial position, it was ending the week on Friday, March 14, as a lamb en route to slaughter. The company was now in a position where it would have a hard time meeting its financial obligations and would have to declare bankruptcy.

On Sunday, March 16, 2008, in advance of markets opening the next day—and under pressure from federal regulators who feared a broader market impact caused by the run on Bear Stearns spreading to others—the firm was acquired by JP Morgan for $2 a share, a sale price representing less than 10 percent of what Bear Stearns had been worth merely two days earlier.

On March 20, 2008 (less than week after the company was sold), Christopher Cox, chairman of the Securities and Exchange Commission, publicly acknowledged that Bear Stearns was the victim of a loss of investor confidence, not a loss of capital, that was driven by rumors of the firm suffering from a liquidity crisis, despite the fact that on March 10 it had $18.1 billion under its roof.

In a widely distributed statement, Cox wrote, "Notwithstanding that Bear Stearns continued to have high quality collateral to provide as security for borrowings, market counterparties became less willing to enter into collateralized funding arrangements with Bear Stearns."

Perception had indeed supplanted reality.

UNDERSTANDING THE SEVENTH COMMANDMENT— RESPOND WITH OVERWHELMING FORCE

Bear Stearns collapsed in a week for failing to adhere to the seventh commandment of damage control:

Respond with overwhelming force.

With crisis as a state of nature, what is perception and what is reality is a distinction without meaning, because the perception can become the reality.

There are no Marquis of Queensberry rules here defining the conduct by which all will play. Whether it is inaccurate information that has been inadvertently communicated, but nonetheless seized upon by your core audiences, or your opponents intentionally disseminating inaccurate information to cause you harm, you have to overwhelm this bad information with the good information in order to win the battle over competing storylines.

In a crisis, when the perception of a situation is not in alignment with the real story, the responsibility is on you to make sure you identify a winning message that pounds home the actual facts and allows you to connect the reality with the perception—and then respond with overwhelming force in order to change the perception to match the reality.

If you do not respond with overwhelming force, you will be run over.

IDENTIFY THE BOTTOM LINE

It's not good enough in a crisis to say "all is okay" when respected voices (and in some cases disrespected voices) are suggesting something is wrong—it only creates the impression that you are ducking and dodging, bobbing and weaving, to avoid the real issue. Moreover, to mitigate against doing more harm, you simply cannot have various positions that create inconsistencies or, even worse, misrepresentations that will further rattle your already spooked and skittish core audiences. Rather, you have to identify your bottom line and consistently deliver it to your core audiences.

Bear Stearns, from the very beginning up until it was too late, failed to fully appreciate the magnitude of the situation the firm was facing, and in particular, that in 2008, with concerns about exposure to toxic mortgages and other issues, that the company's core audiences—clients, lenders, employees, analysts, and the press—were already on edge and needed some serious hand holding. By vacillating in terms of its responses—going from not acknowledging the rumors at the beginning of the first day to denying them at the end of that day—Bear Stearns never provided a strong, consistent, effective bottom line to trump the rumors that were swirling.

To deliver an effective bottom line, you will need to identify a message that is sustainable, is backed with proof points, and can provide a platform from which to add information as it becomes available.

A sustainable bottom line is one that you absolutely, positively know will stand the test of time and scrutiny by your core audiences. The bottom line must also be idiosyncratic to the particular situation. We have already touched on several of these bottom lines:

- It could be an apology and a commitment to do better.
- It could be a pledge of cooperation with a promise to be held accountable.
- It could be a decisive action that draws a line between the past and future.
- It could be the aggressive dissemination of hard and irrefutable information that kills a dangerous rumor.

Whatever the bottom line is, you will need to make it real. There have to be more than just words supporting your arguments—you need to also supply information that aligns with the words, provides context to the words, and puts the issue in your rearview mirror.

When JetBlue stranded thousands of passengers, the CEO issued an apology and announced a new set of policies.

When Hewlett-Packard discovered its CEO was having an inappropriate relationship with a company consultant, which also involved falsified expense reports, the CEO had to resign.

When Major League Baseball said it wanted to address steroid abuse in the sport, it conducted a comprehensive review, a report was made public, and the organization instituted new policies.

And, not only must you make the bottom line real, but it must serve as a foundation that you can build upon as the situation evolves and more information becomes available. Thus, Major League Baseball began with a bottom line built around the commitment to conduct a comprehensive review—and then built upon it once the review was completed by identifying specific policies that it would pursue to clean the game of performance-enhancing drugs.

SHOW MESSAGE DISCIPLINE

Message discipline means a commitment to making sure that the bottom line is effectively projected. The repetition can be as important as the message. Consistency can be as critical as content. And the right forums from which you communicate can be as valuable as the substance of what you say.

Bear Stearns simply did not have the message discipline to deliver its bottom line, as reflected by Ace Greenberg's freelancing on March 10 and the decision by CEO Alan Schwartz to do the CNBC interview on Wednesday, March 12. While the substance of Greenberg's comments may have been accurate, and even if his instinct that the company needed to be aggressively engaging was right, the fact that he, as opposed to the company's current leadership, said it, the way it was said, and how it was said, all contributed to the impression that Bear Stearns did not have its act together. Thus, in addition bringing the rumors into the public sphere, Greenberg's statement also intensified the speculation that Bear was in trouble. Similarly, while the notion of affirmatively trying to get ahead of the rumors on Wednesday morning made a lot of sense, CNBC proved to be a tough forum, given the nature of the initial questions asked, the challenges Schwartz had in communicating (in answering the question he repeated the attack, which gave the rumors more credence), and, through no fault of his own, the breaking news of another crisis that degraded his capacity to deliver his bottom line.

When it comes to who will deliver the crucial information, when it will be delivered, where it will be delivered and how often it will be delivered—there must be message discipline.

The bottom line is the bottom line and needs to be delivered relentlessly to your core audiences with precision. Saying it once in a statement in the face of an onslaught will not always suffice. You need to say it as many times, and as loudly as it takes to blow out the fuse before it reaches the powder keg. And regardless of the question you are asked, seek out the bottom line like a cruise missile locking onto to its target.

If asked to appear on a program that you do not think will give you a fair shot, insist on a different one. Look for a venue that is a respected entity that will promote credibility. And in this era of social media, you can produce your own content and distribute it—why go across town to take live, unfair questions when you can go on YouTube and/or put out your own blog postings?

When taking questions, remember that the focus needs to be on the bottom line and not playing a game of Whac-A-Mole. When answering questions, you are not compelled to answer every question. If at all possible, resist being manhandled into accepting the premise of a question, being dragged into unfriendly territory by an unfriendly host, repeating the negative, or answering a hypothetical.

MAKE SURE EVERYONE IS SINGING OFF THE SAME SHEET OF MUSIC

Once you have identified your bottom line and the organization is disciplined in delivering this bottom line, it is absolutely critical that you make sure *everyone is singing off the same sheet of music*. An organization that relentlessly pushes out the same bottom line information accomplishes two important credibility-building results. First, the organization pounds home information designed to impact the perceptions of its core audiences. And, second, the mere fact that the organization is continually pounding home the bottom line at every level, at every opportunity, and by every member of the organization conveys that the organization has its act together.

Bear Stearns suffered organizationally. From the very beginning when Ace Greenberg was freelancing, to the firm's CEO being stuck in Florida, to the disconnect between what was being said publicly and what was happening internally, the company was hurt by the organizational incapacity to deliver a credible bottom line.

Credibility will be enhanced if from the top to the bottom of the organization, you make sure everyone is singing off the same sheet of music. Each and every member of an organization is a potential spokesperson (they have spouses, significant others, relatives, and friends). Therefore, whether it is the CEO, the business development folks, the sales force, the HR department, or the investor-relations team—everyone should be on the same page. Arm them with regular briefings, talking points, frequently asked questions and answers, a website, and so on, so that they can get to the bottom line when delivering the bottom line. The more the bottom line is disseminated at every level of an organization, the more credible it will be.

Whether it is an external audience or an internal audience, they should be receiving the same bottom-line information. Giving one bottom line to an external audience and another one to an internal audience will create dissonance and lead to questions about consistency, and even about the accuracy of what is being communicated.

Finally, match up the most credible people in the organization with those core audiences who will find them the most credible. The employees may want to hear from the Board. The lenders will likely be interested in talking to the chief financial officer. The shareholders will want to know what the CEO has to say.

To respect the seventh commandment, follow these three steps:

1. Identify the bottom line.
2. Show message discipline.
3. Make sure everyone is singing off the same sheet of music.

RESPECTING THE SEVENTH COMMANDMENT—THOSE WELDS ARE GOOD WELDS

The Bay Bridge connecting Oakland to San Francisco is one of the longest bridges in the world and, with over a quarter of million people a day driving across on it, one of the busiest. In 1989, a portion of the bridge collapsed during the Loma Prieta earthquake, which led to a significant seismic retrofit and the decision to build a replacement for the eastern span of the bridge.

So on April 6, 2005, when the *Oakland Tribune* reported that the FBI was investigating complaints made by a group of welders that the welds being used in the new construction were faulty, it was major news in the Bay Area and soon became a national story.

The welds in question were buried in pylons far below the bed of the bay, making the ability to confirm these allegations very difficult. Moreover, since the welds in question were essential to the integrity of the pylons that were providing the foundation of the new span of the bridge, it was immediately apparent that if the allegations were true, this development represented a significant safety issue—and one that could only be addressed at great cost and time.

The reporting of the faulty weld allegations, and also an alleged effort to cover up the shoddy work with false record documentation, quickly became the lead story in the region's papers, on the local TV news, and on the radio. In the Bay Area, as with much of California, traffic is almost always a leading news story—and adding in a potential public safety issue, with a scandal to boot, quickly made this a Category 5 on the news hurricane scale.

In the initial report in the paper that sparked the fire, the construction consortium overseeing the bridge, KFM, did not comment or offer information to combat the allegations. However, as the story grew into a crisis, the construction consortium took decisive action, including documenting their quality and oversight protocols, publicly releasing the actual records, inviting in state and federal inspectors, and pledging full cooperation with the investigators. Concurrent with this aggressive response by the contruction firm, subsequent reporting revealed that among the construction workers who had made the allegations were welders who had been let go because of concerns about the quality of their work.

At the center of everything the construction firm did and said was a commitment to "fully cooperate" with the various government agencies responsible for public safety; this was their number one priority.

Several weeks later, after third-party government agencies made public their findings that the welds had indeed passed inspections, the construction company was able to expand upon its bottom-line commitment to cooperation, saying: We are cooperating fully and the welds are good welds.

The company recognized that all of the other issues, including the backstory of the disgruntled welders making false claims, were a distraction, and stayed focused on their bottom line:

The company exercised tremendous *discipline in sticking to the message*—regardless of the nature of the question or the issue.

- If the company was asked about its program, it said: "We are cooperating fully . . . the welds are good welds."
- If they were asked about the fired welders, it said: "We are cooperating fully . . . the welds are good welds."
- If asked about the FBI investigation, it said: "We are cooperating fully . . . the welds are good welds."
- It was joked that if the construction firms were asked whether the sun comes up in the east, they would say: "We are cooperating fully . . . the welds are good welds."

Everyone at the company, from executives in its corporate headquarters, to the engineers, to crews on the line, to the government lobbyists, to the communications personnel, all repeated the same message. And this reflected the company's understanding that anyone associated with the bridge was a potential spokesperson, whether authorized or not, and a potential validator of the actions taken, whether informed or not. Keenly aware of this, the company engaged in a series of briefings that emphasized their simple message; the firm produced talking points and fact sheets that stressed this basic point; and all of its written or verbal communications further pounded the message.

The company successfully provided substantive information, while identifying a bottom line that was sustainable, and was a foundation to which information could be added, and which resonated with their core audiences. To bolster their words, the construction firm released studies and reports by third parties confirming the integrity of the welds; walked those interested through their training and oversight protocols; and welcomed government regulators conducting a review of the welds.

The entire organization demonstrated message discipline. Such an approach was a special challenge for engineers, who not only often *are* the smartest guys in the room, but are trained to think in a very linear way and make decisions based on an analysis of data and an application of formulas.

The company effectively backed up its own solid documentation with information generated by others that was especially credible, such as the governmental agency reports, and the validation of other construction workers who spoke out on their own and disputed the allegations of the disgruntled workers. Everyone stayed focused on singing off the same sheet of music.

It was clear that the message had broken through when at a Starbucks coffee shop in San Francisco several months after the crisis hit, two women waiting in line to place their order were overheard discussing their commute over the Bay Bridge. One woman said, "I hear the welds on the bridge are good welds." And the other woman responded by saying, "I hear the same thing." When the message comes bouncing back in the coffee line at Starbucks, you know it has worked, and you know your coffee that day will taste much better.

THE SEVENTH COMMANDMENT APPLIED TO AN EVERYDAY CRISIS—SCHOOL DAZE

On June 28, 2008, at 9:52 A.M., the parents of approximately 150 pre-kindergarten children attending school in Northern California, received the following email (pseudonyms are used for all names and the children's center, and some identifying details been changed):

From: Molly Johnson

Subj: [MRCC]: (no subject)

Date: Thu Jun 12, 2008 9:52 am

To: [parent lists]

Dear Parents,

We had to make an extremely difficult decision today. Amy has turned in her resignation effective immediately, and we had to ask [her] to leave today for safety reasons. I cannot explain more than we were considering the health and welfare of the children, parents, and staff of the MRCC. I apologize for what seem drastic measures, but again we had no choice. We will move quickly to fill the position to maintain the stability and consistency for your children.

Thank you for your understanding,

Molly

Molly Johnson

Executive Director

Maple Road Children's Center

Under an hour later, at 10:51, the next email came over the transom:

From:	Molly Johnson
Subj:	[MRCC]: (no subject)
Date:	Thu Jun 12, 2008 10:51 am
To:	[parent lists]

Dear Parents,

I know many of you are concerned about my earlier Email. I am talking to the Sheriff's dept. representative right now and all safety issues are being handled quickly and efficiently. I will guarantee the safety of all of our children and members of MRCC with great diligence. I apologize if you were concerned about this being an issue of health hazard to your children. There is no disease to be worried about. Simply a safety issue that has been dealt with. If you have any further questions, please call me.

Thank you,

Molly Johnson

Executive Director

Maple Road Children's Center

Fifteen minutes after the second email, a third email was fired off in response to questions from parents.

From:	Molly Johnson
Subj:	Re: [MRCC]: (no subject)
Date:	Thu Jun 12, 2008 11:07 am
To:	[James Hanson; cc: parent lists]

The person in question was in the yellow room. She has been escorted off premises, the police are involved, the lock codes will be changed. There was a verbal threat that needed to be dealt with immediately. No actual physical threat.

Not surprisingly, concerned parents began showing up at the school. They found the locks had been changed, and the teachers did not know what was going on. Other parents could not get through to the school by telephone. And all this was happening with no additional explanations or information.

For a parent, any issue involving your child's safety is a major crisis—and any issue involving law enforcement and your child's safety is of even greater concern. The school's response, by not identifying a bottom line, reflecting even a modicum of message discipline, or having everyone singing off the same sheet of music, did nothing to allay parent concerns and only served to make a bad situation even worse.

Now, in stark comparison, consider how the elementary school principal in a neighboring town responded to a similar situation (pseudonyms are used):

Date: November 17, 2011 2:22:52 PM PST
To: TES-Lists:(all);
Subject: Stranger safety

Dear Parents,

I wanted to make you aware of an incident that occurred yesterday evening around 5:30 pm near our school. Two Madison Middle School students were approached by a white male with a goatee driving a silver or gray Toyota minivan as they waited to be picked from the Madison after school program.

This person asked the students to get into his car which they did not. The students immediately left the area and contacted school personnel who in turn contacted the police. The police responded and made a report.

The students are safe and did the right thing.

Please remind your children about the importance of being aware of their surroundings, not accepting rides from strangers, staying in groups and having a plan if they are approached by someone.

If you have any questions or concerns please do not hesitate to contact me.

Jana Nelson, Principal

The email was very clear and provided enough details and specifics that parents, the core audience here, had the information they needed. The incident necessitated only one email, which proactively and affirmatively described what had happened. And those parents who called the school or went to the school found a situation well in control, with various members of the school briefed and delivering a consistent message.

The elementary school principal receives an A with regards to the seventh commandment—respond with overwhelming force.

The principal was able to identify the bottom line—"The students are safe and did the right thing." The parents were informed and set at ease because the school showed message discipline in how the information was presented and packaged—namely one cogent email. And unlike the preschool example, the information was handled in a way to ensure confidence in those charged with taking care of children, because the organization was singing off the same sheet of music.

COROLLARY TO THE SEVENTH COMMANDMENT— NO MESSAGE HANDCUFFS

History is replete with individuals who identified a simple message, but either were just so tone deaf, or gave responses so inappropriate to the circumstances, that their messages served as handcuffs.

There was Al Gore's "no controlling legal authority" statement, repeated seven times by the vice president at a White House press conference in 2007 about charges he had broken the law relating to soliciting Democratic campaign contributions (the phrase, while being legally accurate, was politically tone deaf, as it made him look evasive).

Or consider BP CEO Tony Haywood's infamous line in the midst of the massive Gulf oil spill, "I want my life back," (which may have been accurate, but was completely inappropriate and five months later he had his wish—and was out of his job).

Responding with overwhelming force only works if you have actually identified a winning bottom line. Pounding a losing bottom line, even if it is technically accurate, will naturally be counterproductive.

When it comes to determining your message, it is best to adhere to the words of the late, great UCLA basketball coach John Wooden: "Be quick, but don't hurry." However, if you find that your message is not working, do not hesitate to change it—even if it means taking a hit for being inconsistent (which you will).

If you do discard your initial message, it will be twice as important to make sure that you get it right the second time.

And when your message is a winning message—pound it in the service of responding with overwhelming force.

FOURTEEN
COMMANDMENT VIII
FIRST IN, FIRST OUT

I have always depended on the kindness of strangers.
—Blanche DuBois, *A Streetcar Named Desire*

THE EIGHTH COMMANDMENT—FIRST IN, FIRST OUT

Minimize the harm posed by the crisis through controlling the flow of information in order to transition out as a featured player in the storyline as quickly as possible. As there are often multiple other actors in a crisis that can become the "stars" of the scandal, have the discipline to execute actions designed to limit your time in the spotlight. Minimizing your exposure to the spotlight will avoid protracted scrutiny and facilitate the building of credibility. And when you are not on stage performing a solo, it is easier to rebuild trust.

DISRESPECTING THE EIGHTH COMMANDMENT—THE ROGER CLEMENS BEANBALL

Major League Baseball had a major problem. From investigative news reports, interviews with former and current players, and just physical observations of the players on the field, it was clear that steroids and other so-called performance-enhancing drugs (PEDs) had found their way into the game. Fans were angry, politicians were angry. Sports talk radio was especially angry. They all sought integrity in a sport revered as the national pastime, but where drug use had become widespread, and, in addition, undermined the sanctity of cherished records. In response, the commissioner of Major League Baseball asked former U.S. senator George J. Mitchell to lead an investigation into the drug crisis.

On December 13, 2007, Senator Mitchell, the former Senate Majority Leader, released his findings on the use of PEDs in professional baseball. The comprehensive opus, running hundreds of pages, was known as *The Mitchell Report.*

In the wake of fans' and politicians' demands, coupled with the federal government's criminal investigation into steroid use involving San Francisco Giants superstar Barry Bonds (who had broken hallowed records in the sport: the single-season home run record and subsequently Hank Aaron's career home run record), this report represented baseball's effort to once and for all address the issue. Bonds had been at the center of the steroids controversy since 2003 and was indicted for perjury and obstruction of justice in 2007, related to the government's investigation of a medical laboratory in the Bay Area believed to have been at the center of a PED ring (he was ultimately found guilty of one count of obstruction of justice).

The Mitchell Report, which went to great lengths to explain its methodology and approach before disseminating its findings, named names— including the names of teams; insiders in the sport, such as trainers who provided the PEDs; and eighty-nine current or retired players who were identified as having used PEDs. Senator Mitchell (whose impeccable credentials included being a former prosecutor and federal judge) stated that for each of the players named, he had relayed the allegations and afforded them the opportunity to respond prior to the report being completed.

Among the named players, were some of the leading figures in the sport including all-stars Andy Pettitte and Roger Clemens. With regards to Clemens, by then a pitcher who had finished the 2007 season with the New York Yankees, and who in his mid-forties had seemingly defied nature with a late career renaissance, *The Mitchell Report* cited the allegations of former Yankee trainer Brian McNamee, who said he had provided steroids to three Yankees— including Andy Pettitte and Roger Clemens. McNamee claimed that he had injected Clemens with the anabolic steroid Winstrol during the 1998, 2000, and 2001 baseball seasons.

In each of those seasons, Clemens, nicknamed "the Rocket," had put up some impressive statistics—all the more impressive for his age at the time:

- In 1998, at thirty-six years old, pitching for the Toronto Blue Jays, he had twenty-six wins and six losses.

- In 2000, at thirty-eight, then pitching for the New York Yankees, his record was thirteen wins, eight losses.
- In 2001, at thirty-nine, his record was twenty wins, three losses.

While some of the players named in the report stepped up and acknowledged their culpability, and some tried to not comment at all, none came anywhere close to matching Clemens's response— whether on his own or through his agent or his lawyer, Roger Clemens hurled beanball after beanball back at *The Mitchell Report.*

His agent, Roger Hendricks, issued a statement from Clemens in response to *The Mitchell Report:*

> I want to state clearly and without qualification: I did not take steroids, human growth hormone or any other banned substances at any time in my baseball career or, in fact, my entire life.

The Rocket's lawyer, Rusty Hardin, also disputed the allegations by attacking the credibility of the trainer, Brian McNamee, calling him a "troubled man" who had named Clemens and fellow pitcher Andy Pettitte because he was "threatened with criminal prosecution."

Clemens himself released a YouTube video asserting he had never used PEDs, and on January 6, 2008, he looked the American people in the eye in an interview with Mike Wallace on *60 Minutes* and vehemently denied he had used banned substances. Rather, he contended, his success was the product of "hard work," and that all he had been injected with were B-12 vitamin shots. Additionally, Clemens fired off a defamation suit against his former trainer and released a tape recording of a call he had with McNamee in which the trainer did not refute Clemens's denials of steroids use (Clemens's suit was later dismissed in federal court, and McNamee filed his own suit against Clemens). And piling on, Clemens's agent put out a comprehensive 18,000-word statistical analysis purporting to show that Clemens's pitching was in line with the performance levels of other pitchers.

Sports Illustrated characterized the response as "the Clemens PR machine revs into full gear."

Clemens had spent all but three of his twenty-four years in the major leagues pitching in the American League, where the pitchers do not come up to bat to hit. There had been grumblings about the fact that Clemens, who liked to make batters uncomfortable by throwing close and inside, was able to get away with his pitching style because he rarely had to face pitching himself—and deal with balls thrown high, hard, and inside in retaliation.

Well, in a crisis, if a star player in the drama throws hard, high, and inside, they need to realize that those who they are throwing at can also throw back. Which is exactly what happened to Roger "the Rocket" Clemens.

The rebuttals came flying.

In response to his agent's release of the statistical analysis of Clemens's pitching record, academics from the University of Pennsylvania released their own report, documenting that "something unusual happened in Clemens' career as he entered his 30s." And shortly after Clemens's *60 Minutes* assertion that he had only been injected with vitamin shots, public reports sourced to "lawyer with knowledge of details of the case" revealed the trainer had testified that Clemens had been injected with PEDs, and not B-12 vitamin shots, alleging that Clemens had suffered from an abscess on his buttocks (the implication being that one would get an abscess from a steroids injection, but not a vitamin shot).

And then Congress got into the act, investigating the use of steroids in sports, including holding a hearing where they called on Clemens to appear. A little more than a month after his *60 Minutes* star turn, Clemens agreed to testify under oath—thereby assuring that his time in the spotlight was going to be longer and more intense. Despite eighty-nine players being named in *The Mitchell Report,* Roger Clemens had, by his own doing, become the superstar of the investigation.

Rusty Hardin, Clemens's lawyer, explained the decision to agree to testify under oath:

> This should show you that he believes strongly that he's telling the truth . . . Everybody's said we're insane lawyers for allowing this. No sane man would subject himself to that unless he deeply believed he was telling the truth.

However, in advance of the congressional hearings, in early February Andy Pettitte, a friend, former teammate, and training partner of Clemens, told federal investigators (and later Congress) that Clemens had discussed being injected with the drug HGH by Brian McNamee.

Shortly after Pettitte's congressional testimony, Clemens, himself testified under oath before the House Government and Oversight Committee that he had not taken steroids—directly contradicting the sworn testimony of his teammate. To Congress, the media, and the fans, Clemons defiantly stated:

> I have never used steroids, human growth hormone or any other type of illegal performance-enhancing drugs. I think these types of drugs should play no role in athletics at any level, and I fully support Sen. Mitchell's conclusions that steroids have no place in baseball. However, I take great issue with the report's allegation that I used these substances. Let me be clear again—I did not.

McNamee, sitting at the same witness table two seats over from Clemens, provided congressional testimony that was starkly different:

> I have helped taint our national pastime . . . When I told Sen. Mitchell that I injected Roger Clemens with performance-enhancing drugs, I told the truth. I told the truth about steroids and human growth hormone. I injected those drugs into the body of Roger Clemens at his direction . . . Unfortunately, Roger has denied this and has led a full-court attack on my credibility.

On August 19, 2010, a federal grand jury indicted Clemens on multiple counts related to his representations before Congress, including obstruction of Congress, perjury, and making false statements. While a jury ultimately acquitted him of the charges, in 2012, Clemens was the one player who emerged as the star of *The Mitchell Report*—which was a direct result of how he responded.

Of the teams, personnel, and players named in *The Mitchell Report*, Roger Clemens was the only one to fire back at Mitchell in such a manner.

Of the three players named by Brian McNamee in *The Mitchell Report*, Roger Clemens was the only one to claim under oath he did not take steroids.

And of these three players, Roger Clemens was the only one indicted.

UNDERSTANDING THE EIGHTH COMMANDMENT— ROGER CLEMENS STRIKES OUT

The Rocket struck out in mastering the disaster from *The Mitchell Report*, and he did so because he violated the eighth commandment of damage control: *First in, first out.*

A crisis, frequently, will have a cast of characters. It is often the case that some of those characters will bring increased attention on themselves.

Seek out actions who allow you to avoid being a star actor. It is better to be a supporting actor that fades away or, even, is entirely behind the scenes when the curtain goes up on a scandal that includes you in the script.

In our age when fifteen minutes of fame (or infamy) is now even shorter, leverage the fleeting nature of the spotlight, the cluttered information environment, and the limited attention space of even core audiences to help make sure you have as short a run of the show as possible.

Roger Clemens had been the star his whole career—whether at the University of Texas, in Boston when he played for the Red Sox, or with the New York Yankees, he was always the center of attention. And when it came to *The Mitchell Report*, Clemens made sure that he was going to continue to be the star—even of his own demise.

Simply put, there was no reason that Roger Clemens needed to join Barry Bonds as the star of the steroids era. While Clemens was certainly among the biggest stars named in *The Mitchell Report*, he had a lot of company. There were eighty-eight other former and active players, multiple teams, and other leading figures in baseball prominently featured in the report.

Moreover, the report was released in an environment where there were additional big-name players who had been tainted by the alleged use of steroids, including superstars who prior to their association with steroids appeared bound for the Baseball Hall of Fame: Mark McGwire (who held for a time the single-season home run record), Rafael Palmiero (one of a small number of players to record 3,000-plus hits and 500-plus home runs), and, especially, Barry Bonds (a seven-time league most valuable player, and the single-season and career home run king).

By the time *The Mitchell Report* was released, the steroids scandal had already burned many professional athletes. In fact, the report itself was an effort in damage control by Major League Baseball to lay all the cards on the table—and pivot out of the so-called steroids era.

Further, Clemens's career had already effectively come to an end following the 2007 season, where he played only a portion of the schedule before being hurt. He was in his mid-forties, and even prior to the release of the report, it was assumed by many inside the game that he had played his last season.

In short, when Clemens was named in *The Mitchell Report*, there was no reason for him to pursue a course of actions that turned him into the singular star of *The Mitchell Report,* including agreeing to testify before Congress. While respecting Clemens's desire to assert his innocence, he could have done so in a manner that would not have put him on a path to a criminal indictment. Clemens could have simply issued a statement reiterating that he did not use steroids and stopped short of challenging the credibility of the report and engaging in a series of very pointed and personal attacks on McNamee that left his former trainer no choice but to fire back and effectively "volunteer" himself to be a featured witness providing sworn testimony before Congress. It was how Clemens responded that turned him into the star of this crisis. And it is important to note that *The Mitchell Report* did not subject Clemens to a criminal inquiry—rather, it was the way Clemens responded that generated a criminal investigation that resulted in an indictment.

Clemens could have simply proclaimed his innocence; given his stature and the fact that he played in New York, the world's media capital, the media onslaught was guaranteed to be unpleasant. He needed to come to terms with the knowledge that his reputation was going to be tainted, and move on. It would have been fine for Clemens to generally dispute the conclusions, and in a non-vitriolic manner attack McNamee. Clemens could have asserted that he never tested positive for PEDs and that the allegations came from someone potentially facing criminal prosecution, and therefore under pressure to name names. But his response to the report not only negated his ability to get off the stage quickly and let other active players suspected of steroids deal with the issue—in fact, he elbowed his way onto the stage with Bonds. And while the jury of his second trial found him not guilty, he could have asserted his innocence in a matter that would have allowed him to avoid being criminally indicted in the first place.

By revving up the Clemens PR machine, Roger Clemens's approach was the equivalent of three strikes and you're out when it came to adhering to the principles of survival.

Strike one was that his aggressive response only served to do more, not less, harm, as it led to greater public, brand, and legal exposure—when he should have been looking to diminish the harm by taking cover behind the fact that the issue, as made clear by the report, was larger than just him.

Strike two was Clemens's and his advisors' failure to exercise a disciplined approach when it came to minimizing the time he spent in the crosshairs of the scandal, by avoiding making new news, so that the report could be characterized as old news.

And *strike three* was creating a multi-front war that led the Rocket to pick fights that only served to undermine his credibility, including the fateful decision to testify under oath before Congress and challenge the testimony of others, which contributed to his criminal indictment.

MAKE THE ISSUE BIGGER THAN JUST YOU

In a crisis, there are likely to be multiple actors and larger public policy or societal issues that go far beyond you or your organization. Your objective should be to present your actions against the bigger issues, and to expand the issue to minimize your own actions. If you can *make the issue bigger than just you,* you can limit the harm by contextualizing the crisis against a larger societal backdrop.

In the Enron crisis, there was the company, there was the accounting firm, there were the banks—and there was the broader public policy issue of what was permissible under U.S. security laws.

In the BP oil spill, there was the oil company; there was Transocean, which operated the Deepwater Horizon offshore oil rig; there was the government's decision to allow the company to manage the crisis; and then there was the larger public policy issue of offshore oil drilling.

In the Major League Baseball steroids scandal, there were the players, there were management personnel, there were the teams, and there was the larger issue of whether the league had looked the other way, believing that the drug-enhanced performances were bringing excitement, fans, and revenue to the sport.

The irony in the Clemens situation is that *The Mitchell Report* was intended to be professional baseball's effort at damage control by making the issue larger than any one player or team; it was intended it to be an acknowledgement of a system-wide failure, so the sport could move on.

Roger Clemens needed to recognize that not only was the issue bigger than him, and not only was the report bigger than him—the fact that it was bigger than him was the very shield he needed to wield to avoid starring in the center ring of the steroid circus. By failing to appreciate this, Clemens did tremendous self-inflicted harm.

There are several actions to consider in a crisis when working to cast the issue as bigger than yourself:

- *Evaluate* who else is embroiled in the scandal and determine whether they are likely to become the bigger player in the story going forward, which, in turn, will impact how aggressively and at what level you engage. In the Clemens case, because Barry Bonds had been indicted, and since *The Mitchell Report* effectively raised questions about all of Major League Baseball, there were others who were far more likely than Clemens to be the media's focus in the days and months ahead.
- *Determine* whether there is a way to position your role as being the consequence of a larger systemic breakdown or a larger problem.
- *Analyze* what role you will play in the matter in the future, in order to calibrate your response. It was clear the next chapter of the scandal would feature the still-active players who were named and would have to face the music in February and March when spring training began. However, since Clemens was going to retire he would not face similar pressures. And, in terms of legal exposure at the time of the report, it was Barry Bonds who had been indicted and who would have to go through the criminal justice process, not Clemens.

If others are destined to be in the spotlight—let them have it. And as Blanche DuBois depended on the "kindness of strangers" in *A Streetcar Named Desire*, you can, too.

MOVE ON, IT'S OLD NEWS

As examined earlier, we live in a constant state of crisis in part because of the number of outlets that convey information, the velocity with which it's conveyed, and the interactive nature of information. However, these same dynamics can also facilitate your ability to swiftly get out of the spotlight. The information environment is highly cluttered, with one story replacing another very quickly. Between the traditional media outlets, online alerts, Twitter, and so on, the public is overwhelmed by the amount of information being projected and directed at them on a daily basis.

As a result of so many individuals, businesses, and organizations having been embroiled in crises, audiences have become conditioned to expect and accept scandal. The fact that you are facing a crisis is a little like being told that the family dog occasionally drinks water out of the toilet bowl. It is unpleasant and not a discussion for polite company, but not exactly a shock either.

And because of the saturation of information, people have short memories. As a personal illustration that fame and infamy can be fleeting, consider our experience following the turmoil of the 2000 presidential campaign. In the immediate months after the Bush-Gore election, a campaign in which we were on national television on a daily basis, and especially so during the recount, we were recognized publicly wherever we went. In fact, when in West Palm Beach, Florida, during the recount we were mobbed to the point of being followed into restrooms by those seeking photos and autographs. However, about six months after the campaign ended, people we met would have some vague recollection of knowing us from TV, but would be unable to pinpoint exactly why. And then, a year from the election, the recollection was of having met us somewhere in the distant past—high school? College? A wedding?

In a crisis, the vicissitudes of the Information Age can put you in the center of a scandal in a nanosecond—however, these same realities can also allow you to move through the scandal swiftly if you use them as a shield. There is no better way to get yourself off center stage then by having the discipline to not add news to your story, so that as quickly as possible you are able to cast your particular story as just old news. And the quicker you can make your story stale, the quicker you will be able to move on.

Roger Clemens seemingly did everything possible to create fresh news on a regular basis, which only served to keep him as the scandal's marquee star. The attacks on Brian McNamee, press conferences, his agent's report on his performance, YouTube videos, the decision to testify before Congress—all of these activities provided new information that directly restricted his ability to cast the issue as old news. *The Mitchell Report* was released in December 2007—and five years later Roger Clemens was still in the middle of the story.

In a crisis, if you are able to control the flow of information and have the fortitude to resist making news, you will quickly make the issue history. And to turn the scandal into old news, you must be disciplined about not adding in new facts or new drama—stick to your position. When asked about the issue, your answer should always remain the same. And you will need to make sure that you are actually moving forward and engaging in your professional life, or whatever is next.

We gauge the success of a scandal becoming old news by how it is covered in the press. Typically, when the scandal is fresh, it will appear in the first few paragraphs of a story. Then, if the subject of the crisis has been successful in getting the information out at the front end, and is disciplined about not adding additional elements, the reporting of the issue will move to the middle of the story. Next, assuming the discipline is maintained and no new news is injected into the matter, references to the subject will migrate to the newspaper jump page (the section of the news story which is not on page one). And, finally, if the discipline is maintained, it will, like an old movie star, fade away from memory.

AVOID CREATING A MULTIPLE-FRONT WAR

In politics, it is said that if you want to have a long career, never run for an office that you cannot afford to lose. In other words, if you want to be mayor, don't run for dog catcher, because if you lose the dog catcher race, your credibility as a candidate will be so diminished that you will have a difficult time running for any other office. The damage control analog to this political maxim is that when you are in a crisis, never pick a fight with an opponent you cannot afford to lose to, because in picking the fight, you are effectively putting your credibility on the line—you have a lot to lose and very little to gain. Rather, the smart play is to *avoid creating a multi-front war* that distracts you from your mission of restoring trust with your core audiences, and drains resources on fights against opponents with whom you don't need to be fighting.

In a crisis, you are typically at your weakest moment when the public is questioning your credibility. A key to surviving is rebuilding trust, which means being exceptionally careful in avoiding actions that further expose your weakened credibility.

In *The Mitchell Report*, the smart players and the smart teams named were the ones who did not seek to aggressively challenge or engage the report. However, because Clemens so vigorously challenged the findings, the others were able to get off the stage very quickly, including Major League Baseball itself, leaving the spotlight nearly solely on Clemens. It was Clemens's decision to attack his former trainer, Brian McNamee, and testify before Congress that opened him up to a multi-front war.

Clemens made a series of decisions that effectively created multiple fights on multiple fronts—all of which had a much bigger downside than upside for him. By trashing his former trainer Brian McNamee, he forced McNamee to fight back, which he did by giving sworn testimony to government officials, testifying before Congress, and engaging with the press. And for Clemens, the decision to testify before Congress—under oath—opened up an entirely new front that ultimately resulted in a criminal indictment.

In a crisis, thoroughly think through your actions, and if you can avoid a fight, avoid it.

Do not pick a fight where you have more to lose than your opponent. Roger Clemens had a lot more to lose than Brian McNamee.

And don't engage in a battle that creates a bigger war. The decision to testify created a legal war for Clemens. Generally speaking, it's a pretty sure sign that your damage control approach has not worked when the very actions you pursue lead to a criminal indictment that otherwise would not have occurred.

To respect the eighth commandment, follow these three steps:

1. Make the issue bigger than just you.
2. Move on, it's old news.
3. Avoid creating a multiple-front war.

RESPECTING THE EIGHTH COMMANDMENT— A ROD'S HITS FOR THE DAMAGE CONTROL CYCLE

On February 7, 2009, *Sports Illustrated* rocked the sports world with a story documenting that 104 Major League Baseball players had tested positive for steroids in 2003, including New York Yankees superstar Alex Rodriguez—who had denied using steroids in a *60 Minutes* interview with CBS anchorwoman Katie Couric.

Forty-eight hours after the *Sports Illustrated* story appeared, a tearful A Rod sat down for in an exclusive interview with ESPN's Peter Gammons and acknowledged:

> When I arrived in Texas in 2001, I felt an enormous amount of pressure. I felt like I had all the weight of the world on top of me and I needed to perform, and perform at a high level every day . . . Back then, [baseball] was a different culture . . . It was very loose. I was young. I was stupid. I was naive. And I wanted to prove to everyone that I was worth being one of the greatest players of all time. I did take a banned substance. And for that, I am very sorry and deeply regretful . . . I am sorry for my Texas years. I apologize to the fans of Texas.

However, when reports of his steroid use were first surfacing, Rodriguez lashed out at a *Sports Illustrated* reporter, who had exposed his name, and went on to accuse her of breaking into his house and stalking him. *Sports Illustrated* denied the charges and stood behind their reporter and the professional manner in which she reported the story.

Rodriguez was already a divisive figure within baseball as the consequence of his historic $275 million contract, and with this forthright admission of steroid use, he was immediately and persistently hammered, as one person after another, in baseball and beyond, lined up to take their whacks at him.

Baseball commissioner Bud Selig lambasted Rodriguez, saying he had "shamed the game."

Tom Hicks, then owner of the Texas Rangers, for whom Rodriguez was playing at the time he used the steroids, stated, "I feel personally betrayed. I feel deceived by Alex."

Calling the news "depressing," even President Barack Obama commented, "If you're a fan of Major League Baseball, I think it tarnishes an entire era, to some degree . . . And it's unfortunate, because I think there were a lot of ballplayers who played it straight."

Just over a week later, at the start of spring training in Florida, A Rod apologized to his teammates and then held a press conference. Facing a media mob, he choked up as he spoke. And as he came clean, he even apologized to those reporters he had previously attacked for their reporting on his steroid use. And he said he had called Katie Couric to apologize for his *60 Minutes* interview.

Then, with the exception of putting out a vanilla book on his career that had been scheduled for release before the controversy, Rodriguez shut up, moved on, and focused on playing baseball.

Where Roger Clemens took actions that led to an extended turn as the star of the scandal, Alex Rodriguez understood that the best approach was to pursue a game plan that would limit his time as a featured player. When A Rod acknowledged his steroids use, apologized for it, and put it in the context of a "loose" baseball "culture,"—he was able to effectively *make the issue bigger than just himself*. In using such an approach, especially with the ongoing controversy surrounding Barry Bonds and Roger Clemens, A Rod was able to move from the sunshine of the batter's box and back into the dark of the dugout—and, in doing so, he ensured he was not doing more harm to himself.

By shutting up, moving on, and concentrating on playing baseball, A Rod was able to make his steroids use old news as quickly as possible. And even when the *Sports Illustrated* reporter who had broken the original story authored a book expose on Rodriguez a few months later, A Rod maintained his discipline and refrained from commenting. His commitment to such a disciplined approach allowed Rodriguez to move through the scandal as quickly as possible—and, thus, he controlled the damage.

Finally, Rodriguez did everything he could to *avoid creating a multi-front war* and, thereby minimized the number of battles he was fighting. In apologizing to the public, his teammates, and the press, Rodriguez, now a serial apologizer, showed that he understood the need to minimize the number of fights in which he was engaged at this moment of weakness, so he could bolster his credibility and put himself in a position to engage in the game that really counted: re-establishing that he was a trustworthy person.

By fall 2009, the Yankees were World Series champs—and Alex Rodriguez, following a tremendous performance in both the playoffs and the World Series, earned the Babe Ruth Award for the Most Valuable Player of the post-season.

And, as ESPN had reported on the crisis when it began, it provided a good sense of how it had ended:

> Alex Rodriguez looked at the award he just received from Babe Ruth's granddaughter with big eyes and a broad grin. It was as if he almost couldn't believe it was his. "Postseason MVP. Wow," Rodriguez said. Pausing for effect he added, "What's next, the good guy award?" Less than a year ago, it would have been difficult to decide which would be more preposterous for the troubled star to earn.

Two ball players, two immense talents. Roger Clemens struck out, Alex Rodriguez hit a homer. And the determining factors had little to do with ball control; they had everything to do with damage control.

THE EIGHTH COMMANDMENT APPLIED TO AN EVERYDAY CRISIS—KIPP CHARTER SCHOOLS

Over the last twenty years, charter schools have become a focus of great debate in education reform. Many charter schools have been extremely successful, changing the lives of students and families, while other schools have not. However, in many communities, local school districts and school boards consider charter schools unwelcome competition and have sought to thwart their ability to operate, even when the schools are high performing and are actively promoted by parents in the community.

Among the most successful charter schools are those that are part of the Knowledge Is Power Program (KIPP). The national network, which establishes schools by providing expertise and educational philosophy to efforts headed by local communities, has over one hundred public charter schools in twenty states, educates over 30,000 students, and operates almost exclusively in historically underserved and poor communities. KIPP's success has been remarkable; their college matriculation rate is approximately double the national average for students from low-income families, and with an extended school day and a college-prep focus their schools have demonstrated that the so-called achievement gap can indeed be closed. At the core of KIPP's philosophy is a commitment to success represented by its motto—"No Excuses."

Because of KIPP's success, due in a large part to the fact that their schools are operated and managed by local people, who are typically enormously dedicated to the program, KIPP had never needed to close a school down because it lacked a suitable facility—until 2007.

In June 2007, the parents of children attending KIPP Harbor Academy in Anne Arundel County, Maryland, received a letter from Jallon Brown, the school's founder, which read:

> It is with immense sadness that we announce that KIPP Harbor Academy must permanently close its doors this summer . . . This situation is very disappointing to me and my staff as we worked tirelessly to put all of your children on the path to college.

Brown's letter to the parents explained in detail that the space the school had been renting at a local college was not adequate to educate the number of students and grades consistent with the KIPP model, and that the local school district had refused to provide the needed space (even though there was available room for KIPP in a local middle school).

Brown effectively communicated to her core audience—the parents—in person and in writing, because she understood that the issue was going to cause profound concern, as reflected by the sentiments of Heather Trotman, who was quoted in *The Baltimore Sun:*

> I really don't care if it's in a barn, in someone's backyard, as long as we have a space. I'm very upset. We don't even know what our options are. KIPP was our choice.

KIPP's national organization made clear that the Anne Arundel school board's approach was not in the best interests of the children. Steve Mancini, KIPP's national public affairs director, explained:

> It's a Sophie's choice: close it or keep the school open and say, "Sorry, there's no room for you," to our rising seventh-graders . . . This is unprecedented for us. Every community we've been in has embraced us . . . Not here."

The local school board was left sputtering, trying to explain the unexplainable. A spokesman for the board struggled to defend the decision, issuing an odd and inherently contradictory statement:

> They were unable to find a home for two years, what if they couldn't find one again? Do we kick them out? That was a big concern for the board. Anybody's assertion that the school district has been against KIPP is just plain wrong. We've done everything we could.

Education reform advocates seized on the closure of the school as emblematic of larger education reform issues in Maryland, where state law does not require local school boards to provide buildings for housing public charter schools such as KIPP—despite their success and the dedication of the students and parents. Commenting on this, John Hussey, of the Center for Education Reform, said:

> It's a symptom of Maryland's charter school law, which we ranked as sixth weakest of 41 charter school laws in the country . . . In this case, it essentially comes down to lack of facilities assistance. And as we've seen here, the local school boards have been hostile toward charter schools.

A *Washington Post* editorial summed up the situation:

A pioneering KIPP charter school may have to close down in Anne Arundel County. Not because it failed students and not because the parents were dis-affected but because it couldn't find a place for its thriving program. That county officials sat on their hands until it was too late speaks to the antipathy many traditional educators have for charter schools. The losers will be mi-nority and low-income children.

In its closing the KIPP Harbor Academy, the school's founder and KIPP officials understood the importance of the eighth commandment and engaged in a series of steps that minimized the role of the school or the KIPP organiza-tion being the star of this crisis—and effectively shined the spotlight on the other actors in the drama.

By announcing the decision to close the school and specifically explain-ing the reasons for the closing, the focus of the crisis moved from the school founder and KIPP to the actions of the local school board and the broader issues of Maryland law. In this way, Brown and KIPP effectively ensured sure they were not doing any more harm to themselves, as they broadened the issue in order to make it bigger than themselves—shining the light on the school's board's resistance to competition and Maryland's education policy toward charter schools.

And, further, Brown and KIPP avoided creating a multi-front war with the parents. By being direct with the statement that the school was closing and that the blame lay squarely with the school district, they made sure there was nothing left to fight over.

By living up to its core value of "No Excuses," KIPP was able to get out of this local crisis by limiting its time as the star of the scandal and putting the spotlight where it belonged: on the local school district.

COROLLARY TO THE EIGHTH COMMANDMENT— KNOW WHEN TO HOLD 'EM, KNOW WHEN TO FOLD 'EM, AND KNOW WHEN TO RUN

In a crisis, there will be times where the dynamic of your situation is such that your ability to control the flow of information in order to minimize your star turn is constrained—and your options are limited.

Such situations boil down to three basic scenarios.

SCENARIO I—KNOW WHEN TO HOLD 'EM

If the dynamic is such that engaging in the crisis could pose a bigger threat to your future than holding back, you will want to consider holding back.

Amazon, the online retailer and one of America's most popular brands, offers a good example of knowing when to hold 'em. In 2011, the state of California, facing a severe budget crisis, and under pressure from traditional brick-and-mortar businesses, sought to collect sales taxes from online retailers, the most prominent being Amazon. The California effort, which was referred to as the "Amazon Tax," was initially strongly resisted by Amazon, and the company spent $5 million to collect signatures for a ballot initiative seeking to ban the tax-collection policy.

Polling data suggested that Amazon would have had a strong chance to rescind the tax, but it became clear that such a campaign would make taxing online retailers a national issue, and thus pose an additional threat to the company's brand. In particular, the high-profile nature of the policy debate was taking place amid a larger debate about corporate responsibility, as manifested in the extreme by the Occupy Wall Street movement.

Amazon ultimately chose not to pursue the ballot initiative and instead sued for peace. The company struck a deal with the state of California, which Amazon characterized as a "win-win," that would allow the state to begin collecting a sales tax a year later.

The decision to hold back and not pursue a ballot initiative was a smart decision by the company. While Amazon could have won the battle at the voting booth, the ballot initiative would have exposed the company to losing the war and posed a powerful thereat to its highly valuable brand image.

SCENARIO II—KNOW WHEN TO FOLD 'EM

In a case where you cannot explain the unexplainable or defend the indefensible, you just have to put your cards on the table, apologize, and beg for forgiveness.

On March 12, 2008, New York governor Eliot Spitzer, a former federal prosecutor and hard-charging state attorney general, knew when to fold 'em. Following a *New York Times* report from two days earlier documenting his use of prostitutes and a related federal investigation, he apologized and resigned from office.

Saying he was "deeply sorry," Governor Spitzer faced the media and offered these words:

> I cannot allow for my private failings to disrupt the people's work. Over the course of my public life, I have insisted—I believe correctly—that people take responsibility for their conduct. I can and will ask no less of myself. For this reason, I am resigning from the office of governor.

Spitzer understood that he faced a situation where it was going to be impossible to explain the unexplainable and defend the indefensible. And as opposed to going through a gauntlet of public humiliations and then being forced to resign, it was better to resign at the front end and avoid such a process.

Eight months later federal prosecutors announced they had decided not to pursue a criminal case against Spitzer, with many speculating that the decision was influenced by the fact that Spitzer resigned from office once the information had become public—as opposed to fighting the matter.

SCENARIO III—KNOW WHEN TO RUN

In a situation where damning information that is not survivable under any circumstances becomes public, you have to realize the gig is up.

Going back to baseball, Mark McGwire, the former All-Star, provides an illustration of knowing when to run. In 2005, McGwire was one of many players and executives called to testify under oath before Congress about the use of steroids in baseball.

In the congressional hearing, McGwire refused to answer questions; instead, he offered a variety of non-substantive answers that left little doubt:

> I'm not here to talk about the past. I'm here to be positive about this subject.
>
> That's not for me to determine.
>
> I'm retired.

After this debacle of a hearing, McGwire effectively disappeared from the public, living in a gated community and spending his time playing golf. For five years he was not seen or heard from in any meaningful way—and in that time period public awareness and knowledge of the extent of steroid use in baseball changed significantly. When McGwire eventually reappeared, after being named the batting coach for the St. Louis Cardinals in 2010, he stated:

> I wish I had never touched steroids. It was foolish and it was a mistake. I truly apologize. Looking back, I wish I had never played during the steroid era.

McGwire knew when to run.

When considering the eighth commandment, it is important to understand whether the situation you face will even allow for you to be able to limit your time in the spotlight. Sometimes, you just need to know when to hold 'em, know when to fold 'em, and know when to run.

FIFTEEN
COMMANDMENT IX
NO SWIFTBOATING

I'm shocked, shocked to find that gambling is going on in here!
—Capt. Louis Renault, *Casablanca*

THE NINTH COMMANDMENT—NO SWIFTBOATING

In situations where there is a self-interested person or entity responsible for a crisis becoming public or pushing the story of the crisis, the harm can be limited by exposing the entity and their self-interested agenda. A disciplined focus is needed to document and then reveal the unclean hands of such parties. One's own credibility can be enhanced by exposing that those behind a crisis have ulterior motives.

DISRESPECTING THE NINTH COMMANDMENT—
THE ORIGINAL SWIFT BOATERS

There may be no better example of the failure to expose a self-interested entity seeking to inflict damage than the "swiftboating" in late summer and early fall 2004 of the Democratic presidential nominee John Kerry.

Senator Kerry is a highly decorated Vietnam veteran who, by any objective standard, served the United States with honor and courage. After his graduation from Yale he volunteered to go to war, where he became the commander of a Navy Swift boat. These boats, as their name suggests, were highly mobile and frequently took enemy fire. The senator, like many presidential candidates from George Washington through John F. Kennedy, had deployed his military record to project his character as someone who could be trusted by the

American people to be their commander in chief. This was especially relevant in the first election following 9/11, where national security was of tremendous concern to American voters—and where the election would turn in large part on who the voters trusted would best keep them and their families safe from terrorists.

Throughout the campaign, Senator Kerry presented his service in Vietnam as a touchstone of his candidacy. This was stressed right from the start as he launched his campaign with a speech in front of the U.S.S. *Constitution* in historic Boston Harbor. Then, during the Democratic primaries, with his campaign in a dog fight for survival, he again looked to his military service. Several weeks before the critical Iowa caucuses, the senator had an emotional reunion with James Rassman, a former Special Forces soldier whom in March 1969 an injured Kerry had personally rescued from the water of the Bay Hap River, saving his life, and for which Kerry received a Bronze Star in recognition for his heroism under enemy fire. The reunion was an enormous boost to the senator and a major factor in the campaign regaining the momentum that would eventually propel him to becoming the Democratic nominee.

Kerry's campaign advertisements featured an eight-millimeter film of the then navy lieutenant in the jungles of Vietnam—a real life *Apocalypse Now.*

The campaign also regularly incorporated members of the senator's Swift boat crew into their events, including bringing these Swift boat veterans around the country on the campaign's airplane.

And, in late summer 2004, as he stepped up to the podium at the Democratic National Convention in Boston to make his acceptance speech, the senator snapped off a sharp salute to the American people and stated—"I am John Kerry and I am reporting for duty." It was a powerful and emotional moment, in the convention hall and around the country. The senator and his campaign were poised for the fall campaign and in a strong position—based in a large part on the senator's connection to his heroic military record, where he fought for the country and put his crew first, with the idea that the American people could trust him to fight for them and put their families first.

In short, the Swift boat storyline was at the core of the Kerry candidacy—it represented the campaign's family jewels.

The Kerry campaign made the senator's military record a foundational aspect of his candidacy, as reported in a May 2004 *Washington Post* story:

The senator from Massachusetts is trying to show that he and his party are more committed to national defense, veterans and patriotism than Bush and the GOP . . . Since Vietnam, Democrats have suffered politically from perceptions of weakness on national security issues, polls have shown. . . . With voters consistently telling pollsters Iraq and terrorism are among their top concerns this year, Kerry is calculating that only by shedding this image can Democrats win the White House in wartime, according to advisers. To do this, Kerry has adopted tough rhetoric when talking about Iraq, al Qaeda and homeland defense and has wrapped himself in red-white-and-blue symbolism."

And the strategy worked, as polling showed that the senator had narrowed a gap with President Bush on the issue of who voters trusted more on national security issues. Coming out of the Democratic Convention in Boston, Senator Kerry had moved into a virtual tie with President Bush, in part because of the gains he made with voters on the issue of trust, especially as it related to national security. The Associated Press reported:

While in Boston, a heavy emphasis on the Democrat's sterling war record impressed male voters, according to an Associated Press poll, improving his ratings on honesty, intelligence, likability and even Bush's strongest issue— the ability to protect the country.

But then, on August 5, 2004, Senator Kerry's political jewels came under attack from a group of political snipers calling themselves Swift Boat Veterans for Truth, led by Houston lawyer John O'Neill, a former Swift boat commander who served in Vietnam after Kerry's tour of duty had ended. The organization, which represented itself as an independent group of Vietnam veterans, launched a TV attack ad challenging Senator Kerry's military record and storyline. The one-minute advertisement, which ran in several hotly contested states, was entitled *Any Questions,* and featured testimonials from Swift boat veterans who had served in Vietnam at the same time as the senator, and raised questions about Kerry's integrity and honesty.

These Swift boaters formally launched their group in May 2004 as a 527 organization (a designation in the tax code that allows an entity to engage in a campaign as an independent organization, not aligned with any one candidate), and claimed to represent 250 veterans who had served on Swift boats in Vietnam.

When the group was formed the Kerry campaign refused to fire back. And when the attack ads went up, the senator's team continued to keep its powder dry. They reasoned that Kerry's war credentials were impeccable, impressive, and assiduously documented.

The swiftboaters' campaign escalated as they began throwing bombs in the form of a book, *Unfit for Command: Swift Boat Veterans Speak Out Against John Kerry*, co-authored by O'Neill and Jerome Corsi. The book, which offered a different version of the senator's service in Vietnam, was based on alleged interviews and other sources of information, and was a full-out character assassination of Senator Kerry, especially when it came to whether he was honest, had integrity, and could be trusted. The book's release and the initial attack ad on Senator Kerry were then followed by several other attack ads—all seeking to raise questions about the senator's character.

The conservative media, from Fox News to right-wing radio outlets to the influential Drudge Report website, began firing away.

The book became a best-seller.

The swiftboat attacks became a central focus on the campaign trail for much of August—a critical month that would set the campaign agenda for the fall sprint to election day.

And from the Kerry campaign, nothing. For weeks, as the Swift boat organization savaged him, the lid on the Kerry arsenal remained sealed tight. His team still reasoned that the claims were so thoroughly without merit that there was no need to hit back. It was not until several weeks after the Swift boat group had launched their attacks that the Kerry campaign finally took off the gloves and filed a Federal Elections Commission complaint, questioning the ties between the group and partisan Republicans.

But by this time, the damage had been done.

A *Los Angeles Times* poll conducted before the Swift boat attacks and after, found the ad campaign "appears to be hurting the Democratic nominee." In what was a very close race, the newspaper's polling showed that Kerry's two-point lead before the attacks had turned into a three-point deficit. Almost 70 percent of those polled had seen or heard about the attacks, and gave Bush an advantage of 46 percent compared to 38 percent on the issue of who best "has the honesty and integrity to serve as president."

Pundits, voters, the press—even his opponents—all were perplexed as to why the Kerry campaign took so long to fight back.

News reports during and, in particular, after the campaign indicated that while the senator wanted to fight back from day one, his campaign staff made the decision not to engage the swiftboaters out of a concern that responding would have created still more attention for a group that was not worthy of such attention. This approach was informed by their experience when they ignored the group's launch in May, and the swiftboaters had received little attention. The Kerry campaign believed that no one—especially the press—would take these demonstrably false attacks seriously.

In fact, the Kerry campaign, and others, knew early on that these swiftboaters were not who they purported to be and that their assertions were riddled with factual inaccuracies.

There were veterans featured in the attacks who had, in fact, not served with Kerry. A number of the former soldiers making the accusations had actually not been present at the events for which they attacked the senator. Others were making assertions that contradicted their prior statements regarding Senator Kerry's conduct. And, moreover, there were many other vets who had served with Kerry who offered their versions of the facts, which were entirely consistent with the senator's.

Even a cursory background check revealed that the swiftboaters were clearly not independent:

- The group included a number of Republican operatives with links to the Republican Party working on the swiftboaters' behalf.
- The leader of the swiftboaters, John O'Neill, was an active Republican from Texas who had contributed money to Republicans.
- The campaign ads were reportedly paid for by top Republican donors, including Bob Perry, a major Bush contributor who gave over $4 million to the swiftboaters.
- *The New York Times* reported that "records show that the group received the bulk of its initial financing from two men with ties to the president and his family—one a longtime political associate of Mr. [Karl] Rove's, the other a trustee of the foundation for Mr. Bush's father's presidential library."

- The Bush campaign's lawyer also served as the lawyer for the swiftboaters.
- The book on John Kerry's service was co-authored by O'Neill and Jerome Corsi, a right-wing columnist, and published by Regnery, a politically active, conservative publishing house.

And by the time the Kerry campaign finally emerged from its bunker and began firing back, it was too late.

The damage had been done.

In a little over three weeks, from early August until the end of the month (and beyond) the swiftboat attacks hit their target.

The senator's post-convention poll standings were degraded.

The campaign was put on the defensive.

Basic questions were raised about John Kerry's character on the very issue that represented the core of his candidacy, whether he could be trusted on national security issues. And perhaps most damning of all, his failure to fight back caused voters to worry about whether he could indeed be trusted to fight for them, if he wasn't even willing to stand up and fight for himself on an issue that was so deeply personal.

UNDERSTANDING THE NINTH COMMANDMENT—NO SWIFTBOATING

Senator Kerry's campaign not only broke the ninth commandment of damage control—it facilitated the introduction of a new concept into the American lexicon:

No swiftboating.

In New England, there is a saying that if you go to bed at night and there's no snow on the ground, and you wake up the next morning to see snow on the ground, you can safely conclude that it snowed.

When it comes to damage control, if you go to bed at night and you are not in a deep hole, and you wake up the next morning to find yourself peering up out of a deep hole, you can safely conclude that someone spent the night digging that deep hole for you—and to their benefit.

And you simply can't curl up and go into a fetal position—you have to climb out of the hole, stand tall, and fight back against those who are trying to take you down.

EXPOSE THE HIDDEN HANDS

In a crisis there are those who are the subject of the crisis, and then there are those who benefit from your crisis—your political opponent, your business competitor, a colleague vying for a promotion.

And like Claude Raines in *Casablanca* feigning shock at the mention that gambling was indeed taking place at Rick's Café Américain, you, too, should never be shocked, *shocked* to learn of self-interested parties in the middle of your crisis. It is incumbent upon you to *expose the hidden hands* and, in doing so, limit the harm by raising issues about their motivations. Some examples of hidden hands:

- Purportedly, it was Eric Mangini, the former New England Patriots assistant coach who became the head coach of the rival New York Jets, who in 2007 was among those responsible for alerting National Football League officials that the Patriots taped the practices of their opponents.
- It was short-sellers with direct financial interests who were pushing out information on Bear Stearns's financial viability in 2008.
- When it came to issues related to copyrighted material on the Internet, in 2012, Silicon Valley social media companies were known to have been behind the scenes helping to fan the flames of public opposition to legislation designed to address piracy protections being pushed by the Hollywood film and entertainment industry.

Thus, it should come as no surprise that those who stand to benefit from a crisis are often the very ones who either played a role in the outing of the crisis, or are stirring the pot. In each of the above examples, the storylines would have been recast if those with hidden agendas had their roles exposed—and the harms represented by these crises would have been limited.

The Kerry campaign needed to have engaged the Swift boat group with its own counter-offensive, designed to expose the attacks as a sophisticated assault against the senator's character. And they needed to show how it was being organized, funded, and promoted by partisan political opponents—and not, as was claimed, by independent, uninterested parties.

Equally important, the campaign should have made this information public at the point of attack, in order to blunt the impact from the very beginning. Had the Kerry campaign accurately shown who the Swift boat organization really was, the harm to Senator Kerry's character would have been limited, as the public would have discounted the charges as having come from highly partisan opponents.

RESEARCH COUNTS

To expose the hidden hands stirring the pot in your crisis, you have to do your research, and do it thoroughly. The moment you find yourself in a crisis, try and discover if someone is directly or indirectly involved in promoting the matter, then determine their real agenda and, as comprehensively as you can, compile this information so it can be disseminated to your core audience. Understand that the quicker you can assemble and distribute the information documenting the unclean hands, the quicker the storyline will be recast—and the sooner you can limit your harm. It does no good, as illustrated by the Kerry campaign, to have assembled the research, but not to have deployed it at the moment of the attack.

NO FREE LAYUPS

Pat Riley, the legendary five-time NBA champion head coach, had a rule: *No free layups.* In other words, you simply cannot let the opposition take easy shots at will without making them feel some pain. In a crisis, the No Free Layups rule translates into making sure that if there is someone with unclean hands benefiting from the damage, you must publicly expose their conflict, put them on the defensive, and hit them where it will, in fact, hurt.

While the folks behind the Swift boat attacks were various Republican apparatchiks—the true beneficiary of their actions was the Bush-Cheney campaign. And both President Bush and Vice President Cheney had tremendous exposure on the issue of their military records. President Bush had spent the Vietnam War in the National Guard serving in Alabama, and there were serious questions about whether, as the son and grandson of prominent politicians, strings had been pulled for him to avoid combat. Meanwhile, Vice President Cheney had avoided military service altogether by applying for, and securing, five deferments. When asked about his deferments, Cheney was quoted by *The Washington Post* as saying, "I had other priorities in the 60s than military service." We point this out not to refight the campaign, but to underscore the point that the Kerry campaign had plenty of material by which to block the attack, by making sure their political opponents were not able to take any free shots. Senator Kerry's campaign could easily have pointed out the swiftboaters' Republican connections, and, using the unclean hands as a hook, directly confronted Bush and Cheney about their military service records.

To make sure your opponents get no free layups, look for ways to connect the dots between those who are stoking the fire of the crisis and those who are benefiting. Much like in Watergate where the key source Deep Throat counseled *Washington Post* reporter Bob Woodward to "follow the money," you should follow the trail to discover who is benefiting from your crisis and draw the connections. Moreover, after the dots have been connected, do not be shy about showing the contrast between your record and the record of those with the unclean hands.

MAKE THE TRUTH CLEAR FOR ALL TO SEE

We cannot tell you how many times we have heard some version of the following phrases from a frustrated client who has just retained us because they are drowning in the middle of a crisis:

- Doesn't the truth matter?
- I feel like I am Alice in Wonderland!
- Why are people saying all these lies about me?

A crisis is not a Harvard-Yale debate where there are impartial judges, a neutral audience, and an objective scoring system. A crisis is akin to a steel-cage wrestling match with low blows and eye gouging. Your core audiences behave like the Romans at a gladiator match (and predisposed to turn their thumbs down). The judges, to the extent there even are judges, are like the Russian ice skating judges you see at the Olympics who are anything but impartial. In a crisis, you will often feel like the only survivor on a deserted island, and, therefore, the burden is on you to *make the truth clear for all to see*, including calling out those with the unclean hands behind the crisis, if you want to taint the attacks while maintaining your credibility.

Senator Kerry's campaign seemed to operate under the naive belief that a presidential campaign is an intellectually honest exercise where a third-party arbiter—the press, in this instance—would step in and cry foul on the pernicious Swift boat attacks. They waited for the cavalry, but the cavalry never came. And by thinking that the press would eventually step in, the campaign imperiled its own credibility, as voters were more struck not by the substance of the attacks, but by the lack of a substantive counterpunch. And as a consequence, the truth was compromised.

When the facts are on your side, force feed the facts. Impose your will on the story by providing on-the-record statements that force your core audiences to pay attention to the facts. Do not hesitate to directly challenge, question, or counter-attack those who stand to benefit from your crisis. (As discussed previously, you must be sensitive with whom you are picking a fight—but if the fight is with someone with a direct interest in the crisis who is standing to benefit in some way, and your very survivability is at stake, then this is a fight you must wage.) Be vigilant in looking for the underlying truths. Did someone cut a deal with prosecutors to get a lesser sentence? Is the restaurant across the street seeking to scoop up your customers? Is an opposing coach trying to raid your recruits? Is a competitor trying to steal your best employees? Whenever there is something to be gained at your expense, there will often be plenty of people willing to spread whatever lies will advance them and sink you.

To respect the ninth commandment, follow these three steps:

1. Expose the hidden hands.
2. No free layups.
3. Make the truth clear for all to see.

RESPECTING THE NINTH COMMANDMENT—FAHRENHEIT 9/11

The mood in Michael Moore's studio offices in New York City was very glum in early May 2004. Walt Disney Studios, as a result of acquiring Miramax Films, owned the distribution rights to *Fahrenheit 9/11*, the director's scathing polemic on the Iraq War, and Disney had decided to block the release of the film.

The folks supporting Michael Moore, including his agent, Hollywood power broker Ari Emanuel, were suggesting that Disney had concerns about the controversial political nature of the film and the impact it could have on the company. For Moore and his production team, who had spent several years of their lives working on the film—this was a major crisis. Disney's blocking of the film's distribution could be interpreted as a reflection on the quality of their work. Their careers were potentially going to be hurt. And for Moore, this was especially painful—a film that he believed to be an important statement on significant societal issues was not going to be made available to the public.

Among the glum faces, there were a few who could barely contain their glee—pumping their fists and hooting with laughter—to the glares of others in the room who could not understand such a celebratory mood in the face of a terrible crisis.

What did those few know that the others did not?

Simply put, a number of those in the room realized that if—with an emphasis on *if*—it became public knowledge that a leading entertainment company was refusing to distribute a film out of concern about the movie's political impact, then the crisis was going to turn into the cinematic opportunity of a lifetime.

Anyone who remembers the history of films such as *Deep Throat* or *The Last Temptation of Christ* knows that the moment the public is told they cannot or should not see a film, the film is guaranteed to have a much larger audience than it would have had otherwise.

Within hours of the Disney decision, a rising-star *New York Times* reporter, Jim Rutenberg, who covered media and entertainment, became aware of the decision to torch *Fahrenheit 9/11*. The paper interviewed Emanuel, who directly pointed to the politics behind the studio's decision to block the film. And on May 5, 2004 (ironically, about the same time the swiftboaters formally launched their organization), the *Times* gave the story a "big ride" breaking news, with the front-page headline:

DISNEY IS BLOCKING DISTRIBUTION
OF FILM THAT CRITICIZES BUSH

The story detailed Disney's concerns about *Fahrenheit 9/11* and, in particular, focused on Emanuel's assertion that partisan politics were behind the decision to block the film, because of a connection to the company's financial interests:

Disney came under heavy criticism from conservatives the previous May after the disclosure that Miramax had agreed to finance the film when Icon Productions, Mel Gibson's company, backed out.

Moore's agent, Ari Emanuel, said Michael D. Eisner, Disney's chief executive, asked him last spring to pull out of the deal with Miramax. Emanuel said Eisner expressed particular concern that it would endanger tax breaks Disney receives for its theme park, hotels, and other ventures in Florida, where Bush's brother, Jeb, is governor."

And then all hell broke loose.

The wire services jumped on the story.

The cable outlets breathlessly pumped it up.

The online world went nuts—even the conservative Drudge Report broke the story with its infamous siren alert, denoting an especially hot story.

In the fevered news cycles that ensued, Michael Moore took to the soap box—retaining super-lawyer David Boies, holding press conferences with members of Congress, and appearing on numerous media outlets—with his message focused on how it was the Bush administration that was benefiting from the suppression of his film.

Under extreme pressure, it was ultimately resolved that *Fahrenheit 9/11* would be released by other distributors. The film went to Cannes, the world's most venerable film festival, and became the first documentary in more than forty years to win the Palme d'Or, the festival's award for the best film. And all of this was no doubt helped by the controversy over Disney's attempted censorship.

As the film had its initial screenings and the story around it unfolded, groups began appearing out of the woodwork to try to discredit factual assertions in the film. In fighting off these attacks, Moore's team assembled a fact bible to back up the claims he presented, relied on experts, and aggressively defended the facts in the film.

Fahrenheit 9/11 opened a little over a month after Cannes as the number one film in America, with moviegoers standing in line for hours to get tickets, and it earned more in its opening weekend than any other theatrically released documentary in history. The film went on to shatter all existing records for documentaries, grossing more than $220 million.

Michael Moore and his team understood how not to be swiftboated—even before swiftboating had become part of the vernacular. The Moore team knew there was an ulterior motive behind the decision not to distribute the film, and, through Ari Emanuel, made this information available, which allowed Moore to minimize the harm that would have been done. Instead, they recast the storyline to their great benefit (thereby avoiding potential harm), and they did this by providing information about the hidden agendas of those behind the attempt to bury the film. By exposing the hidden hands, Moore recast the story from one of a film being consigned to the trash heap of history, to a film that made history.

Moreover, by having a person associated with the film, Ari Emanuel, providing specific details, the *Fahrenheit 9/11* team was able to force feed the facts regarding those who had sought to pull the film from distribution. In making it clear that there was going to be a political price to pay for taking a kill shot at the movie, Moore showed there were no free layups when it came to his film.

Finally, Moore took steps to make the truth clear for all to see. He had the facts to back up *Fahrenheit 9/11*'s assertions against those trying to discredit his film. Moore and his team's willingness to force feed the facts, and frontally engage those coming after them, served to marginalize the impact of the attacks and, correspondingly, enhance the film and its director's credibility.

THE NINTH COMMANDMENT APPLIED TO AN EVERYDAY CRISIS— WHAT HAPPENS IN NAPA DOESN'T STAY IN NAPA

A group of local developers in Napa, California, filed plans in 2007 with the planning commission and the county to transform an unused old factory located alongside the Napa River into a mixed-use residential housing development. The group, Napa Redevelopment Partners, was led by Keith Rogal, a very respected Napa-area businessman.

However, this was the town of Napa, in the heart of the nation's most prestigious wine region, and the community had strong environmental and land-use feelings that translated into strict development laws, reflecting a prevailing culture generally in opposition to development. Thus, the project generated angst. Immediately.

Napa County environmental organizations expressed concern.

The local paper, the *Napa Valley Register*, wrote articles looking at the project's size and scope.

A number of elected officials and others made their reservations public.

In particular, a local lawyer, James Marshall, emerged to spearhead what was thought to be a grassroots effort to pursue a local ballot initiative that would stop the proposed development of the former Napa Pipe factory site. Marshall's initiative and campaign was known as the Responsible Growth Initiative.

Given the prevailing public sentiment on development and polling data on the issue, the ballot measure was expected to easily pass.

Keith Rogal and his team were in a tough spot. They had bought a property that would otherwise have limited value. They had raised money from investors to pursue the project. The developer's plans were under attack. Their small business was in a serious crisis. And if the initiative passed, their project would be stone dead.

They decided to fight back to try to limit the harm being done—and then things got interesting. Very interesting.

Rogal's local development team began poking around, doing some research, and asking questions. In doing so, they determined that the small-town lawyer leading the fight against them had no prior record of involvement or opposition to land-use issues in the community or county.

And, in turn, the local press began asking why this lawyer was engaged in such an action. Was there someone or some group with an ulterior motive behind the effort?

Soon, the talk on the streets of Napa was less about the merits of the development project and more about who was behind the effort to kill the deal. By taking steps to expose the hidden hands, Rogal and his partners recast the matter from being about local developers, to who were the hidden hands stirring the pot.

Under mounting public pressure generated by the developers, Marshall eventually acknowledged that there were others behind the opposition effort, though he would not acknowledge whom.

The *Napa Valley Register* reported under the headline "Unknown Identity of Anti–Napa Pipe Plan Backers":

> The people behind the Responsible Growth Initiative—an initiative based on 1980's Measure A—want to remain hidden for now. The money behind a new push to get the voter approved slow-growth initiative on the June ballot remains a mystery, just as paid signature gatherers are spreading out around Napa shopping meccas.

As paid signature gathers from nationally known signature-gathering firms, prominent statewide ballot consultants, and out-of-state operatives appeared in Napa to try and kill the development, others in the community who were concerned about the anonymous nature of the campaign directly challenged Jim Marshall and the Responsible Growth campaign by filing complaints with local election officials regarding the campaign's finance reporting.

At this point, the funding for the opposition began to dry up, as it became clear that this was not going to be a free shot where whoever was really behind the ballot initiative could continue to anonymously fund it.

Meanwhile, proponents of the development project formed their own group called Keep Napa Napa, which involved Keith Rogal and his development partners but also included a large contingent of everyday Napans. The group force fed the issues, making it clear that the political operatives who had been working against the project were from out of town, were associated with conservative causes such as the highly controversial opposition to gay marriage, and had been involved in pro-development activities in other parts of the state on behalf of big-box stores. All of this raised questions about the true motives of Jim Marshall and his backers. Keep Napa Napa had the discipline to pursue an approach whereby those entities behind the initiative had no free layups. The result was that environmental and other progressive organizations that could have joined the effort against the development backed away, and elected officials became wary of associating themselves with the ballot initiative.

The local paper reported on the updates:

> The local proponents of the informally named Responsible Growth Initiative are paying hired guns to gather signatures to place the initiative on the June ballot—hired guns strongly linked to conservative causes. . . . The conservative ties are surprising considering the initiative is aimed at limiting a major residential development, as slow-growth initiatives are more commonly pushed by environmental and other left-wing groups.

Napa's local radio personalities and bloggers were soon focusing on the opposition—and directly challenging their credibility—while the supporters of the development project, by organizing a large and diverse group of actual Napa citizens, saw their credibility bolstered. And by the end of the campaign, a large group of voters had aligned themselves in opposition to the measure.

Those fighting the ballot initiative included the Napa Chamber of Commerce, Napa Valley Vintners, the Napa County Democratic Party, and Save Napa's Agricultural Gateway—all of this representing a huge sea change from where the issue began. And the area's two local newspapers, the *Napa Valley Register* and the *St. Helena Star,* also joined in opposition to the initiative.

Keith Rogal and his team improved their credibility by making the truth clear for all to see, and in the battle for public trust the scales shifted in their favor.

On June 3, 2008, Napa voters went to the polls and rejected the initiative.

Keith Rogal and his small-town development team changed the story by making sure they were not swiftboated.

COROLLARY TO THE NINTH COMMANDMENT— NO CIVILIAN CASUALTIES

During the 2012 Republican presidential primary campaign, there was an awful lot of talk about sex.

First, there was pizza executive Herman Cain's imbroglio involving his efforts to comfort various women in distress, including two who had received cash settlements related to sexual harassment claims and a third who said she had a thirteen-year affair with the candidate.

Then there was Newt Gingrich's former wife asserting that the former Speaker of the House of Representatives wanted an open marriage when he was in the midst of an affair with the woman who would become his third wife.

Next came former senator Rick Santorum, who essentially came out against sex altogether in the discussion of whether religious organizations' health care plans should be required to cover contraceptives under President Obama's national health care plan.

The Republicans, who have suffered in recent years from a gender gap in presidential elections, seemed to be affirmatively engaging in steps to do more harm to themselves, leading top Republican consultant Alex Castellanos to observe, "Republicans being against sex is not good. Sex is popular."

Conservative talk radio host Rush Limbaugh, apparently believing he was riding to the sound of the guns in defense of his fellow conservatives, and, presumably, trying to make sure they were not being swiftboated by a pro-sex Democratic lobby, joined the fray. In February 2012, he attacked Sandra Fluke, a Georgetown law student who two weeks earlier had testified at a congressional hearing in support of mandated private health insurance for contraceptives.

Limbaugh's comments were exceedingly harsh, calling Fluke as a "slut" and "prostitute":

> What does it say about the college coed Susan Fluke [he misstated her name], who goes before a congressional committee and essentially says that she must be paid to have sex? What does that make her? It makes her a slut, right? It makes her a prostitute. She wants to be paid to have sex . . . Can you imagine if you're her parents how proud of Sandra Fluke you would be? Your daughter goes up to a congressional hearing conducted by the Botox-filled Nancy Pelosi and testifies she's having so much sex she can't afford her own birth control pills and she agrees that Obama should provide them, or the Pope . . . So, Ms. Fluke and the rest of you feminazis, here's the deal. If we are going to pay for your contraceptives, and thus pay for you to have sex, we want something for it, and I'll tell you what it is. We want you to post the videos online so we can all watch.

Limbaugh's comments generated an enormous backlash.

Women's groups such as the National Organization for Women were enraged.

Georgetown's president John DeGioa strongly came to Fluke's defense, describing Limbaugh's statement "as misogynistic, vitriolic, and a misrepresentation of the position of Sandra Fluke." And he did so in an email sent to everyone on Georgetown's campus.

President Obama called to comfort the law student, commending her for speaking out about the concerns of American women. And, especially meaningful for Fluke, the president told her that her parents should be proud of her.

Limbaugh had an audience of over 15 million listeners a week, yet dozens of his corporate advertisers, who had stuck with him through earlier incidents, fled. Women veterans called for his program to be dropped from Armed Forces Radio. Even some fellow Republicans claimed he had gone too far.

Why was this comment—among all the incendiary comments Limbaugh had made over the years—the one that seemed to be the most problematic?

For one very simple reason: He took a shot at a civilian.

In a crisis, you need to make sure you are not being swiftboated—but you also need to distinguish between legitimate combatants and noncombatants.

Planned Parenthood is a combatant. A college student is not.

Firing at civilians is wrong and it backfires. Many have learned this the hard way:

- The University of California, Davis, police who pepper sprayed students at a peaceful protest. The video of the police officer casually spraying the students became an Internet meme that quickly went viral.
- The creators of a smear campaign launched in 2000 at John McCain, who was challenging George Bush for the Republican presidential nomination. During the South Carolina primary battle, there was the outrageous allegation that Senator McCain's adopted daughter was fathered by the senator out of wedlock.
- A respected Democratic political consultant questioning the choice of Mitt Romney's wife, Ann Romney, to be a stay-at-home mother.

In all of these instances the public felt a line had clearly been crossed and those involved felt the blowback.

Swiftboating has become a fact of life. In a crisis you have to be aware of it, and you have to deal with it with research, savvy, and discipline. Follow the ninth commandment: no swiftboating—and also keep in mind its important corollary: no civilian casualties.

SIXTEEN
COMMANDMENT X
THEY DISSEMBLE, YOU DESTROY

Somebody messes with me, I'm gonna mess with them.

—Al Capone, *The Untouchables*

THE TENTH COMMANDMENT—THEY DISSEMBLE, YOU DESTROY

Fight back when the opposition dissembles—it will mitigate additional harm by shifting attention away from you and onto those who have prevaricated. In seizing upon your opponent's discrepancy, you must have the discipline to focus like a laser on the specific, provable inaccuracy, which in turn will allow you to change the storyline by calling into question all of their representations. By showing your opponents have engaged in a misrepresentation, you will undermine their credibility and, in turn, create a favorable compare-and-contrast dynamic with your own credibility.

DISRESPECTING THE TENTH COMMANDMENT— DON'T BE "SNOOKERED"

On July 1, 2010, at its annual convention, the NAACP passed a resolution calling on "Tea Party leaders to repudiate those in their ranks who use racist language in their signs and speeches."

The NAACP resolution followed a disturbing year-long series of documented incidents where individuals who appeared at Tea Party events engaged in a range of racist, anti-gay, and anti-Semitic conduct.

On July 19, 2010, two videos, along with a blog post, appeared on the late Andrew Breitbart's influential conservative website Big Government and quickly migrated to widely read conservative websites such as FoxNews.com. The Breitbart videos purported to document remarks made by a Department of Agriculture official, Shirley Sherrod, in a March 2010 address to the NAACP. The videos appeared to show Sherrod, an African American woman, who was the Georgia state director of rural development, acknowledging that she discriminated against white people. The accompanying blog post explicitly called out the NAACP on the grounds that it was an organization "now holding itself up as the supreme judge of another groups' racial tolerance":

> In the first video, Sherrod describes how she racially discriminates against a white farmer. She describes how she is torn over how much she will choose to help him. And, she admits that she doesn't do everything she can for him, because he is white. Eventually, her basic humanity informs that this white man is poor and needs help. But she decides that he should get help from "one of his own kind." She refers him to a white lawyer.
>
> Sherrod's racist tale is received by the NAACP audience with nodding approval and murmurs of recognition and agreement. Hardly the behavior of the group now holding itself up as the supreme judge of another groups' racial tolerance.

FoxNews.com picked up the posting and drew the connection between the NAACP's Tea Party resolution and Sherrod's speech:

> Days after the NAACP clashed with Tea Party members over allegations of racism, a video has surfaced showing an Agriculture Department official regaling an NAACP audience with a story about how she withheld help to a white farmer facing bankruptcy.

This was followed by reports on other mainstream media and online outlets such as the CBS News affiliate in New York City and *The Atlanta Journal-Constitution*.

The Drudge Report headline read: "SHOCK: Video Suggests Racism at NAACP Event."

The same night as the videos were posted, Fox News dedicated much of its primetime to the subject, including top-rated Bill O'Reilly calling for Sherrod to resign. The Fox News star lead off his show that night with the question, "Is there racism in the Department of Agriculture?"

Then the NAACP itself criticized Sherrod:

> Racism is about the abuse of power. Ms. Sherrod had it in her position at USDA. According to her remarks, she mistreated a white farmer in need of assistance because of his race. We are appalled by her actions, just as we are with abuses of power against farmers of color and female farmers. Her actions were shameful. While she went on to explain in the story that she ultimately realized her mistake, as well as the common predicament of working people of all races, she gave no indication she had attempted to right the wrong she had done to this man. The reaction from many in the audience is disturbing. We will be looking into the behavior of NAACP representatives at this local event and take any appropriate action.

Before the story broke on Breitbart's site, Sherrod had warned her employer, the Department of Agriculture, of the misleading tapes. But as the story continued to escalate in response to what was being reported on Fox and other media outlets, in an apparent panic, officials at the Department of Agriculture called Sherrod twice on her ride home from work that night—leading her to pull her car to the side of the road and swiftly write and email in her resignation. Agriculture secretary Tom Vilsack subsequently stated the department's position:

> Yesterday, I asked for and accepted Ms. Sherrod's resignation for two reasons. First, for the past 18 months, we have been working to turn the page on the sordid civil rights record at USDA and this controversy could make it more difficult to move forward on correcting injustices. Second, state rural development directors make many decisions and are often called to use their discretion. The controversy surrounding her comments would create situations where her decisions, rightly or wrongly, would be called into question making it difficult for her to bring jobs to Georgia. Our policy is clear. There is zero tolerance for discrimination at USDA and we strongly condemn any act of discrimination against any person. We have a duty to ensure that when we provide services to the American people we do so in an equitable manner.

But equally important is our duty to instill confidence in the American people that we are fair service providers.

By the end of the day, the NAACP was in retreat, the Department of Agriculture was playing defense, and Sherrod had lost her job.

However, over the next few days, the rest of the story began to emerge.

Crucially, the entirety of Sherrod's speech became available, which provided context for the excerpted remarks and told a very different version of the story. The full transcript of her remarks made clear Sherrod was talking about an event that had taken place almost twenty-five years earlier, and at a time when she was not even working for the Department of Agriculture. Further, Sherrod's speech made the point that poverty affects all races—and spoke to how she had come to learn this lesson by specifically helping a white farmer who was in peril of losing his land.

The incident Sherrod referenced was related to her past, when she worked for a non-profit organization that focused on supporting black farmers, where she was asked to help a white farm family. Sherrod explained how her work on behalf of the white family helped her understand the effects of poverty on all races. As the result of her work, she and this white family went on to become life-long friends.

In the days following Sherrod's resignation, the white farmer, Roger Spooner, spoke out in her defense, saying, "If we hadn't have found her, we would have lost everything, I'm afraid."

As the speech at the heart of the controversy became fully available, and the details of the original story understood, everyone was forced to backtrack. *The New York Times* observed, "Shirley Sherrod, had gained instant fame and emerged as the heroine of a compelling story about race and redemption. Pretty much everyone else had egg on his face."

O'Reilly apologized, saying, "I owe Ms. Sherrod an apology for not doing my homework, for not putting her remarks into the proper context."

A chastened Secretary Vilsack offered her a new job and said, "This is a good woman, she's been put through hell and I could have and should have done a better job."

And at the NAACP, where it all began, the organization claimed it had been "snookered."

But by this point the damage to the NAACP and Department of Agriculture had been done—and Sherrod had lost her job as a result of a story that was false from the onset.

UNDERSTANDING THE TENTH COMMANDMENT— THEY DISSEMBLE, YOU DESTROY

In forcing Sherrod to resign based on a misleading video posted by an opponent, the Department of Agriculture and the NAACP violated the tenth commandment of damage control:

They dissemble, you destroy.

In May 1987, President Ronald Reagan's former Secretary of Labor, Raymond Donovan, stood on the steps of a New York courthouse, following his acquittal on larceny and fraud charges related to allegations of contract rigging, and plaintively asked, "Which office do I go to to get my reputation back?"

The best way to get your reputation back in situations where it has been hijacked, is to not allow it to be hijacked in the first place.

And you do this by fighting back against those who lie, distort, misrepresent, or dissemble.

SEIZE ON A DISCREPANCY

As discussed in the previous chapter, often in a crisis there is an opposing party with something to gain that is promoting, if not directly behind, the scandal. In such a situation, opponents typically overplay their hands and engage in clear misrepresentations in their ardor to promote the scandal. The moment your opponent puts forth a misrepresentation is the moment you *seize on a discrepancy,* turn the tables, and limit the damage—including the damage to your reputation. And you do this by shifting the focus from you to your opponent.

In the Shirley Sherrod incident, the Department of Agriculture and the NAACP were not only "snookered"; the two organizations collectively squandered the opportunity to seize upon the fact that an avowed opponent released a video edited in a highly misleading manner designed to create a blatant misrepresentation. In fact, the entire "scandal" was the product of an excerpted video and accompanying blog post that made the exact opposite point of what Sherrod actually conveyed in the totality of her remarks.

In seeking the opportunity to seize upon a discrepancy, go through the checklist of *who, what, when, where,* and *how.*

Consider *who* is putting out the negative information. Is the information coming from an objective source or is it being promoted by an entity with a specific agenda? Andrew Breitbart's blog post should have made it clear that the video was not coming from an objective news source, but rather, from an individual with an agenda.

Look at *what* is being distributed. Is the information being presented in its entirety or is it being shown in a way to cast you in the worst possible light? Since this video was a very brief excerpt of a much longer speech, its authenticity needed to have been questioned.

Examine *when* the information is made available. Is information being released at a time designed to inflict maximum damage to you, and maximum benefit to your opponent? The fact that the Sherrod video was from a speech she made four months previously and dealt with an incident that took place twenty-five years earlier, and then suddenly appeared almost immediately following the NAACP passing a resolution related to the Tea Party, should have been a clear warning sign.

Determine from *where* the information came. Did the story come from an organization or media outlet with a specific bent? Since the video was posted by an avowed opponent of the NAACP, seeking to attack the organization for its Tea Party resolution, this was an indication that it was far from reliable.

And, finally, think about *how* the information was released. Is the information being communicated in ways that should raise questions? The fact that ideological pundits at Fox News and other conservative outlets jumped on the video should have pointed to a coordinated attack by the opposition.

FOCUS LASER-LIKE ON A PROVABLE MISREPRESENTATION

In a crisis, there is typically a flurry of information being disseminated and multiple charges and attacks coming from different directions. In such a situation, it is imperative to identify what you can prove beyond a shadow of a doubt is inaccurate. In our experience it is best to have the discipline to focus like a laser on one glaring inaccuracy, blow it up, and then use the inaccuracy to change the storyline by calling into question all of the representations made by your opponents.

In the videos that were released by Breitbart, there were a number of inaccuracies. However, above all else, there was the underlying fact that the videos had been edited in such a way as to express the exact opposite of what Sherrod had communicated. It was Breitbart whose conduct could have been called into question, had the Department of Agriculture or the NAACP focused their responses on this glaring inaccuracy—an inaccuracy that should have been immediately seized upon by both groups, as the Department of Agriculture had been specifically forewarned by Sherrod as to the existence of the misleading tapes and the speech itself had taken place before the NAACP, which, with even with a minimal level of due diligence, could have discovered that the tapes were deceptively edited.

To change the storyline as the result of a discrepancy, you will need to have the discipline to *focus laser-like on a provable misrepresentation.*

First, make sure that the inaccuracy can be proven beyond a shadow of a doubt.

Second, elevate this specific inaccuracy so it breaks through the media noise and becomes a defining aspect of the crisis. If you have a variety of issues—some of which are clear and some that may be in a gray area—you will dilute the impact of the attack. The counter-offensive needs a sharp point to break through.

And, third, deploy the inaccuracy so that it is used to call into question everything else that is being said by your opponent in order to create a chilling effect on others who would otherwise repeat it, promote it, or believe it.

Often, your situation can be profoundly impacted by the ability to inject additional information into a story. In a crisis where your opponents have provided only a small piece of the narrative, the failure to present the whole story can create a dynamic where there is an implicit misrepresentation—and you can seize on this opening by detailing the entire story, which serves to both change the storyline and raise questions about the false nature of the initial information.

The ability to provide this additional information gives you the opportunity to alter the narrative or storyline of a crisis, especially if the initial negative information being disseminated against you comes from a suspect entity—as the combination of the tainted origin and incomplete nature of the original information will cause people to question the source behind the story. Paul Harvey, the legendary syndicated radio host, featured a regular segment entitled "The Rest of the Story." In a crisis, consider what information can be given to tell the rest of the story, and in doing so, you can fundamentally change or redirect the arc of the story.

Even a cursory review of the initial Sherrod videos released on the conservative website should have revealed that the "rest of the story" was not being communicated—given that the incident being discussed took place more than two decades ago—long before Sherrod was even an employee of the Department of Agriculture.

In the opening moments of a crisis, have the discipline to review the information with a level head and determine if what is being put forth reflects the entire story. Even if the entire story is negative, you can still raise questions about the motives of your opposition so long as you have the discipline to put out the whole story.

PICK A FIGHT WITH THE RIGHT ENEMY IN THE RIGHT WAY

In the "First In, First Out" chapter, we looked at how Roger Clemens picked a fight with his former trainer—a fight he could not afford to lose. However, in a crisis, if there is an opponent, there is the opportunity to reshape the story if you *pick a fight with the right enemy in the right way.* This will allow you to build up your credibility by drawing a favorable compare-and-contrast situation.

Both the Department of Agriculture and the NAACP had an opponent worth picking a fight with—Breitbart. His website had purposefully put up a misleading video on racism, and the evidence of his deception could be clearly documented. In revealing this falsehood, the NAACP, in particular, was in an exceedingly strong position to pit its credibility against that of Breitbart.

In order to pick the right fight, with the right opponent, on the right issue, there are three elements that need to be in place:

First, you must be sure beyond a shadow of a doubt that your opponent is dissembling—and be able to prove it.

Second, there must be an identifiable enemy benefiting from your distress.

And, third, by creating conflict and calling attention to the position of your adversary, you must benefit from the compare-and-contrast scenario (so don't pick a fight with Mother Theresa, but do pick a fight with Big Tobacco).

To respect the Tenth Commandment, follow these three steps:

1. Seize on a discrepancy.
2. Focus laser-like on a provable misrepresentation.
3. Pick a fight with the right enemy, in the right way.

RESPECTING THE TENTH COMMANDMENT—RATS

It was the second full week of 2000 and Al Gore and George W. Bush were locked in a battle for the presidency that would end up being among the closest

American elections in history. On a daily basis, the two campaigns were trading volleys—each trying to gain the upper hand. And given the closeness of the race, both campaigns were in a constant crisis mode. How effective their attacks and counter-attacks were at any given moment could tilt the polls and impact the direction of the race and ultimately help decide who would hold the world's most powerful office. Gore was especially feeling the heat. The Bush campaign and the Republican National Committee (RNC) had a significant financial advantage that they were deploying with great effect by releasing a constant bombardment of negative television ads.

One thirty-second ad would become a national story, leading the television news, featured on the front pages of newspapers across the country, and dominate the campaign for a week. This memorable commercial, attacking Gore's health plan proposal, paid for by the RNC and run frequently in a number of crucial battleground states, included a tagline stating: THE GORE PRESCRIPTION PLAN: BUREAUCRATS DECIDE.

The ad initially caught the eye of the Gore campaign because of what was readily apparent in the message of the commercial. Based on polling and focus group research, the Gore campaign knew this "Bureaucrats" ad was effective for three reasons: First, in race where the meta-narrative held Gore to be competent but unlikable, and Bush to be likeable but not particularly competent, the ad was designed to degrade voter perceptions of Gore's core strength of competency (by suggesting that the Gore plan was not effective). Second, in a dead-even race in which both campaigns were engaged in intense combat for the small number of undecided voters in a handful of key swing states, and in which health care was a major issue, the commercial served to undermine Gore's health care plan by playing to voter fears of government regulators replacing doctors. Finally, in several key battleground states the fact that third-party candidate Ralph Nader was on the ballot had moved these states from close but leaning towards Gore, to what were now considered toss-ups. This ad had the potential to affect the decisions of a small but critical voter cohort who would otherwise be voting for Gore by pushing them to Nader. From the campaign's tracking, it was known that since the commercial had gone into rotation on August 28, it had been run over 4,000 times in sixteen states, including major battleground states such as Ohio, Pennsylvania, Michigan, and Florida.

However, what ultimately captured the Gore campaign's attention and made the ad a national story was what was *not* readily apparent. An eagle-eyed supporter in Washington State saw the spot on TV and realized that the ad contained a hidden message—the word RATS—which was derived from the last four letters in the tagline BUREAUCRATS, and conveyed subliminally in a single frame of the commercial. This was a case of subliminal advertising, a form of advertising where extremely briefly displaying words or images can affect ideas or behavior—even if the recipient is not aware they have been targeted. Subliminal advertising had a long and controversial history, and the fact that it was being deployed in a presidential campaign to attempt to subconsciously influence voters represented a potentially explosive story—given that it would raise questions about the ethics of the Bush campaign, which would be especially damning for a candidate whose campaign narrative was based on Bush being the likeable guy.

The Gore campaign recorded the ad in several markets around the country and, after careful review, confirmed that it indeed contained the subliminal message. Sensing an opportunity to go on the offensive, they reached out to *The New York Times* and tipped the paper to the story, including bringing the reporter into a production studio to show the ad in a slowed-down version, demonstrating how the chyrons in a commercial (the words that appear on the screen) are produced frame by frame, and providing production experts to attest to the process—all designed to anticipate the Bush defense and make clear with facts that the word "RATS" was in all likelihood no mistake.

Shortly after midnight on Monday morning, September 12, 2000, the paper's lead campaign correspondent Rick Berke, one of the most respected political reporters in the country, broke a page one story online (and where he made clear that the Gore campaign had brought the ad to the paper's attention in a "slowed down version"), "At first glance the television commercial on prescription drugs looks like a run-of-the-mill attack advertisement . . . But then if you watch very closely, something else happens. The word 'RATS,' a fragment of the word 'BUREAUCRATS,' pops up in one frame."

The *Times* story, which detailed the controversial history of subliminal advertising, quoted the president of the prestigious advertising firm Young & Rubicam (that helped lead the Bush campaign's advertising consultants), who said, "Are you serious? That's unbelievable . . . I hope we haven't stooped to that. That's pretty bad. I thought it was illegal anyway."

Following up after the story appeared, in the very early morning hours, the Gore campaign, using *The New York Times* reporting as validation, conducted a series of individual briefings with members of the national press corps traveling with the campaign. They walked reporter after reporter through the issue, including showing them the ad frame by frame and documenting how such a subliminal message could not have been inadvertent, but rather had to have been purposefully placed.

By the time daylight broke, the Bush campaign was put squarely on the defensive with the burden of proof shifted to them to explain the word "RATS"—and they were caught completely unprepared.

When asked about the ad during an appearance on ABC's *Good Morning America,* then governor Bush claimed not to know anything about the story, let alone the ad. This was met with an incredulous response given the prominent play of the story in the country's leading newspaper and the fact the campaign was being besieged with questions on the issue. Bush's answer was a lose-lose proposition for his campaign—either the Republicans had engaged in questionable conduct, and he was lying about it, which undermined his positioning as the "likeable" candidate, or he was ignorant of a story that was rocketing around the nation, and in which case his ignorance of the facts amplified with a very large megaphone that he was indeed not ready for prime time—how could he go on network TV and not be prepared to answer the question that was the issue of the day? And in a later press appearance, Bush famously was unable to correctly pronounce the word "subliminal"—saying it as "subliminable."

Between the *Times* story and Bush's seeming non-denial denial, the story was now officially out of control—and it got worse.

The Bush campaign tried to counter-attack the Gore campaign, saying, "It sounds like happy hour over at the Gore campaign. It's a bizarre allegation. It's ridiculous and it's not true."

In response, the Gore campaign released the names of experts and a number of treatises on the ethics of subliminal advertising and they held to their position that this was a deliberate use of a widely deplored form of advertising.

And the story was now wildly out of control.

The Republicans, arguing that the RATS slide was one frame out of nine hundred, that appeared only for 1/30th of a second, claimed that there was no subliminal advertising in the ad and stated they were not going to pull the ad.

At the same time, Democratic surrogates all over the country launched into Bush for engaging in a deliberate effort to mislead voters and called for the ad to be pulled.

By now the story was a full-blown crisis for the Bush campaign.

The Republican political consultant who made the ad, at first said the use of the word "RATS" was "purely accidental," but then later tried to defuse the issue by referencing the "hidden" message in the Beatles song "Strawberry Fields Forever" saying, "If you play the ad backwards, it says 'Paul is Dead.'"

Democrats increased the pressure and called on the Federal Communications Commission (the government agency responsible for overseeing broadcast transmissions) to investigate the use of subliminal advertising.

ABC's George Stephanopoulos said of the Bush operation, "It is becoming the gang that can't shoot straight."

CNN reported, "After a series of missteps and distractions, members of the Bush camp may be expressing their frustration today with a single word: 'RATS.'"

Even Republicans were quoted saying that RATS could not have been inadvertent.

Later cited by noted presidential campaign correspondent Roger Simon in his book on the 2000 campaign, *Divided We Stand,* as "one of the most successfully planted stories in campaign history," the RATS controversy was truly a made-for-TV event. It was in the midst of a close, contentious campaign; it had a visual component; it was bizarre; it had legal implications; it appeared to be a novel effort to influence voters; and it had very public denials and non-denials.

The Gore campaign responded to the crisis posed by an effective Republican negative attack ad with a clear understanding of and respect for the tenth commandment: If they dissemble, you destroy.

First, the Gore team was able to seize on a discrepancy in the negative ad. Rather than issuing a general statement saying the ad was not credible, the Gore campaign identified a specific key discrepancy in the Bush story (the RATS frame), and demonstrated to the press how the word "RATS" could not have appeared by mistake by walking reporters through how an ad is created frame by frame, showing how the chyrons are produced, and providing experts who could attest to the fact it was unlikely just a simple error. Recognizing that the bizarre nature of the issue could have been dismissed or brushed aside if they had just made a broad allegation, Gore's team was forceful in establishing the existence of the subliminal message through the use of experts and a frame-by-frame presentation of the commercial. Thus, when Republicans claimed that RATS was merely one frame out of nine hundred or shown for

1/30th of a second, the press had already been prepared to understand that this was consistent with how subliminal advertising is designed to work. They further relied on the validation of *The New York Times* to pound home that this was indeed subliminal advertising, which in turn focused the story on being about the ethical conduct of their opposition, and not a back-and-forth on the merits of the actual message of the ad—and in doing so, reduced the immediate damage from by the barrage of powerful negative commercials directed at Gore. The subsequent flood of free press coverage reporting on the RATS advertising controversy both drowned out the actual message as well as tainted the ad in the eyes of voters. In short, by jumping on the discrepancy, the Gore campaign had engaged in a bit of political jujitsu, turning the negative ad on Vice President Gore into a self-inflicted negative ad against Governor Bush.

Second, Gore's campaign team had the discipline to bring a sustained laser-like focus on a provable misrepresentation: the Bush campaign's claim of not having engaged in subliminal advertising. When the Republicans attempted to sidestep the controversy or defuse it, the Gore campaign drove the issue with a singular focus on demonstrating that their opponent's denials were not credible. In doing so, Gore effectively made the entire back-and-forth contingent on whether or not there was a subliminal message. By focusing sharply on one immutable, irrefutable, and undeniably false representation, Gore called into question the entire commercial and, more broadly, the credibility of the Bush campaign.

And third, the Gore campaign was able to pick the right fight with the right enemy in the right way: Engaging in a fight that made clear that the Bush campaign, which was seeking the support of voters on the basis of Bush being the more likeable candidate, was in fact engaged in conduct designed to trick the voters. Gore did not make this a fight about the broader subject of the ad—rather, he made it a fight about the specific ethics of using subliminal advertising on unsuspecting voters. His campaign successfully argued this was not about the Republicans attacking Gore on health care, it was about them trying to influence voters in an unethical manner.

By the end of the day, Bush said the ad was being pulled.

The Gore campaign, while outmanned and outgunned in terms of money it could spend on advertising, on this issue fought back and won the battle in no small part because they had respected our the tenth commandment: If they dissemble, you destroy.

THE TENTH COMMANDMENT APPLIED TO AN
EVERYDAY CRISIS—DOGGIE DAMAGE CONTROL

It was the day before Christmas 2007, and Chris and his immediate family were having a picnic at the Buena Vista park near their house in San Francisco. Present were two parents (Chris and Andrea), a four-year-old and two-year-old, and their dog, Lola. At the time, Lola was a seven-year-old mutt who had been rescued from the pound the day before she was scheduled to be put down. As a puppy, Lola had been used as the bait in pit bull rings—and bore both the physical and emotional scars from such a traumatic puppyhood. Thus, while fantastic with kids, she was wary of other dogs, and great care was taken to keep her on a leash and under supervision.

As the kids played in the playground, Lola was tethered by her leash to a post outside of the playground. While putting out the spread for their little picnic in the park, another dog, off-leash in contravention of the city's ordinances and, seemingly, without an owner (or, as they say in San Francisco, "a people companion"), approached. Lola barked a few warning barks at the dog, which continued to come forward and was aggressively barking back. As the other dog got inside Lola's physical space, Lola, in dog speak, made it clear that she did not want to engage and that the intruding dog should back away, which it did, but only momentarily. By this point, Andrea and Chris were scrambling to get between Lola and the other dog. However, the other off-leash dog, whose owner was still nowhere to be seen, came charging at Lola, precipitating a flurry of growling and snapping teeth. By the time the two dogs were separated, the unleashed dog had clearly gotten the worse of the exchange.

With the two kids scared and crying over the melee, Chris went back into the playground to console them and Andrea stayed with the dogs, attempting to console the now-bitten, whimpering, unleashed interloper.

At this point, a highly agitated middle-aged woman, who subsequently became known as Cruella de Vil, arrived on the scene and immediately began berating Andrea over the incident—despite the fact that it was Cruella's dog who had been off leash and unattended while she was nowhere to be seen, and had not even been present for the fracas.

After trying to reason with the woman to no avail and get her to focus on her dog, Andrea returned to Chris, the kids, and Lola. Cruella, leaving her dog, came into the playground area and proceeded to inform Andrea and Chris, in front of their kids on Christmas Eve, that she was "law enforce-ment" and that she was going to take action to have Lola destroyed. In a very calm but firm way, Andrea provided her name and told Cruella that she needed to back away, and, if she so desired, she should pursue this matter in a formal manner. Predictably, the kids, especially their four-year-old, were greatly distressed by the exchange, and under the impression that Lola was in great peril as the result of Cruella's threats.

As their family left the playground, Lola in tow, a man who had been with his children on the playground came over to Andrea and Chris and indicated he had seen the entire incident. He offered to serve as a witness should he be needed—and provided his name and contact information. His version of the fight, as he recounted it, reflected an objective understanding of what had transpired, and he was clearly appalled by the conduct of Cruella.

Leaving the playground, Andrea and Chris assumed that this was the last of the matter given that their dog had been on a leash and tied up and the other dog had been off leash, unattended, and had initiated the confrontation.

However, a few weeks later, a notice from San Francisco Animal Control stating that Lola was being formally pursued by Cruella. An animal control law enforcement officer would serve as an adjudicator of the situation, and both sides were compelled to come in and present their cases.

Lola, and by extension Lola's people companions, were going to doggie criminal court!

At this point, Andrea and Chris swung into action.

The formal charging documents from animal control included the name of the woman whose dog had instigated the melee. A quick online search indi-cated that she was not, in fact, law enforcement (she had been a federal pros-ecutor), and that she was a part-time law professor.

The gentlemen who had offered to be a witness was tracked down and he turned out to be a respected reporter for the *San Diego Union-Tribune*—a professional at observing and reporting on events.

On the day of the proceedings, Cruella came in, along with a group of supporters, and prosecuted her case as if it was a federal criminal trial. She had exhibits documenting the medical nature and costs of Lola's bites to her dog. She presented a version of events that effectively made Lola out to be the aggressor responsible for the fight—omitting the key fact that her dog was off leash and Lola was on leash. And she even presented a dossier of online stories about Chris's background as a "political attack dog" and attempted to suggest that somehow Lola was guilty by virtue of her association with him—despite the reality that she was in fact a "mama's dog"!

When it came to their defense, Andrea and Chris had a very simple one-two-three punch.

First, Andrea and Chris were able to seize on a discrepancy (one of many) in Cruella's version of events—most specifically pointing out that it was Lola who was on leash, and her dog that was not on leash, which immediately altered the terms of the matter and reduced Lola's exposure.

Second, a comprehensive letter from the *Union-Tribune* reporter was produced, which, in addition to noting his background as a professional recorder of events, provided a detailed minute-by-minute tick-tock of the incident that completely corroborated the information provided by Andrea and Chris—and, in doing so, demonstrated the power of a disciplined commitment to a laser-like focus on a provable misrepresentation.

And, to an audible gasp from Cruella's cadre of supporters, realizing that this was an opportunity to pick the right fight with the right enemy, Andrea and Chris released a letter of complaint that they had recently sent to the State Bar of California related to her representations of being a member of law enforcement, knowing that the law enforcement officials presiding over the dog court would be sensitive to a civilian holding herself out as "law enforcement."

The "judge," while admonishing both sides and issuing warnings, made it clear that Lola was a free dog.

In the pursuit of Lola's exoneration, Andrea and Chris had applied the tenth commandment of damage control to an everyday situation: If they dissemble, you destroy.

By deploying the *Union-Tribune* reporter's account of the incident, Andrea and Chris were able to seize on discrepancies between Cruella's version of the incident and what truly happened, including the fact that of all the parties involved—man, woman, children, and dogs—it was Cruella's behavior that was the most egregious. In seizing on these discrepancies, the damage to Lola was limited, and the focus was turned to Cruella's own conduct—i.e., to all present it was clear that this woman was a nut job.

In having the discipline to focus on the specific issue of who was on leash and who was off leash, Andrea and Chris were able to effectively call into question Cruella's version of events, and shift the burden in terms of who was ultimately the responsible party, despite the fact it was her dog who had received the worse of the exchange.

And, finally, we looked to pick the right fight, which would create a favorable compare-and-contrast situation when it came to their credibility versus her credibility. The complaint made to the California Bar served as a vehicle to communicate in dog court—where the presiding judge is, in fact, an actual member of law enforcement—that this was a woman whose dissembling about her credentials raised serious questions about her credibility, and in doing so bolstered credibility.

COROLLARY TO THE TENTH COMMANDMENT— DON'T BE TOO QUICK TO JUDGE, TOO SOON TO ACCUSE

The National Enquirer first reported in October 2007 that former democratic vice presidential nominee John Edwards had an affair and fathered a child at the same time that his wife, Elizabeth Edwards, was battling terminal cancer. John Edwards fired back at the tabloid for having "made up" the story and went on to state: "The story is false. It's completely untrue, ridiculous."

When Jose Canseco, the former Major League Baseball star, went public with charges that a majority of players in the sport used steroids, and disclosed names, he was widely attacked inside the game. But several years later, Canseco was a star witness at a congressional hearing on the topic, as many of the players he claimed to have been on the "juice" subsequently were positively identified as steroid users, including some of the same players who had attacked Canseco in the past.

In each of these cases, folks who were seeking to limit their damage seemed to approach the situation by readying and firing—but without aiming.

In following the tenth commandment's edict, keep in mind that this is not horseshoes or hand grenades—close does not count.

In the 1990s, many of President Clinton's political opponents and critics found themselves on the losing end of highly charged attacks and counterattacks—as they opened themselves up to having their fundamental credibility challenged because they were simply *too quick to judge and too soon to accuse*.

In 1996, the highly regarded Pulitzer Prize–winning author and former *Wall Street Journal* reporter James Stewart published *Blood Sport: The President and His Adversaries*. The book was intended to be an objective and comprehensive investigation of the various allegations leveled against the Clintons from their Arkansas days, including the specifics of the land deal known as Whitewater.

The highly anticipated hardcover was to be released with a significant bells-and-whistles roll out, befitting a book from such a high-profile author focusing on a sitting president and the first lady on the eve of a re-election campaign.

In particular, partisan opponents of the Clintons were poised to aggressively use the book to justify additional investigative hearings designed to inflict political damage on the Clintons in the context of the 1996 presidential campaign.

The key participants were ready for war.

The president's team, anticipating the worse, was prepared to question the credibility of the reporting.

The proponents of the book were poised to seize on the revelations to question the credibility of the Clintons.

And the author was going to need to protect the integrity of his reporting in a book that was going to get significant attention and scrutiny, as it was investigating the conduct of the president and the first lady of the United States.

This was a crisis for all sides, and whoever prevailed would have their credibility enhanced while the others would see their credibility tarnished. And one particular charge in the book became the central flash point.

As part of the release of the book, ABC's influential news program *Nightline* featured an exclusive interview with the author. In the nationwide broadcast, he indicated the book would make public the suggestion that First Lady Hillary Clinton broke the law in 1987 when she filed a loan renewal application related to the Whitewater land-development scandal, as it included a "false financial document" that inflated the worth of the land investment.

This allegation sent the Clinton haters into high gear. Here was definitive proof that laws had been broken.

For the book's author, given that the document was in black and white, this appeared to be very solid ground on which to establish the credibility of his reporting. And for the Clintons, this appeared to be a very damning charge.

However, there was one problem.

One big problem for the opponents.

And one very big problem for the credibility of the book.

The allegation was flat-out wrong.

The author was too quick to judge, too soon to accuse.

In fact, Hillary Clinton had provided the accurate information, it was just on the backside of the form, which the author and the Clintons' partisan opponents failed to examine.

This key fact was seized upon by the Clinton White House and documented by reporters closely covering the story. *The Atlantic* wrote how the incident played out:

> Whoops... Hillary Clinton was right and Stewart was thumpingly wrong. He had failed to read the back of the personal financial statement for the loan-renewal application, where she had explained the valuation in detail. In capital letters at the bottom of the document, where Stewart could hardly have missed it, was the warning "both sides of this statement must be completed."

This inaccuracy became a defining moment in the rollout of the book. And while the book found audiences with those predisposed to oppose the Clintons, its impact with the broader public was greatly limited. The damage had been controlled.

In a crisis, if you are going to seize on a discrepancy, you have to be damn sure that you are right and they are wrong, as you are laying your credibility cards on the table and playing all in. But if you have the cards—and play them right—this is a highly effective route to damage control.

SEVENTEEN
THE DAMAGE CONTROL SURVIVAL KIT

Ride the light, baby.

—Carlos Santana

SO THERE WAS CHRIS—DAYS BEFORE ELECTION DAY 2000—STANDING IN THE DUSTY TWI-light shadows of the Los Cruces, New Mexico, Public Schools Sports Stadium. Vice President Al Gore was set to address a Latino rally. In a nip-and-tuck election, where it was clear every vote was going to count, the Gore campaign was seeking to turn out the Latino vote in hopes of winning New Mexico, which had emerged as a critical piece of the campaign's Electoral College strategy. Appearing with the Democratic nominee were a group of prominent Latinos who had come to participate in the rally, including singing legend Carlos Santana.

The White House motorcade had come to a stop to unload the vice president, his Secret Service detail, his staff, and the traveling Latino dignitaries, and in the not-so-far distance a cloud of red dust was rolling its way toward Chris. At first glance, it might have appeared to be a herd of charging cattle—but, in fact, it was the presidential campaign press corps charging from the bus that brought up the rear of the motorcade.

These distinguished members of the Fourth Estate, rushing forward with cameras, boom mics, ladders, and recorders in hand, were on the move because major news had crossed the transom that could alter the course of the election, and the press wanted an immediate reaction—a story had just broken on a local Fox News affiliate in Portland, Maine, that then governor George W. Bush had been arrested many years earlier for driving under the influence.

And Chris was on the spot. The press was going to want to know what the campaign knew. When the campaign knew it. What the campaign was going to say about the revelation.

Standing next to Chris, as he gazed out at the marauding media herd, happened to be Santana, dressed entirely in black. He looked at Chris, looked over at the approaching swirl, looked back to Chris, and offered seven words that Chris took to be guidance, and that have lived with him forever: "Ride the light, baby. Ride the light."

While Carlos Santana's counsel is certainly profound, in an effort to offer what is a more prosaic prescriptive approach, please find the User's Manual in the next chapter, which summarizes the thoughts offered in this book, including The Survival Principles and The Ten Commandments of Damage Control, along with their accompanying corollaries.

Our hope is that this User's Manual will serve as a quick reference point for those who may be facing a crisis—big or small.

And, of course, if you prefer, you can go into the night and follow the course laid out by Santana:

Ride the light, baby. Ride the light.

EIGHTEEN
THE USER'S MANUAL

THE SURVIVAL PRINCIPLES

DO NO HARM—It's Not the Crime, It's the Cover-Up

- Don't Chase the Story, Get Ahead of the Story
- Avoid Over-Spin, Focus on Counter-Spin
- Don't Lay the Blame on Others, Accept Responsibility

DISCIPLINE—It's Not Personal, It's Strictly Business

- Commit to Preparation
- Exercise Mental Toughness in the Fog of a Crisis
- Think Long Term

CREDIBILITY—I Want the Truth!

- Accurate Information Is the Coin of the Realm
- Manage Expectations
- Control the Flow of Information

THE TEN COMMANDMENTS OF DAMAGE CONTROL

I. FULL DISCLOSURE

Everything that can come out, will come out. All too often it's the drip, drip, drip that causes most of the lasting damage.

But you only get one bite at the apology apple.

II. SPEAK TO YOUR CORE AUDIENCE

Determine the key points to get across and stay focused on them. Reiterate your message at every opportunity. Discipline is crucial.

But do not pander.

III. DON'T FEED THE FIRE

It's human nature to succumb to the pressures of the moment that push you into making the situation worse. Resist that pull.

But the prevent defense can keep you from winning.

IV. DETAILS MATTER

Be prepared with detailed answers to tough questions. The smallest discrepancy can get magnified into the biggest problem.

But you are not in a confessional.

V. HOLD YOUR HEAD HIGH

Original actions may seem insignificant compared with mistakes made after the fact. Seize the moment to put out the entire story.

But there are no second acts.

VI. BE STRAIGHT ABOUT WHAT YOU KNOW, WHAT YOU DON'T KNOW, AND WHAT YOU ARE GOING TO DO TO FIX THE PROBLEM

Your credibility is at stake—and the public can easily discern hedged answers and half-truths. When you don't have answers, create a process to ascertain the answers, and make clear how you will fix the problem going forward.

But don't pick a fight you can't win.

VII. RESPOND WITH OVERWHELMING FORCE

Identify the most important groups you're trying to reach and what it is they need to hear. Keep it simple and keep saying it.

But no message handcuffs.

VIII. FIRST IN, FIRST OUT

You can reduce your exposure by getting your story out there quickly and candidly. Often there are multiple players in a crisis, so let others become the star of the scandal.

But know when to hold 'em, know when to fold 'em, and know when to run.

IX. NO SWIFTBOATING

Your setback is your rivals' opportunity—and that setback often comes from those with unclean hands. Get on top of your story and your message before they do, because they'll try to make you look worse. Expose the real agenda of your opposition.

But no civilian casualties.

X. THEY DISSEMBLE, YOU DESTROY

If your opponents engage in misrepresentations about you, your organization, or your company, go after them—hard. You protect your reputation—and undermine theirs.

But don't be too quick to judge and too soon to accuse. Damage control is not horseshoes or hand grenades, close does not count. You must have the opposition dead to rights if you call them out.

ACKNOWLEDGMENTS

WE ARE EXTRAORDINARILY GRATEFUL TO ALL OF THE FOLLOWING FOR THEIR TREMENDOUS HELP WITH this book.

Mel Berger at William Morris Endeavor

Marina Brodskaya

Emily Carleton at Palgrave Macmillan

Andrea Evans

Misha Guttentag

Sasha Guttentag

Rod Kramer

Laura Lancaster at Palgrave Macmillan

Dominic and Quincy Lehane

Linda Lichter

Susha Roy

INDEX

ABOUT THE AUTHORS

CHRISTOPHER LEHANE

Named a "Master of Disaster" by *Newsweek* and "Master of the Dark Arts" of politics by *The New York Times,* Christopher Lehane is a partner in the strategic communications firm Fabiani & Lehane, which provides high-level counsel to corporate, entertainment, political, and professional sports clients facing complex challenges typically involving some combination of the law, finance, government affairs, and communications. His firm has represented the likes of Goldman Sachs, Lance Armstrong, and Hollywood studios. Lehane, whose career began in Democratic politics and who continues to be active as a political consultant, served in various positions in the Clinton-Gore Administration during the 1990s, including Special Assistant Counsel to President Bill Clinton, Press Secretary for Vice President Al Gore, and Counselor to Housing and Urban Development Secretary Andrew Cuomo (later the Governor of New York). A lecturer on crisis management at the Stanford University Graduate School of Business, Lehane is a regular commentator and speaker on the art of damage control. He graduated from Harvard Law School in 1994 and from Amherst College in 1990 and lives in San Francisco, California, with his wife, Andrea, and two sons, Dominic and Quincy.

MARK FABIANI

Mark Fabiani's La Jolla–based company has since 1997 provided strategic advice and tactical execution to clients facing complex financial, communications, government affairs, and legal challenges. In 2000, Fabiani served as the Deputy Campaign Manager for Communications and Strategy for former Vice President Al Gore's presidential campaign, in the closest presidential election in modern history. From 1994 through 1996 Fabiani was Special Counsel to President Bill Clinton and provided legal, communications, and political counsel to the President and First Lady of the United States. Fabiani also served for four years as Deputy Mayor of Los Angeles and Chief of Staff to Los Angeles mayor Tom Bradley. Fabiani, who graduated Cum Laude from Harvard Law School in 1982, has also served in senior positions at the United States Department of Justice and the Department of Housing and Urban Development. Fabiani lives in La Jolla, California, with his wife June and three children, Joseph, Isabella, and Lucca.

BILL GUTTENTAG

Bill Guttentag is a two-time Oscar-winning feature film and documentary writer-producer-director. His films include the dramatic features *Live!*, starring Eva Mendes and Andre Braugher and *Knife Fight* starring Rob Lowe, Julie Bowen, and Carrie-Ann Moss. His documentary features include *Nanking*, which premiered at the Sundance Film Festival and *Soundtrack for a Revolution*, which had its international premiere at the Cannes Film Festival.

In 2003 he won an Academy Award for the documentary *Twin Towers*. He has also has received a second documentary Oscar, three additional Oscar nominations, a Peabody Award, three Emmy Awards, two Writers Guild Award nominations, and a Robert Kennedy Journalism Award. His films have been selected for the Sundance Film Festival three times, and have played and won awards at numerous American and international film festivals.

He has directed documentary films for HBO, ABC News, CBS, and other networks. He was also an executive producer and creator of the non-fiction series *Law & Order: Crime & Punishment*, which ran for three seasons on NBC. His first novel, *Boulevard*, was published by Pegasus Books/W.W. Norton in 2010. He was a John S. Knight journalism fellow at Stanford University, and since 2001 he has been a lecturer at the Graduate School of Business at Stanford.